Hand Coding

Coded UI

(An Evaluation Journey from Inception to Completion)

G. Suden

ISBN-13:   978-1547000852
ISBN-10:   1547000856

Printed by CreateSpace, An Amazon.com Company
Order online at https://www.createspace.com/7208560

Available from Amazon.com, Amazon Europe, other online stores and retail outlets.

To my parents, wife and my amazing kids for giving me the support and drive to finish this book. I love you all!

Acknowledgements

The author is thankful to Lovleen, Simran and Kanwal for copy editing the manuscript.

Contents

List of Figures

Overview

THIS book is aimed at testers who want to try their hands at automated testing using Coded UI, which is available as part of Microsoft® Visual Studio® (Enterprise Edition). Coded UI has empowered developers and automation testers to work using the same automation tool and language, hence enabling them to collaborate more efficiently and effectively. Moreover, Coded UI can be used for both Web and Windows-based Applications which enables automation testers to devise a single Automation Framework that reuses common code and libraries. This makes the test automation more efficient, reduces the test automation effort, lowers the cost of maintenance and also provides a higher Return On Investment. Therefore, in my view, if you are planning to use Coded UI for automation, it will be a right step forward in your world of automated testing.

You will find a lot of books which go through mainly the theoretical aspects of automation and provide only a few code snippets on how automation is performed in reality. There is a famous saying *'In theory, theory and practice are the same. In practice, they are not'*, so I thought I should write a book which explains how automation is *practically* done rather than just explaining it in theory. Moreover, I'm a big fan of *hand coding* the *test automation code* as opposed to using the auto generated *Record and Playback* code. Initially this project started as a Coded UI evaluation exercise, however over time, it developed into an entire Automation Framework which **hand codes** the **Coded UI** automation code. This *hand coding* approach can be applied to any project which aims to use Coded UI as the test automation tool.

This book provides a step by step guide that will teach you how to setup the Automation Framework from scratch using Coded UI. As mentioned before, the book concentrates on the 'practical side' of automated testing rather than the 'theoretical side'. It includes complete listings of the *hand coded* automation code for the demo Website, Windows-based applications (Windows Forms and WPF Applications) and Web Service that have been developed for you to test against. The code listings explain the logic of individual tests, repositories and generic functions.

This book is divided into ten chapters as follows:

- Chapter 1, *Getting Started*, introduces reasons to use automation in our testing. It highlights the reasons why we should avoid the *Record and Playback* approach. It also provides the *Golden Rules* one should follow when automating tests.

- Chapter 2, *Automation Approach*, covers the importance of having a framework, the driving force behind a successful automation. It also discusses the components of an Automation Framework using Coded UI. A demo website has been setup to help you learn the practical Web Testing scenarios listed in the book. We will setup the project structure required to create our Coded UI Automation Framework. We will also learn about the UI Control hierarchy and how to identify them in Coded UI.

- Chapter 3, *Web Based Application - UITestControls*, starts with creating our first automated test using UITestControls. We will learn how the Coded UI project structure, which we have setup in the previous chapter, hangs together to give us an Automation Framework on which we can build robust and easily maintainable code. We will expand our Automation Framework by learning how to enable the inbuilt logging mechanism provided by Coded UI.

- Chapter 4, *Web Based Application - HtmlControls*, covers automating the Web Testing scenarios using HtmlControls. We will add a number of important features to the Automation Framework such as logging to the Standard Output window, CSV files (so that you can refer back when required), saving screenshots etc. The chapter also covers how to automate data entry, verification and negative tests using HtmlControls. Finally, we will expand our Automation Framework to create a Test Result Summary report at the end of the test execution.

- Chapter 5, *Automate With Databases*, covers automating tabular and summary reports in the demo website again using HtmlControls. We will learn how to perform various automated verification tasks using a database.

- Chapter 6, *Data Driven Testing*, describes how to perform data driven testing using external data files (instead of using hard-coded data in the test). We will cover both XLS and XLSX Excel® formats for automation purpose. Before we finish this chapter, we will add more features to the Automation Framework e.g. adding a test step failure threshold, logging failed test steps only and comparing decimal numbers with a defined tolerance.

- Chapter 7, *Cross Browser Testing*, covers testing our demo website with different browsers using Coded UI. We will cover Mozilla Firefox, Google Chrome, Internet Explorer and Microsoft Edge web browsers. We will also see a practical example on how to make our test scripts browser compatible so that we can run them on multiple browsers.

- Chapter 8, *Web Services Testing*, deals with automating the testing of web services in Coded UI. We will write a sample working web service and automate its testing via different methods namely WebRequest, HttpWebRequest and Service Reference.

- Chapter 9, *Windows Forms Application - WinControls*, covers automating Windows Forms Applications using WinControls. The book provides a demo Windows

Forms Application to help you learn the practical scenarios listed in the book. The chapter covers automation scenarios on data entry, verification and drag-n-drop tasks using WinControls.

- Chapter 10, *Windows Presentation Foundation (WPF) Application - WpfControls*, covers automating WPF Applications using WpfControls. The book provides a demo WPF Application to help you learn the practical scenarios listed in the book. The chapter covers automation scenarios on data entry and verification tasks using WpfControls.

Since this book has been designed to be a *Practical Oriented Approach*, we will adhere to the following steps in each section of a chapter (wherever applicable):

✓ define a *Test Scenario* using one of the demo applications - Website, Windows Forms Application, WPF Application or the Web Service.

✓ define the required Configuration Parameters in the *Configuration File*.

✓ write code for the required controls in the *Repository File*.

✓ write code for the required generic functions in the *Utility File* .

✓ write code for the business process in the *Page File*.

✓ write code for the test logic as per the *Test Scenario* (defined in the beginning) in the *Test File*.

✓ finally, execute the test and view the *Outcome*.

Please note that this book aims to teach you how to hand code automated tests in Coded UI using C# and provides you with a framework to achieve this. It is not about teaching you "how to code effectively" in C#. You may find there are another ways to code certain listings shown in the book, so feel free to modify the code and implement this in your framework. In my view, as an experienced automation tester, as long as your code is doing what it is supposed to do and is highlighting bugs or issues in the system you are testing, you are doing a great job. It doesn't need to be a perfectly written piece of code using all the advanced and fancy features of the language. A tester's coding skills do not need to be as comprehensive as a professional programmer to add value. Personally, I don't mind if it takes a few milliseconds, or a few seconds, or for that matter a few minutes to execute an automated test. Once automated, I can add it to my Regression Test Pack and execute it almost without any effort while I'm concentrating on other important tests.

Welcome to the world of *hand coding* your Coded UI tests!

Chapter 1

Getting Started

Getting Started

In this chapter, we will learn about:

- *Why we should automate testing*

- *How not to automate testing*

- *Golden rules for automated testing*

So let's get on with it...

THERE has always been enormous pressure on software organisations to meet delivery deadlines with static or even reduced Quality Assurance (QA) resources. In your time being a QA person, have you ever worked in a project where the development dates have shifted to the right on a project plan? The very first thing that usually happens in such instances is to reduce the testing time! The financial pressures demand cost and resource reductions. This results in an increased risk of software failure. On the other hand, there is always a lot of pressure to deliver new functionalities to keep ahead of the competition. Delivering a bug free system demands good test coverage. Manual software testing with good test coverage is a labour intensive task. This is where the automated testing comes into the picture: *to achieve desired quality goals within the constraints of time and money.* I must emphasise here that the primary goal of automation should be to increase the test coverage and hence the quality, not to cut testing costs.

Once automated tests are created they can easily be repeated to perform frequent regression testing as and when required. Sanity automated tests can be shared with the development team to execute before the builds are made available to the QA team.

☞ If you own my other book "Automated Web Testing", you will find that this chapter is a near repeat of what has already been covered in there. However, the chapter contains very useful information for an Automation Tester and I didn't want the owners of this book to feel left out without having read my previous book therefore I have also included the relevant information from that chapter in this book.

1.1 Why Automate?

The need for speed is practically the mantra of the Information Age. In the real world, automating any part of the testing can pay big dividends. Delivering a product late will result in loss of customers, revenue and market share. However, on the other hand, delivering a defective software product will be even more catastrophic - costing millions or billions and even bringing the entire organisation down. If it doesn't do what it says on the tin then the product may cost you many times more than the entire testing budget!

Thankfully automation usually brings a lot of benefits to the organisation such as:

- **Regression Testing** - Software applications grow in functionality and complexity over time, meaning that the number of tests will also increase. Depending on the impact analysis, even with a very low percentage of code change, the software needs a very high percentage of the regression tests to be repeated. In some cases, 100% regression tests need to be repeated. When testing time is cut-short, regression testing is usually cut-short too to give priority to other important areas. Automation can really help test the new functionality as well as regression test the existing functionality.

- **Test Efficiency and Accuracy** - is usually improved as the comparison of the expected and actual results is performed by computer and thereby eliminating human error. Automated tests are fast and, as we will see later, reuse functions & modules within different tests or on different versions of the software.

- **Test Coverage** - We can achieve better test coverage using automation. We can randomly select records each time we execute a test and thus providing more coverage. Similarly the same tests can be executed when new data arrives.

- **Saves Time and Money** - Automation initially is associated with increased effort however; its benefits will pay off in the long run! Regression testing becomes effortless and is highly beneficial for software products with a long maintenance life.

- **Tester's Motivation** - Manual testing can be error-prone and mundane. The automated testing on the other hand is repeatable, leaving testers to concentrate on other important tasks.

- **Reliable** - Automated testing is reliable. When a tester writes a test for a defect he or she has found, and adds it to the Regression Test Pack; the test just cannot be forgotten. It automatically executes and checks for that peculiar condition where it failed once. A manual tester on the other hand can simply forget to perform this test or may even choose not to perform it due to time pressure or for a number of other reasons.

- **Quicker Time to Market** - In today's competitive environment, time to market is usually the key driver for a number of projects, particularly for the revenue generating products. Automation can help reduce time to market by not only shortening the test cycle but also helps you meet the deadlines with a reliable product.

1.2   How Not To Automate?

There are many ways to approach the test automation and it is highly important to develop an overall approach which suits your project. If you approach automation purely from a *Record and Playback* perspective, you are due for a big surprise later on. In a *Record and Playback* approach, tests are performed manually while the inputs and outputs are recorded in the background. During a subsequent execution, same steps are played back with the same input values and the actual outputs are compared with the stored ones. Any differences are reported as errors.

Although the *Record and Playback* approach will get you on-board with a very little learning curve, there are several disadvantages in using this approach. We shall cover some main ones here:

- It requires all the actions to be recorded manually. For example, for an Employee Data Entry system, all the steps have to be repeated for each employee to be added, updated and deleted.

- The application under test must be stable enough for business transactions to be recorded, leaving very little opportunity for early detection of errors.

- For a highly agile development environment, an object's recognition properties may change which would result in the object being not identified successfully during a playback and subsequently failing the test. This causes scripts to be re-recorded, which is often very costly and time consuming.

- There is no decision making logic in the recorded scripts. For example, if you need to perform different actions based on employee's age group then you would need to record separate scripts because the data is hard-coded in scripts. Moreover, if for some reason you have to re-record a script due to change in age group logic then you would most likely need to re-record all age group logic scripts.

- Web browsers continue to be the primary gateway, channelling the end-user's interactions with the web applications. However different web browsers render the web contents differently and for that reason, web based applications need to be tested on a number of different browsers. If you have recorded a script against one browser, it may not work on some other browser.

- For large applications, test execution performance may decrease due to duplication of objects and hence resulting in a very large repository. This is because the same object may be recorded multiple times in different scripts.

- Recording may not playback successfully because of synchronisation problems, which is a significant issue in automated web testing. The script may be waiting for an object or element to appear on the web page but if it doesn't appear in time, the script may just try to perform action on it resulting in the test failure. These kind of synchronisation points need to be *programmed* into the test scripts via your Automation Framework.

- Recording produces scripts that are difficult to maintain. Amending a recorded script and getting it to replay correctly requires a lot of time and effort. Moreover, as the application's functionality grows, the more tests you record. You will have to re-record scripts due to functionality changes e.g. screens/objects added, modified or removed. Maintenance of these recorded scripts will become an immense burden at some point costing you even more time and money. Maintenance is very important in test automation and this in fact, is one of the main motivation factors to build a robust Automation Framework.

- *Record and Playback* scripts hardly take advantage of code re-use from one test to another. A good Automation Framework, on the other hand, would facilitate code organisation, minimise duplication and make it easier to re-use the existing code. Moreover, with an Automation Framework you can provide meaningful names to the objects instead of auto-generated names which were given to them at the time of recording the script.

- With a basic *Record and Playback* script, if something unexpected happens during test execution, the test will fail. An automated test however, should cope with different events that may happen and not just 'what happened' when the script was recorded. Again this should be *programmed* into the automation script. During a verification test, I may want to continue the test until it has hit a predefined threshold of failures. A basic *Record and Playback* tool may not offer this facility.

Record and Playback is one of the earliest automation approaches but I personally avoid it being my main automation approach for any project. However, this doesn't mean that I don't use it. *Record and Playback* really has helped me a number of times to identify the code and objects when I didn't know how to start automating a piece of functionality! However, in this book we shall develop an Automation Framework which doesn't use *Record and Playback* approach. You will be able to hand code Coded UI scripts which are modular and easily maintainable.

1.3   Golden Automation Rules

Here are some golden automation rules to keep in mind that I have learnt through my experience:

1. Start small and simple first. Don't try to automate the complicated scenarios first if you are just starting off with automated testing. Take smaller steps before you start walking and then finally running.

2. An effective automated test design principle - *always* start the test with a known state.

3. Don't try to automate everything. This may not be practical in your project, so set realistic expectations.

4. It is typically not a single complex test that uncovers a bug. You may need to perform a combination of simple tests to highlight a bug.

5. Once you are confident with the Automation Framework, test cases with high value and low effort should be automated first.

6. Run your automated tests regularly, if possible, with every build. Machines can find flaws.

7. Test your *Test* - make sure you have seen the test case failing at least once - force the failure condition so that you know the coded logic works.

8. No matter how much you automate, you still can't replace manual testing or testers. The purpose of automation is not to eliminate testers but to make better use of their time.

9. Ensure that each test has a specific purpose and identifiable result(s).

10. Log your expected and actual result values during comparison. You never know when you are going to need to look into your test results.

11. All things done well can be done even better. Revising and striving to improve your Automation Framework is a way of improving your skills and driving you on to new heights.

12. Use an Automation Framework that is easy to manage and allows new tests to be added easily.

13. Focus on modularity and re-usability. Build libraries of functions that you can reuse in other projects.

14. Test automation is a long term strategic solution and not a quick-fix to testing. Buying an automation tool is just like buying a treadmill - to lose weight. However if you never use it, the only thing you have lost is the weight of your purse! You must really invest your time and effort to get the real benefits in both cases.

15. Code coverage is not a reliable metric for ensuring end-to-end quality, but should be used as a measure to gauge the effectiveness of test automation.

16. The *test automation code* has to be used for a long term (just like the *production code*) and hence needs to be easily maintainable. So we need to deploy similar principles and practices in programming the *test automation code* (including coding standards) as we use for the *production code*.

Chapter 2

Automation Approach

Automation Approach

In this chapter, we will learn about:

- *The Automation Framework that we are going to develop*

- *The UI Controls and their hierarchy*

- *Setting up the Coded UI project structure*

- *Identifying the UI Controls*

So let's get on with it...

W HAT is an Automation Framework? An Automation Framework is an application that allows you to write tests without worrying about the constraints of the underlying test tools. As in the Software Development Life Cycle (SDLC) to develop software applications, framework design plays a vital role in building the test approach for automation. The need for a well-defined and designed test framework is especially important in automated testing. It is the starting point for success with the automated testing.

A well designed Automation Framework makes the test automation more efficient, reduces test automation effort, lowers the cost of maintenance and also provides a higher Return On Investment (ROI). It is very important to have a framework that enhances efficiency in the development of automated test scripts through modular, reusable and maintainable code. The reusable library of functions is much in the same way as any other software system. A good test Automation Framework should ensure a uniform design across multiple test scripts and should minimise code maintenance overhead.

Easy maintenance of automation code is crucial to test automation. If we cannot maintain the automation code and bring it up-to-date quick enough with the changes in the Application Under Test (AUT), we will not get the payback. Moreover, adding more features to the framework should not disturb existing tests.

Effective test reporting is another important feature and enhances the value of the framework. The framework should support the production of both a summary report - a high level view of all the tests executed as well as a detailed report - providing a step by step view of various steps in the test.

Similarly, log generation is another important part of the test execution. The framework should provide the means to create debug logs which can help find a problem quickly. Execution reports and logs are important for any automation execution and should be stored for future reference.

2.1   Automation Framework

We will develop our Automation Framework using Coded UI as we progress through this book. Figure 2.1 shows our Automation Framework in its simplest form.

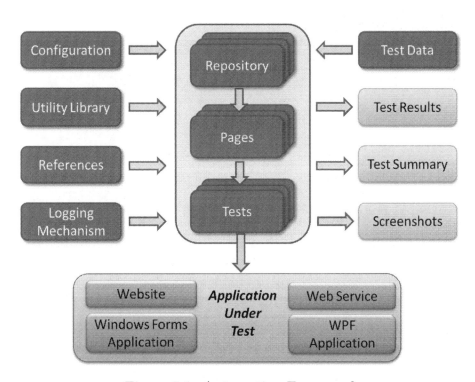

Figure 2.1: Automation Framework

Let me start by briefly explaining the framework components.

2.1.1 Configuration File

The Configuration File is used to store a number of configurable parameters of your framework that are used throughout your testing. Some examples of these parameters are:

```
public const int TIMEOUT_MILLISEC = 60000;
public static string BROWSER = FIREFOX;
```

2.1.2 Utility File

The Utility File holds a number of general purpose functions that are to be used throughout your testing. An example of such a function is:

```
public static void ReportExpectedVsActual(String exp, String act)
```

This function accepts two arguments: the expected outcome and the actual outcome, and reports the result. If the expected and actual outcomes are the same, it will pass the test step, otherwise will fail it.

2.1.3 Reference Files

The Automation Framework uses a number of reference files and libraries e.g. reference to the logging dll, web service etc. You will learn how to reference these files in the framework in later chapters as and when we need them.

2.1.4 Logging Mechanism

Logging Mechanism is the heart of an Automation Framework. This gives us a lot of information about what happens during the test execution. We will learn how to setup the logging mechanism provided in Coded UI by default and also how to setup our own logging mechanism to capture a number of events taking place during the test execution.

2.1.5 Repository Files

The Repository Files contain the repository of all the objects in the Website Under Test or the Application Under Test (AUT). We will create a single repository which will be shared by all tests. The repository of individual web pages or windows will be held in separate files so that they have a logical separation. In our framework code, each repository file will have the prefix "rep" followed by the technology it represents and then followed by the name of the page or window e.g. the repository file name for the website's home page will be repHtmlHome. Similarly the repository file name for the WPF Application's home page will be repWpfHome.

2.1.6 Page Files

The Page Files contain the testing logic for individual web pages or windows (screens). In a page file, we write functions which accomplish business processes for a particular web page or window. For example, the page file for a login page will contain the functions on:

- logging in a user with the given credentials or
- performing an individual action on the login page e.g. click the *Login* button.

The business logic of individual web pages or windows will be held in separate page files so that they have a logical separation. In our framework code, each page file will have the prefix `"page"` followed by the technology it represents and then followed by the name of the page or window e.g. the page file name for the website's home page will be `pageHtmlHome`. Similarly the page file name for the WPF Application's home page will be `pageWpfHome`.

2.1.7 Test Files

The Test Files contain all of your Test Scenarios (tests). One test file may contain one or more Test Scenarios. Each Test Scenario completes a business process end-to-end. Figure 2.2 shows the structure of an automated test script file. As you can see, each test script file has a number of important parts:

- Setup Before Each Test - this is the code that is executed before a test is executed e.g. setting up the logging mechanism.

- Teardown After Each Test - this is the code that is executed after a test completes execution e.g. saving the log file, closing the browser etc.

- Each test will have its own logic to verify. For each test step, once we have derived the expected and actual results, we will make a call to the generic function `ReportExpectedVsActual` to report the outcome of the test step.

- Report Overall Test Result will report the final result of the current test. If any test step has failed, the overall result of that test will be Fail.

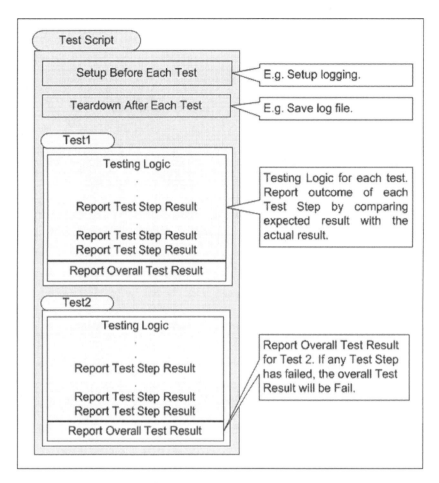

Figure 2.2: Automated Test Script Structure

This structure will be followed for all of our tests. This gives us a consistent approach to writing tests as a result. Don't worry if you don't understand the flow at this stage. Just keep the script structure in mind for the time being. Things will become more apparent when we start writing our first test in the next chapter!

2.1.8 Test Data

There are a number of ways that you can specify the data to be used for a test. We will cover the following three types of data sources for the purpose of our automated testing:

- Specifying the test data in each test also known as hard-coded test data.

- Using data from Excel® files in XLS and XLSX format.

- Using data from database tables.

2.1.9 Test Results

We will learn how to configure the test results produced in Coded UI by default. We will also produce our own test results as per our logging mechanism. This will give us extra information about the test run.

2.1.10 Test Summary

We will produce our own test results summary as the information available from Coded UI in the *Test Explorer* is overwritten at the next run.

2.1.11 Screenshots

Although Coded UI provides the mechanism to take screenshots at various stages of the test execution, there may be instances where you may want to take a screenshot at a certain point during the test execution. Therefore we will add this feature in our Automation Framework.

2.1.12 Application Under Test

There are four type of Applications Under Test (AUT) that we will automate against using Coded UI. These are:

- A Website.

- A Web Service.

- A Windows Forms Application.

- A WPF Application.

2.2 Anatomy of a Coded UI Test

As of yet, we haven't seen a Coded UI Test in this book however, I thought it is more appropriate that I present a quick mapping of our Automated Test Script *structure* (Figure 2.2) with the actual Coded UI Test Script *structure* as shown in Figure 2.3 so that you can correlate the two when we start writing our tests in the next chapter.

- The *Attribute* [CodedUITest] tells the testing framework to recognize the class as a testing extension and maps to the *Test Script*.

- The *Attribute* [TestInitialize] tells the testing framework to call this method before any test is executed and maps to the *Setup Before Each Test*.

- The *Attribute* [TestCleanup] tells the testing framework to call this method after each test is executed and maps to the *Teardown After Each Test*.

- The *Attribute* [TestMethod] preceding each test tells the testing framework that the method should be executed to perform a test and maps to the *Test* or *Test Scenario*.

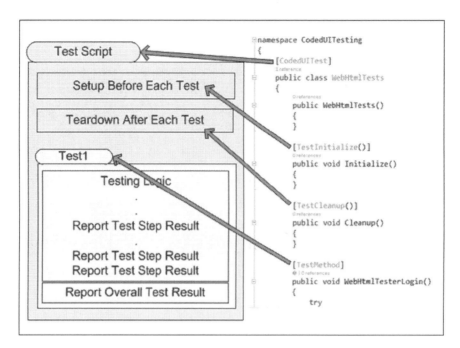

Figure 2.3: Test Attributes

2.3   Understanding UI Controls and Hierarchy

Windows has a Graphical User Interface (GUI) for working with our computer and a Web Browser has a Graphical User Interface that allows us to surf the web. A Graphical User Interface has a wide range of controls like Edit Boxes, Labels, List Views, Tree Views etc. with which a user interacts. Coded UI supports various types of controls used on both the Web Applications and the Windows-based Applications. These controls can be categorised as *generic controls* i.e. `UIControls` or *technology specific controls* e.g. `WinButton` for Windows-based Applications or `HtmlButton` for Web Applications. Figure 2.4 shows various types of controls Coded UI supports and their hierarchy.

As you can see, at the top level are the generic controls called `UITestControls`. They provide properties and methods which are generic to controls across technologies.

At the next level are the technology specific controls:

- `HtmlControls` for the Web Applications (`TechnologyName = Web`).

- `WinControls` for the Windows Forms Applications (`TechnologyName = MSAA`).

- `WpfControls` for the Windows Presentation Foundation (WPF) Applications (`TechnologyName = UIA`).

Note that the technology `UIA` is the successor to `MSAA`.

At the next level in the hierarchy are the specific controls that allow different kind of user interactions e.g. an `HtmlButton` represents a button control to test the Graphical

User Interface of Web pages. Controls at a level inherit all the properties from the higher level.

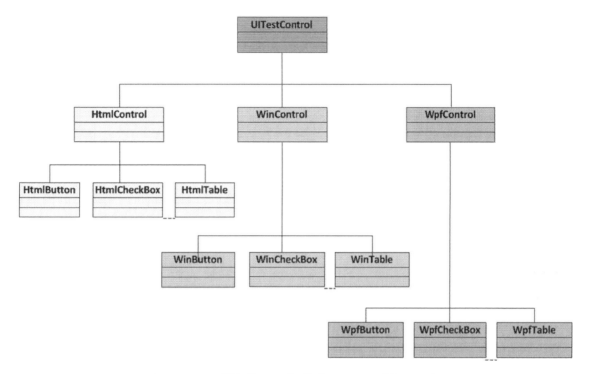

Figure 2.4: UI Controls Inheritance Hierarchy

Each technology has a specified set of properties that can be used to search for controls on the Graphical User Interface. Coded UI chooses only those properties exposed by the technology as the *Search Properties*. We will learn about it in detail in later sections.

2.4   Applications Under Test

This book is less about the theory aspects and more about the practical aspects. The more automation you perform, the more confident you become in automating different kind of applications. In order to impart you a vast automation experience, the book provides four different kind of applications to automate against.

2.4.1   Demo Website - UITestControls and HtmlControls

For automation using `UITestControls` and `HtmlControls`, we will use a demonstration Web Application at `http://testing.arkenstone-ltd.com` as shown in Figure 2.5. The demo website uses a number of controls that are used in most of the websites these days e.g. data entry fields, command buttons, radio buttons, check boxes, tables, static text, images, links etc. We will learn how to automate the testing of these controls using Coded UI.

☞ If you are facing any issue accessing the demo website, please email the 'Book Support Team' at autoweb.testing@gmail.com. Please specify "AutoWeb Demo Portal" in the subject/title of the email.

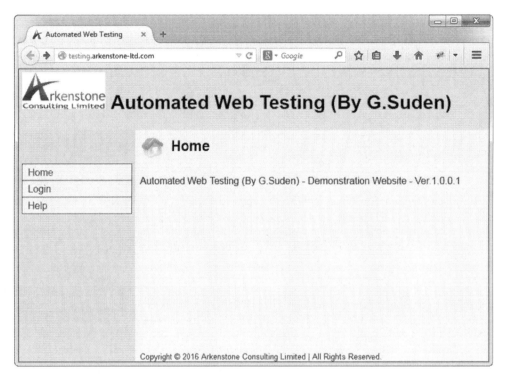

Figure 2.5: Demo Web Application

There are two types of users that exist in the demo website:

- A general or normal user whose credentials are:

    User: Tester

    Password: Tester123

- An administrator user whose credentials are:

    Admin User: Admin

    Password: Admin123

Please note that the credentials are case-sensitive.

2.4.1.1 Site Map

Figure 2.6 shows the Site Map of the demo website. Each of the two user types (Tester and Admin), has a home page with the functionality they have access to. Please spend some time to familiarise yourself with the website as you will use it frequently during the next few chapters.

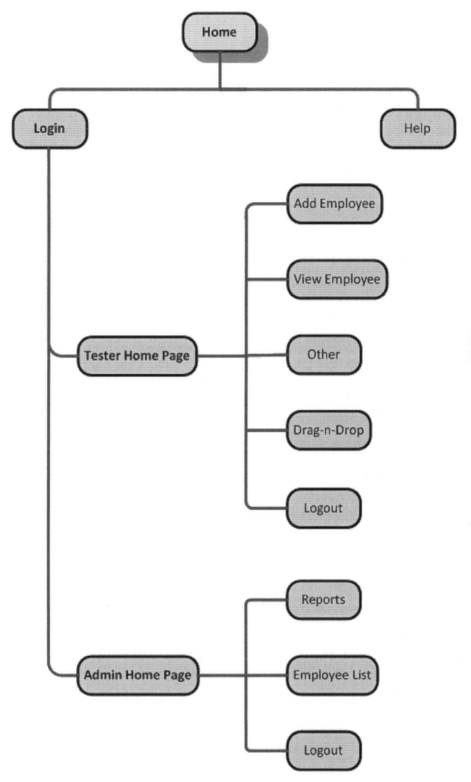

Figure 2.6: Demo Portal - Site Map

2.4.2   Demo Windows Forms Application - WinControls

For automation using `WinControls`, we will use a demonstration Windows Forms Application as shown in Figure 2.7. Similar user credentials exist for this application as on the demo website. A later chapter will detail how to download and compile this application on your workstation for the purposes of automation.

 Note that the menu items in the demo Windows Forms Application are made visible or invisible depending on which user is logged in.

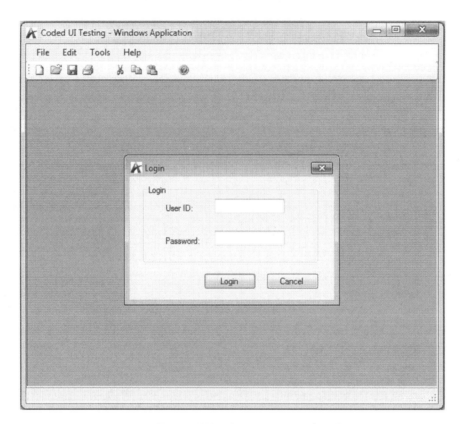

Figure 2.7: Demo Windows Forms Application

2.4.3   Demo WPF Application - WpfControls

Similarly for automation using `WpfControls`, we will use a demonstration Windows Presentation Foundation Application as shown in Figure 2.8. Similar user credentials exist for this application as on the demo website. A later chapter will detail how to download and compile this application on your workstation for the purposes of automation.

 Note that the menu items in the demo WPF Application are made visible or invisible depending on which user is logged in.

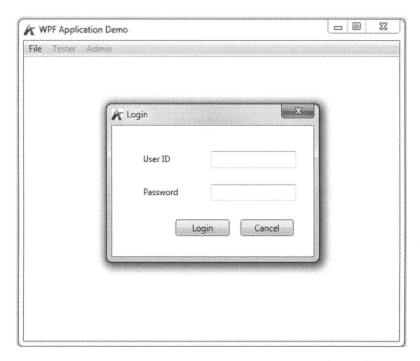

Figure 2.8: Demo Windows Presentation Foundation (WPF) Application

2.4.4 Demo Web Service

Similarly for the Web Services, we will use a demonstration Web Service as shown in Figure 2.9. A later chapter will detail how to build this Web Service on your workstation for the purposes of automation.

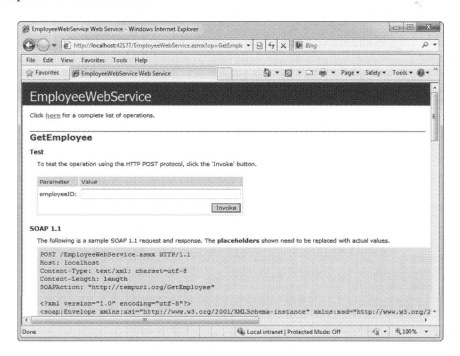

Figure 2.9: Demo Web Service

2.5   Setting Up the Coded UI Project

Let's first of all setup the structure of our Coded UI project using the following steps:

Step 1: Launch Microsoft Visual Studio® from its installed location or from its desktop shortcut.

Step 2: Create a new project.

- Go to *File ⇒ New ⇒ Project...*

- In the left hand pane, navigate to *Installed ⇒ Templates ⇒ Visual C# ⇒ Test*.

- In the middle pane, click on the *Coded UI Test Project*.

- Type the *Name:* as 'CodedUITesting' as shown in Figure 2.10.

- Select the *Location:* as 'C:\'. You can select a different location; however this book assumes you have chosen 'C:\'.

- Leave everything else as default and click the *OK* button.

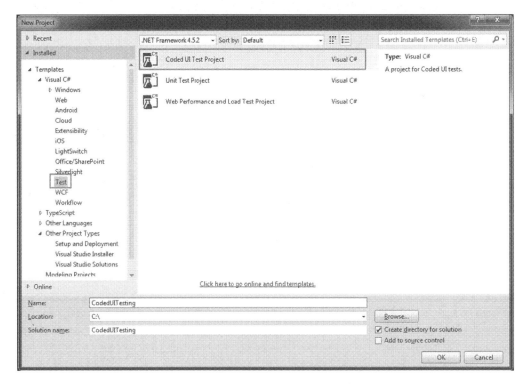

Figure 2.10: Coded UI Project

After the setup completes, you will be shown a window as shown in Figure 2.11. As of now, press the *Cancel* button. We will address this later on.

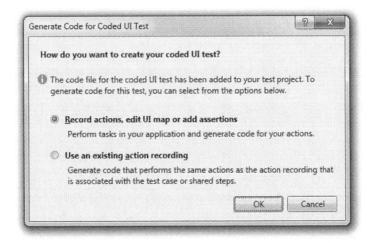

Figure 2.11: Generate Code for Coded UI Test

Step 3: Now let's setup the Coded UI Test File.

- In the *Solution Explorer*, right click on the 'CodedUITests1.cs' and select *Rename* as shown in Figure 2.12.

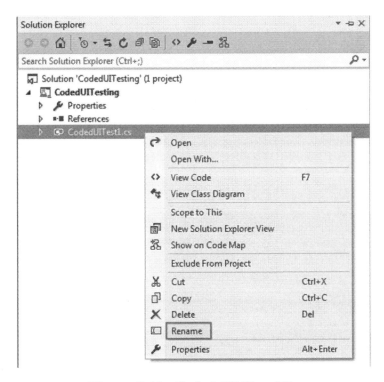

Figure 2.12: Coded UI Test File

- Type the name as 'WebUITests.cs' and press the [Enter] key.

- Select the *Yes* button to rename the class as shown in Figure 2.13.

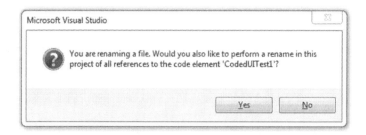

Figure 2.13: Rename - WebUITests File

- Select *File ⇒ Save All*.

☞ While working in Microsoft Visual Studio® it is a good practice to keep saving your work. Use ⎡Ctrl⎤ + ⎡S⎤ to *Save* the current file or use ⎡Ctrl⎤ + ⎡Shift⎤ + ⎡S⎤ to *Save All*.

Step 4: Setup the Repository Folder.

- In the *Solution Explorer*, right click on the *CodedUITesting* project and select *Add ⇒ New Folder* as shown in Figure 2.14.

- Type the *name* as 'Repository'.

Figure 2.14: Add Repository Folder

Step 5: Setup the Pages Folder.

Similarly add the *Pages* folder.

Step 6: Setup the Configuration File.

- In the *Solution Explorer*, right click on the *CodedUITesting* project and select *Add* ⇒ *Class...* as shown in Figure 2.15.

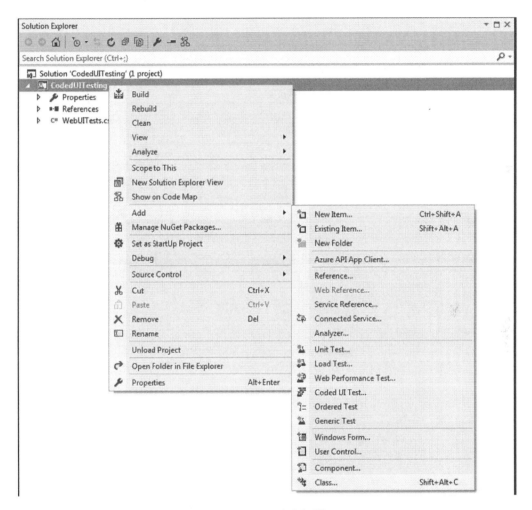

Figure 2.15: Add Class

- Type the *name* as 'Config.cs' as shown in Figure 2.16.
- Click the *Add* button.

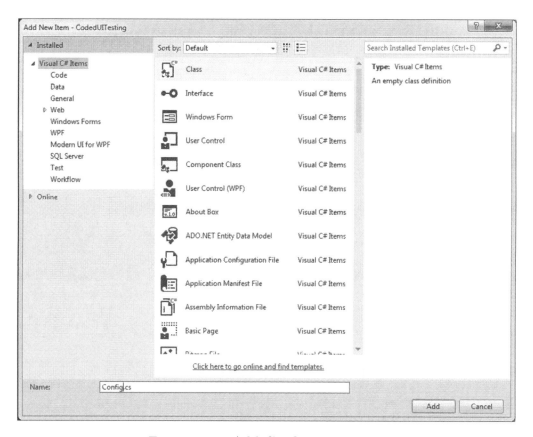

Figure 2.16: Add Configuration File

Step 7: Setup the Utility File.

Similarly add the 'Utility.cs' class.

Once all of the above steps have been completed successfully, the final *Solution Explorer* window will look like Figure 2.17.

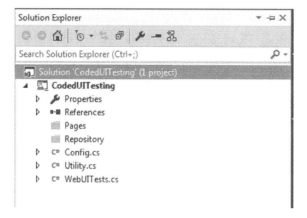

Figure 2.17: Solution Explorer Window

Our basic Coded UI project structure is complete now. We will add more components as we progress through the book.

2.6   Identifying UI Controls

As an Automation Tester, one of the important tasks that you have to perform is to identify UI Controls (also called Elements or Objects) in the Application Under Test. But why do we need to identify objects? Because we need to know which UI Controls need to be interacted with (as part of the Test Scenario) so that you can verify the outcome e.g. enter wrong credentials in the login screen and verify that an error response is generated. So let's learn how to identify these controls.

2.6.1   Coded UI Test Builder

In order to identify controls in the Application Under Test, we will use the *Coded UI Test Builder*.

- In the *Solution Explorer*, double click on the 'WebUITests.cs' file.

- Right click anywhere in the [TestMethod] and select *Generate Code for Coded UI Test ⇒ Use Coded UI Test Builder...* as shown in Figure 2.18.

- Or click anywhere in the [TestMethod] and select menu item *Test ⇒ Generate Code for Coded UI Test ⇒ Use Coded UI Test Builder...*

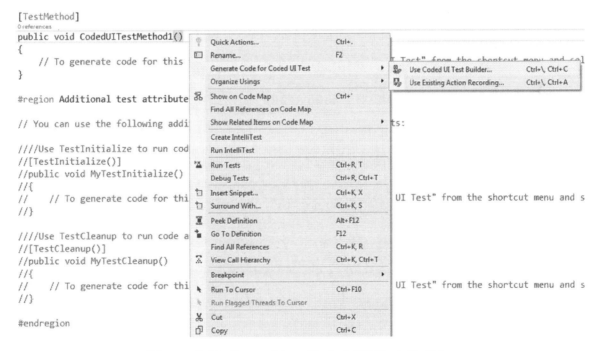

Figure 2.18: Launching Coded UI Test Builder

A new window will launch as shown in figure 2.19.

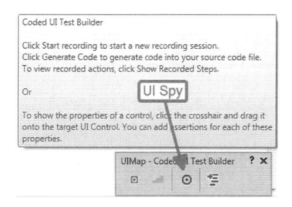

Figure 2.19: Coded UI Test Builder

 If we would have selected the *OK* button in Figure 2.11, this window would have appeared.

We will mainly use the *UI Spy* feature of the *Coded UI Test Builder* to identify UI Controls as we will not be performing any *Record and Playback* of actions.

2.6.2   UI Spy

Let me first of all show you how to identify the control 'User ID' in our demo website.

- Launch the Internet Explorer. I have used IE 11 for this example.

- Navigate to the Automation Portal URL `http://testing.arkenstone-ltd.com`.

- Click the *Login* link on the left hand side.

- Left click the *Circled Dot* icon (the *UI Spy* button) with your mouse (Step ①) and drag the *Crosshair* icon onto the 'User ID' control (Step ②) as shown in Figure 2.20

- Alternatively hover onto the 'User ID' control and press Shift + Ctrl + I .

- A *Control Properties* window will be displayed as shown for (Step ③). This window shows the properties of the UI Control we just spied on.

2.6.3   Control Properties

There are two columns on this *Control Properties* window namely - *Property* and *Value*. *Property* column is the name of the property e.g. `ControlType` and *Value* column is the value of that property e.g. `Edit`. We will use these properties to search for controls on the AUT and we can use any of these properties to search for a control.

An object's properties can fall into two categories namely - *Search Properties* and *Filter Properties*. If the object's *Technology* is `Web` then it can have both *Search* and

Filter Properties associated with it. However, for MSAA or UIA *Technology*, only *Search Properties* are available and are used for the object recognition.

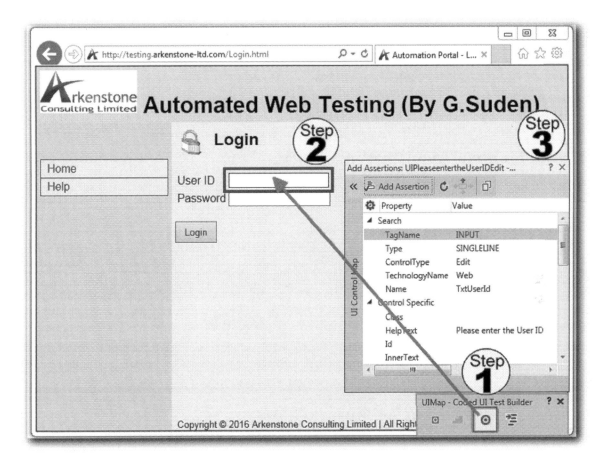

Figure 2.20: Identifying A UI Control

2.6.3.1 Search Properties

These are the set of properties that are used to search for a UI control. If an object can be uniquely identified by its 'Id' then we can use this as the *Search Property* and leave all the other Search and Filter properties for the object identification purpose. A *Property* name is used as a parameter to the SearchProperties class' Add method and the *Value* is also a parameter containing the value of that property name.

```
<UIControl>.SearchProperties.Add(
    UITestControl.PropertyNames.ControlType, "Edit");
```

2.6.3.2 Filter Properties

These are the set of properties that are used to identify a UI control when the *Search Properties* return multiple matches. *Filter Properties* are evaluated one by one in a sequential order. If an object cannot be identified based on one *Filter Property*, then that property is ignored and the Coded UI starts identifying the object based on the next *Filter Property*. A *Property* name is used as a parameter to the `FilterProperties` class' `Add` method and the *Value* is also a parameter containing the value of that property name.

```
<UIControl>.FilterProperties.Add(
    UITestControl.PropertyNames.FriendlyName, "Login");
```

2.6.4   Control Identification Mechanism

During the test execution, search for the control in question is triggered explicitly by a `Find()` method or implicitly by the usage of the control in an action (e.g. click the control) or property validation (e.g. check its value). The search mechanism used by Coded UI is *Breadth-First* which starts with finding the control under the container element. Coded UI first searches for the object having all the specified *Search Properties* using an `AND` operator. Three scenarios can take place during this search:

1. Search finds *no* control using the *Search Properties*.

2. Search finds only *one* control using the *Search Properties*.

3. Search finds *multiple* controls using the *Search Properties*.

When scenario 1 or 2 occurs, Coded UI skips using the *Filter Properties* (even if they are specified) because:

- For scenario 1, there are no controls to apply the *Filter Properties* to.

- For scenario 2, Coded UI has already found our control so there is no need to apply the *Filter Properties*.

However for scenario 3, where the properties specified in the *Search Properties* result in multiple controls, Coded UI uses the *Filter Properties*, one at a time, and repeats the search till it finds the resultant exact control. This can be referred to as an `OR` operation using the `Filter Properties`. In some cases, if Coded UI has exhausted all the *Filter Properties* (one-by-one) but still it can't find the exact one match, it will return the first match.

 Tip: If there is a *Filter Property* that can uniquely identify the object then make that property the *Search Property*.

Coded UI's Control Identification Mechanism is depicted in Figure 2.21.

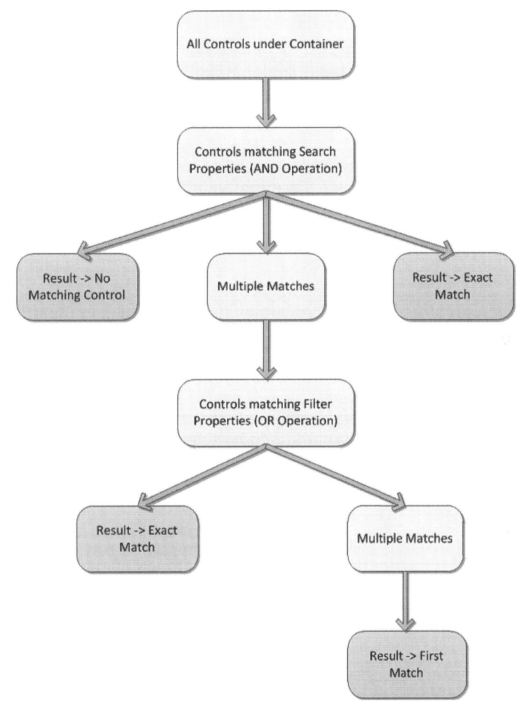

Figure 2.21: Control Identification Mechanism

Chapter 3

Web Based Application - UITestControls

Web Based Application - UITestControls

In this chapter, we will:

- *Learn about a typical 3-Tier Web Application Architecture*

- *Write our first automated Coded UI test using UITestControls*

- *Execute an automated Coded UI test*

- *Enable HtmlLogger to view important information about Coded UI test runs*

- *Add more tests to your test suite*

So let's get on with it...

A Web Application is an application that can be accessed by the users through a Web Browser. Figure 3.1 shows the implementation of a typical 3-Tier Web Application Architecture. Here is the sequence of events that take place when you want to access a website:

- You will be using a *Web Browser* such as Chrome or Firefox on your workstation.

- The *Page Request* of your entered web address is sent to the *Web Server* via your internet service provider.

- The *Web Server* fetches the required data from the *Database Server* e.g. fetch employee details.

- The *Web Server* renders and returns the requested *Web Page* to the *Web Browser* for display.

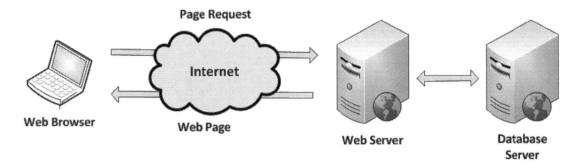

Figure 3.1: Typical Web Application Architecture

As per the famous saying *'An ounce of practice is worth more than tons of theory'*; so without delving into anything else, let's jump straight into writing our first automated Coded UI test and see the automation in action!

3.1 Your First Automated Test

We will perform the following Test Scenario to automate our first test:

- Launch the demo website.

- Click on the *Login* link.

- Login with the user 'Tester'.

- Close the demo website.

3.1.1 Creating The Configuration Parameters

First of all, let's add some configuration variables which we will need throughout our Automation Framework. Double click the 'Config.cs' file in *Solution Explorer* and add Listing 3.1 code to it.

> ☞ Sometimes the code statements we show in the listings may not fit into one line and may go beyond the textual limit of the page. Such code statements are shown with *Soft Returns* - as shown in Figure 3.2 - denoting that the code continues on the next line. This does not mean that you have to press the

key when writing the code in the editor, you can just carry on typing the statement in the same line.

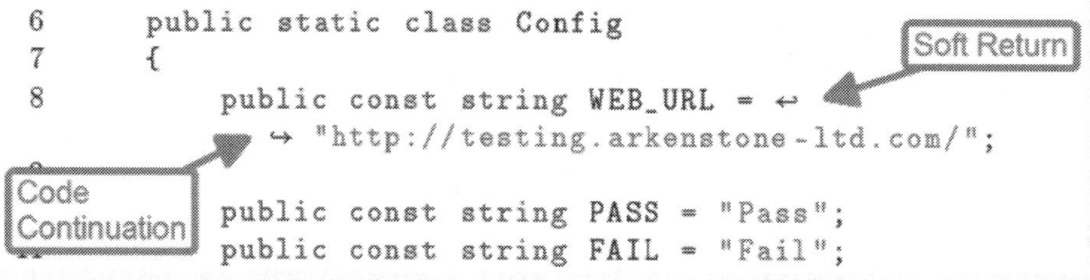

Figure 3.2: Soft Returns - Code Continuation

Listing 3.1: 'Config.cs' - Parameters file

```
1   /*****************************************************************
2    * All rights reserved. Copyright 2017 Arkenstone-ltd.com *
3    *****************************************************************/
4   namespace CodedUITesting
5   {
6       public static class Config
7       {
8           public const string WEB_URL = ↵
                 ↪ "http://testing.arkenstone-ltd.com/";
9
10          public const string PASS = "Pass";
11          public const string FAIL = "Fail";
12
13          public const int TIMEOUT_MILLISEC = 60000;
14
15          public const string UI_TESTCONTROL = ↵
                 ↪ "Microsoft.VisualStudio.TestTools.UITesting. ↵
                 ↪ UITestControl";
16      }
17  }
```

Let me explain the code:

◇ Line 4: The name of our namespace i.e. `CodedUITesting`.
◇ Line 6: Name of the class i.e. `Config`.
◇ Line 8: The URL of the Website Under Test.
◇ Lines 10 and 11: Define the `PASS` and `FAIL` configuration variables used throughout in the framework.

☞ It is a good practice to define such values as string constants because if you need to change their value later on, you can just change them in one place, 'Config.cs' file, and all the other automation code is automatically taken care of.

◈ Line 13: Timeout in milliseconds when waiting for a control to be ready for an action.
◈ Line 15: Defines a string constant for the `UITestControl`.

3.1.2 Defining The Browser Window

Double click the 'Utility.cs' file in *Solution Explorer* and add Listing 3.2 code to it.

Listing 3.2: 'Utility.cs' - Defining the Browser Window

```
1  /*****************************************************
2   * All rights reserved. Copyright 2017 Arkenstone-ltd.com *
3   *****************************************************/
4
5  using Microsoft.VisualStudio.TestTools.UITesting;
6
7  namespace CodedUITesting
8  {
9      public static class Utility
10     {
11         public static BrowserWindow Browser;
12     }
13 }
```

◈ Line 5: The keyword "`using`" states that we are using the
`Microsoft.VisualStudio.TestTools.UITesting` namespace in our program.
◈ Line 11: Defines a `public static Browser` object representing the Browser Window.

3.1.3 Building The Object Repository

We have already learnt that each technology (`Web`, `MSAA` or `UIA`) exposes a set of properties that can be used for control searches via Coded UI tests. In this chapter we will specifically use properties exposed by `UITestControls` only, so that you can get a better understanding of the properties available for automation using these controls.

Launch the *UI Spy* as follows:

- In the *Solution Explorer*, double click on the 'WebUITests.cs' file.

- Right click anywhere in the [`TestMethod`] and select *Generate Code for Coded UI Test* ⇒ *Use Coded UI Test Builder...* as shown in Figure 2.18.

- Or click anywhere in the [TestMethod] and select menu item *Test ⇒ Generate Code for Coded UI Test ⇒ Use Coded UI Test Builder...*

Please note down the following properties of the demo website's *Home* page:

☞ As we have learnt earlier, you can identify a control by one of the following two ways:

- Left click the *Circled Dot* icon (the *UI Spy* button) with your mouse and drag the *Crosshair* onto the UI control.

- Or hover onto the UI control and press [Shift] + [Ctrl] + [I] .

Home Page Controls			
Control	*Type*	*Property*	*Value*
Home	Hyperlink	TechnologyName	Web
		ControlType	Hyperlink
		FriendlyName	Home
Login	Hyperlink	TechnologyName	Web
		ControlType	Hyperlink
		FriendlyName	Login
Help	Hyperlink	TechnologyName	Web
		ControlType	Hyperlink
		FriendlyName	Help

And for the *Login* page as follows:

Login Page Controls			
Control	*Type*	*Property*	*Value*
User ID	EditBox	TechnologyName	Web
		ControlType	Edit
		Name	TxtUserId
Password	EditBox	TechnologyName	Web
		ControlType	Edit
		Name	TxtPassword
Login	Button	TechnologyName	Web
		ControlType	Button
		FriendlyName	Login
		Name	null (no value)

Let's start writing the code for the *Home* page's repository.

- In the *Solution Explorer*, right click on the *Repository* folder.

- Click *Add ⇒ Class...* as shown in Figure 3.3.

- Type the *Name:* as 'repUIHome.cs'.

- Click the *Add* button.

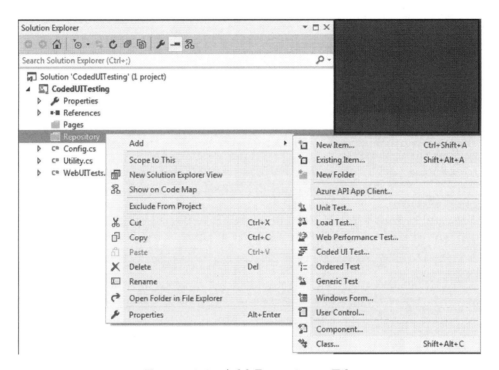

Figure 3.3: Add Repository File

Add Listing 3.3 code to it.

Listing 3.3: 'repUIHome.cs' - UITestControls Home page repository

```
1  /*************************************************************
2   * All rights reserved. Copyright 2017 Arkenstone-ltd.com *
3   *************************************************************/
4
5  using Microsoft.VisualStudio.TestTools.UITesting;
6
7  namespace CodedUITesting
8  {
9      public static class repUIHome
10     {
11         private static UITestControl mLink_Home;
12         private static UITestControl mLink_Login;
```

```
13          private static UITestControl mLink_Help;
14
15          public static UITestControl Link_Home
16          {
17              get
18              {
19                  if (mLink_Home == null ←
                        ↪ ||!mLink_Home.Exists)
20                  {
21                      mLink_Home = new ←
                            ↪ UITestControl(Utility.Browser);
22                      mLink_Home.TechnologyName = "Web";
23                      mLink_Home.SearchProperties.Add( ←
                            ↪ UITestControl.PropertyNames. ←
                            ↪ ControlType, "Hyperlink");
24                      mLink_Home.FilterProperties.Add( ←
                            ↪ UITestControl.PropertyNames. ←
                            ↪ FriendlyName, "Home");
25                  }
26                  return mLink_Home;
27              }
28          }
29
30          public static UITestControl Link_Login
31          {
32              get
33              {
34                  if (mLink_Login == null || ←
                        ↪ !mLink_Login.Exists)
35                  {
36                      mLink_Login = new ←
                            ↪ UITestControl(Utility.Browser);
37                      mLink_Login.TechnologyName = "Web";
38                      mLink_Login.SearchProperties.Add( ←
                            ↪ UITestControl.PropertyNames. ←
                            ↪ ControlType, "Hyperlink");
39                      mLink_Login.FilterProperties.Add( ←
                            ↪ UITestControl.PropertyNames. ←
                            ↪ FriendlyName, "Login");
40                  }
41                  return mLink_Login;
42              }
43          }
44
45          public static UITestControl Link_Help
```

```
46              {
47                  get
48                  {
49                      if (mLink_Help == null ||  ↵
                            ↪ !mLink_Help.Exists)
50                      {
51                          mLink_Help = new  ↵
                                ↪ UITestControl(Utility.Browser);
52                          mLink_Help.TechnologyName = "Web";
53                          mLink_Help.SearchProperties.Add(  ↵
                                ↪ UITestControl.PropertyNames.  ↵
                                ↪ ControlType, "Hyperlink");
54                          mLink_Help.FilterProperties.Add(  ↵
                                ↪ UITestControl.PropertyNames.  ↵
                                ↪ FriendlyName, "Help");
55                      }
56                      return mLink_Help;
57                  }
58              }
59          }
60  }
```

◈ Line 11: Defines a member variable `mLink_Home` for the *Home* Hyperlink. Note that we have declared this as a `private` member and will be accessible only within the body of the class.

◈ Lines 12 and 13: Similarly define member variables `mLink_Login` and `mLink_Help` for the *Login* and *Help* Hyperlinks respectively.

◈ Line 15: Defines the `Link_Home` *property* for the *Home* Hyperlink. Note that we have declared the property with scope `public` therefore it will be accessible outside the body of the class.

◈ Line 17: Defines the `get` accessor method to retrieve the value of the `Link_Home` property. So whenever we reference this property in our code, the `get` accessor will be invoked to read the value of the property.

◈ Line 19: Ensures that `mLink_Home` is `null` or doesn't exist.

◈ Line 21: Initialises a new instance of the `UITestControl` class with the search limitation of `Utility.Browser` window.

◈ Line 22: Sets the `TechnologyName` of the UI Control as noted earlier.

◈ Line 23: Sets the `SearchProperties` of the UI Control as noted earlier. Please note that we have used a strongly typed property name i.e. `UITestControl.PropertyNames.ControlType` of the `UITestControl`. You can use the value `"ControlType"` instead but it is always better to use a strongly typed property name.

◈ Line 24: Sets the `FilterProperties` of the UI Control as noted earlier. Again we have used a strongly typed property name i.e. `UITestControl.PropertyNames.FriendlyName` of the `UITestControl`.

◈ Line 26: The `get` accessor returns the member variable `mLink_Home` as it must return a value of the property type.

◈ Lines 30 and 45: Similarly define the `Link_Login` and `Link_Help` properties for the *Login* and *Help* Hyperlinks respectively and their `get` accessors.

Similarly add class named 'repUILogin.cs' and add Listing 3.4 code to it.

Listing 3.4: 'repUILogin.cs' - UITestControls Login page repository

```
 1  /****************************************************
 2   * All rights reserved. Copyright 2017 Arkenstone-ltd.com *
 3   ****************************************************/
 4
 5  using Microsoft.VisualStudio.TestTools.UITesting;
 6
 7  namespace CodedUITesting
 8  {
 9      public static class repUILogin
10      {
11          private static UITestControl mEditBox_Username;
12          private static UITestControl mEditBox_Password;
13          private static UITestControl mButton_Login;
14
15          public static UITestControl EditBox_Username
16          {
17              get
18              {
19                  if (mEditBox_Username == null || ↵
                        ↪ !mEditBox_Username.Exists)
20                  {
21                      mEditBox_Username = new ↵
                            ↪ UITestControl(Utility.Browser);
22                      mEditBox_Username.TechnologyName = ↵
                            ↪ "Web";
23                      mEditBox_Username.SearchProperties.Add( ↵
                            ↪ UITestControl.PropertyNames. ↵
                            ↪ ControlType, "Edit");
24                      mEditBox_Username.SearchProperties.Add( ↵
                            ↪ UITestControl.PropertyNames. ↵
                            ↪ Name, "TxtUserId");
25                  }
26                  return mEditBox_Username;
27              }
28          }
```

```
29
30        public static UITestControl EditBox_Password
31        {
32            get
33            {
34                if (mEditBox_Password == null || ↵
                   ↪ !mEditBox_Password.Exists)
35                {
36                    mEditBox_Password = new ↵
                       ↪ UITestControl(Utility.Browser);
37                    mEditBox_Password.TechnologyName = ↵
                       ↪ "Web";
38                    mEditBox_Password.SearchProperties.Add( ↵
                       ↪ UITestControl.PropertyNames. ↵
                       ↪ ControlType, "Edit");
39                    mEditBox_Password.SearchProperties.Add( ↵
                       ↪ UITestControl.PropertyNames. ↵
                       ↪ Name, "TxtPassword");
40                }
41                return mEditBox_Password;
42            }
43        }
44
45        public static UITestControl Button_Login
46        {
47            get
48            {
49                if (mButton_Login == null || ↵
                   ↪ !mButton_Login.Exists)
50                {
51                    mButton_Login = new ↵
                       ↪ UITestControl(Utility.Browser);
52                    mButton_Login.TechnologyName = "Web";
53                    mButton_Login.SearchProperties.Add( ↵
                       ↪ UITestControl.PropertyNames. ↵
                       ↪ ControlType, "Button");
54                    mButton_Login.SearchProperties.Add( ↵
                       ↪ UITestControl.PropertyNames. ↵
                       ↪ FriendlyName, "Login");
55                    mButton_Login.SearchProperties.Add( ↵
                       ↪ UITestControl.PropertyNames. ↵
                       ↪ Name, null);
56                }
57                return mButton_Login;
58            }
```

```
59            }
60        }
61  }
```

◈ Note that we have used only the `SearchProperties` to uniquely identify the controls therefore we don't need to specify the `FilterProperties`.

3.1.4 Utility Functions - Click And Set Text

Ok, by now we have defined the repository for the two pages. We will now need some generic functions to perform a few actions on these pages. These are:

Click - Clicks an object on the screen		
Input Parameters	*object*	Object to be clicked
Return Value	*void*	Returns nothing

SetValue - Sets the value of an object on the screen		
Input Parameters	*object*	Object whose value is to be set
	value	Value to be set
Return Value	*void*	Returns nothing

Since these are the generic functions, we need to update the 'Utility.cs' code as per Listing 3.5.

Listing 3.5: 'Utility.cs' - Utility functions Click and SetValue

```
1   /****************************************************************
2    * All rights reserved. Copyright 2017 Arkenstone-ltd.com *
3    ***************************************************************/
4
5   using Microsoft.VisualStudio.TestTools.UITesting;
6   using System;
7
8   namespace CodedUITesting
9   {
10      public static class Utility
11      {
12          public static BrowserWindow Browser;
13
14          public static void Click(Object obj)
15          {
16              switch (obj.GetType().ToString())
```

Chapter 3

```
17              {
18                  case Config.UI_TESTCONTROL:
19                      ((UITestControl)obj).WaitForControlExist( ←
                            ↪ Config.TIMEOUT_MILLISEC);
20                      ((UITestControl)obj).WaitForControlReady( ←
                            ↪ Config.TIMEOUT_MILLISEC);
21                      Console.WriteLine("Click ←
                            ↪ UITestControl: FriendlyName - " ←
                            ↪ + ←
                            ↪ ((UITestControl)obj).FriendlyName ←
                            ↪ + " (Name - " + ←
                            ↪ ((UITestControl)obj).Name + ←
                            ↪ ")");
22                      Mouse.Click((UITestControl)obj);
23                      break;
24
25                  default:
26                      Console.WriteLine("Error, Unknown ←
                            ↪ object type: " + ←
                            ↪ obj.GetType().ToString());
27                      break;
28              }
29          }
30
31          public static void SetValue(Object obj, String ←
                ↪ val)
32          {
33              switch (obj.GetType().ToString())
34              {
35                  case Config.UI_TESTCONTROL:
36                      ((UITestControl)obj).WaitForControlExist( ←
                            ↪ Config.TIMEOUT_MILLISEC);
37                      ((UITestControl)obj).WaitForControlReady( ←
                            ↪ Config.TIMEOUT_MILLISEC);
38                      Console.WriteLine("SetValue ←
                            ↪ UITestControl: FriendlyName - " ←
                            ↪ + ←
                            ↪ ((UITestControl)obj).FriendlyName ←
                            ↪ + " (Name - " + ←
                            ↪ ((UITestControl)obj).Name + ")" ←
                            ↪ + " Value: " + val);
39                      Keyboard.SendKeys((UITestControl)obj, ←
                            ↪ val);
40                      break;
41
```

```
42              default:
43                  Console.WriteLine("Error, Unknown ←
                    ↪ object type: " + ←
                    ↪ obj.GetType().ToString());
44                  break;
45              }
46          }
47      }
48 }
```

◈ Line 6: Additional import required for the types defined in other namespaces to support the new functionality.

◈ Line 14: Defines the `Click` function which accepts an object as an argument and returns a `void`.

◈ Line 16: Gets the `Type` of the current instance.

◈ Line 18: Checks if the object is of the `UITestControl Type`.

◈ Line 19: Waits for the control to exist for the configured amount of time. Note the implicit `cast` to convert the object to type `UITestControl`.

◈ Line 20: Waits for the control to be ready for the configured amount of time.

◈ Line 21: Logs some useful information about the object we are trying to click. This usually helps in debugging script issues. We will discuss more about logging in later chapters.

◈ Line 22: Clicks the object. Again note the implicit `cast` to convert the object to type `UITestControl`.

◈ Line 23: The `break` statement terminates the switch statement in which it appears. Control is passed to the statement that follows the terminated statement.

◈ Line 25: In the `switch` statement, if no `case` label contains a matching value, control is transferred to the `default` section where we log an error message.

◈ Line 31: Defines the `SetValue` function which accepts an object and its value as two arguments and returns a `void`.

◈ Line 39: Uses `Keyboard.SendKeys` to enter the value in the object.

3.1.5 Defining The Page Logic

Let's define the business logic for the *Home* page of our demo website which will have the following actions:

Action	Description
ClickHome()	This action will navigate to the *Home* page.
ClickLogin()	This action will navigate to the *Login* page.
ClickHelp()	This action will navigate to the *Help* page.

Let's start writing the code for the *Home* page actions.

- In the *Solution Explorer*, right click on the *Pages* folder.

- Click *Add* ⇒ *Class...*

- Type the *Name:* as 'pageUIHome.cs'.

- Click the *Add* button.

- Add Listing 3.6 code to 'pageUIHome.cs' file.

Listing 3.6: 'pageUIHome.cs' - UITestControls Home page logic

```
1  /********************************************************
2   * All rights reserved. Copyright 2017 Arkenstone-ltd.com *
3   ********************************************************/
4
5  namespace CodedUITesting
6  {
7      class pageUIHome
8      {
9          public void ClickHome()
10         {
11             Utility.Click(repUIHome.Link_Home);
12         }
13
14         public void ClickLogin()
15         {
16             Utility.Click(repUIHome.Link_Login);
17         }
18
19         public void ClickHelp()
20         {
21             Utility.Click(repUIHome.Link_Help);
22         }
23     }
24 }
```

◈ Line 9: Defines the `ClickHome` function.
◈ Line 11: Calls the generic Utility function `Click` with the repository item for the home hyperlink i.e. `repUIHome.Link_Home`.
◈ Line 14: Defines the `ClickLogin` function.
◈ Line 16: Calls the generic Utility function `Click` with the repository item for the login hyperlink i.e. `repUIHome.Link_Login`.

◈ Line 19: Defines the `ClickHelp` function.
◈ Line 21: Calls the generic Utility function `Click` with the repository item for the help hyperlink i.e. `repUIHome.Link_Help`.

Let's define the business logic for the *Login* page of our demo website which will have the following action:

Action	Description
`LoginUser()`	Action for the user login with given credentials.

Now let's write the code for the *Login* page's logic.

- In the *Solution Explorer*, right click on the *Pages* folder.
- Click *Add* ⇒ *Class...*
- Type the *Name:* as 'pageUILogin.cs'.
- Click the *Add* button.
- Add Listing 3.7 code to 'pageUILogin.cs'.

Listing 3.7: 'pageUILogin.cs' - UITestControls Login page logic

```
1  /****************************************************************
2   * All rights reserved. Copyright 2017 Arkenstone-ltd.com *
3   ****************************************************************/
4
5  namespace CodedUITesting
6  {
7      class pageUILogin
8      {
9          public void LoginUser(string uid, string pwd)
10         {
11             Utility.SetValue(repUILogin.EditBox_Username, ↵
                   ↪ uid);
12             Utility.SetValue(repUILogin.EditBox_Password, ↵
                   ↪ pwd);
13             Utility.Click(repUILogin.Button_Login);
14         }
15     }
16 }
```

◈ Line 9: Defines the `LoginUser` function which accepts two arguments - user id and password.

◈ Line 11: Calls the generic Utility function `SetValue` with the repository item for the user id edit box i.e. `repUIHome.EditBox_Username`.

◈ Line 12: Calls the generic Utility function `SetValue` with the repository item for the password edit box i.e. `repUIHome.EditBox_Password`.

◈ Line 13: Calls the generic Utility function `Click` with the repository item for the login button i.e. `repUIHome.Button_Login`.

3.1.6   Utility Functions - Browser Launch and Close

Almost there but before we can start writing the test, we need to define two more generic functions as follows:

LaunchWebApp - Launches the Web Application in the browser window		
Input Parameters	*none*	No arguments
Return Value	*void*	Returns nothing

CloseWebApp - Closes the Web Application i.e. the browser window		
Input Parameters	*none*	No arguments
Return Value	*void*	Returns nothing

Now add these new functions to the 'Utility.cs' file as shown in Listing 3.8

Listing 3.8: 'Utility.cs' - LaunchWebApp and CloseWebApp

```
1  public static void LaunchWebApp()
2  {
3      Browser = BrowserWindow.Launch(Config.WEB_URL);
4      Browser.Maximized = true;
5  }
6
7  public static void CloseWebApp()
8  {
9      if (Browser != null)
10         if (Browser.Exists)
11         {
12             Playback.Wait(2000);
13             Browser.Close();
14         }
15 }
```

◈ Line 1: Defines the `LaunchWebApp` function.
◈ Line 3: Launches the browser window with the configured web URL.
◈ Line 4: Maximises the browser window.
◈ Line 7: Defines the `CloseWebApp` function.
◈ Line 9: Ensures that the `Browser` is not `null`.
◈ Line 10: Ensures that the `Browser` window exists.
◈ Line 12: Ensures some breathing time (handling synchronisation issue).
◈ Line 13: Closes the browser window.

3.1.7 Writing The Test

Let's now start writing the code for the Test Scenario we defined in the beginning.

- In the *Solution Explorer*, open the 'WebUITests.cs' file by double clicking on it.

- Replace its code with one as shown in Listing 3.9.

Listing 3.9: 'WebUITests.cs' - WebUITesterLogin

```
1  /***********************************************************
2   * All rights reserved. Copyright 2017 Arkenstone-ltd.com *
3   ***********************************************************/
4
5  using Microsoft.VisualStudio.TestTools.UITesting;
6  using Microsoft.VisualStudio.TestTools.UnitTesting;
7
8  namespace CodedUITesting
9  {
10     [CodedUITest]
11     public class WebUITests
12     {
13         public WebUITests()
14         {
15         }
16
17         [TestInitialize()]
18         public void Initialize()
19         {
20         }
21
22         [TestMethod]
23         public void WebUITesterLogin()
24         {
25             Utility.LaunchWebApp();
26
```

```
27              pageUIHome Home = new pageUIHome();
28              Home.ClickLogin();
29
30              pageUILogin Login = new pageUILogin();
31              Login.LoginUser("Tester", "Tester123");
32
33              Utility.CloseWebApp();
34          }
35
36          public TestContext TestContext
37          {
38              get
39              {
40                  return testContextInstance;
41              }
42              set
43              {
44                  testContextInstance = value;
45              }
46          }
47          private TestContext testContextInstance;
48      }
49 }
```

◈ Lines 5 and 6: Imports required to support the functionality.

◈ Line 10: The *Attribute* [CodedUITest] tells the testing framework that the class supplies Coded UI tests and should be recognised as a testing extension.

◈ Line 18: The Initialize() method has the [TestInitialize()] *Attribute* applied to it, which tells the testing framework to call this method before running each test. We will learn more about this *Attribute* as we progress through the book.

◈ Line 22: The *Attribute* [TestMethod] precedes each test indicating that the method should be available in the execution list to perform a test. Therefore, if you don't precede a method with this *Attribute* then it won't appear in the list of tests to be executed.

◈ Line 23: The test method where we will code the Test Scenario.

◈ Line 25: Launches the Web Application.

◈ Line 27: Creates a new instance of the pageUIHome.

◈ Line 28: Clicks the *Login* link.

◈ Line 30: Creates a new instance of the pageUILogin.

◈ Line 31: Invokes the LoginUser function with the *Tester* user's credentials.

◈ Line 33: Closes the Web Application.

◈ Line 36: The TestContext is used to store information that is provided to the Coded UI tests such as the TestName, TestRunDirectory, TestResultsDirectory etc. We will learn how to use these properties in later chapters.

3.1.8   Executing the Test

Finally, we are ready to execute our first automated Coded UI test! Right click anywhere in the [TestMethod] WebUITesterLogin() and select *Run Tests* as shown in Figure 3.4.

Figure 3.4: Run Tests

After building the Coded UI test, the execution will start. Coded UI uses Internet Explorer as the default browser for test execution so you will see the demo website being launched using Internet Explorer. Once the execution is complete, you will see a *Test Explorer* window as shown in Figure3.5.

Click on the WebUITesterLogin test as shown for (Step ①) and then click on the *Output* link as shown for (Step ②).

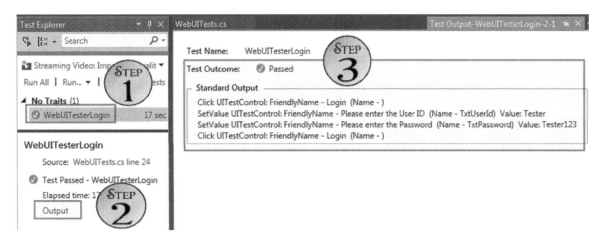

Figure 3.5: View Output

As shown for (Step ③), the *Test Outcome* is shown as Passed and the *Standard Output* window shows the log information that we added in our generic Utility methods.

3.2 Enabling HtmlLogger

Visual Studio® logs important information about your Coded UI test runs in the Html format. There are two ways to enable this logging as covered in the following subsections:

3.2.1 QTAgent32 Config File

For target .NET Framework version 4:

- Navigate to 'C:\Program Files (x86)\Microsoft Visual Studio 14.0\Common7\IDE' folder.

- Open the 'QTAgent32_40.exe.config' file in Notepad or any other text editor.

- Search for the string `"EqtTraceLevel"`. Set its value to "4" as shown below. Use "0" for *off*, "1" for *errors*, "2" for *warnings*, "3" for *info* and "4" for *verbose*.

```
<add name="EqtTraceLevel" value="4" />
```

- Save and close the file.

☞ Documentation on Microsoft's website states that if you are targeting .NET Framework version 4.5 then you need to update the 'QTAgent32.exe.config' file. I had .NET 4.5.2 and updating this file had no affect. However, updating the 'QTAgent32_40.exe.config' file worked fine.

Let's re-execute the test with the changes above. In the *Test Explorer* window, right click on the `WebUITesterLogin` and select *Run Selected Tests* as shown in Figure 3.6.

Figure 3.6: Re-execute Tests

Click on the *Output* link and then the *UITestActionLog.html* as shown in Figure 3.7.

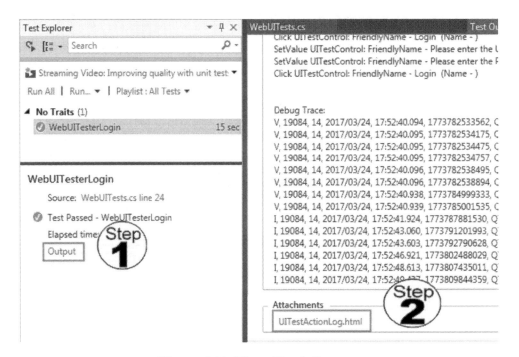

Figure 3.7: View Html Output

You will see an output window as shown in Figure 3.8 which lists each step that was performed during the test execution along with its image!

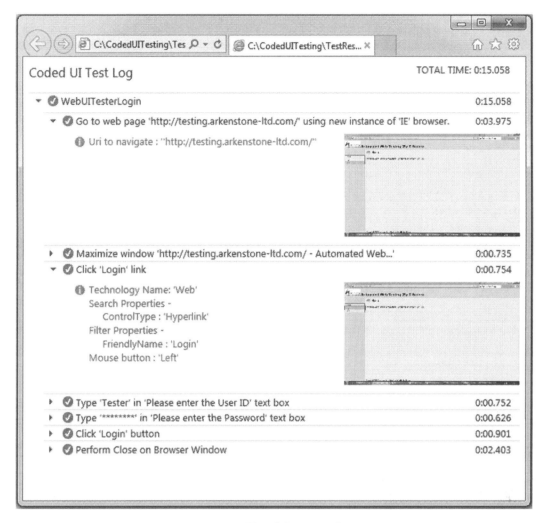

Figure 3.8: Html Logger Output

The html log files are stored in your project folder. In our case, the location of the test result folder will be 'C:\CodedUITesting\TestResults'. You will have to navigate through subfolders to reach the 'UITestActionLog.html' file from *Windows File Explorer*.

> ☞ For our demo purpose, we have used the *verbose* mode i.e. `"EqtTraceLevel" value="4"` which logs detailed information about the test run including a screenshot of each step. However, in the real life testing, you may want to use a lower option as this mode creates large log files and can slow down performance.

3.2.2 App.config File

Another way to enable the HtmlLogger is to add a configuration file 'App.config' to your *CodedUITesting* project.

Before we proceed further, please reopen the 'QTAgent32_40.exe.config' file and set the "EqtTraceLevel" value to "0".

- In the *Solution Explorer*, right click on the *CodedUITesting* project.

- Click *Add* ⇒ *New Item...*

- Scroll down to the *Application Configuration File* as shown in Figure 3.9.

- Click the *Add* button.

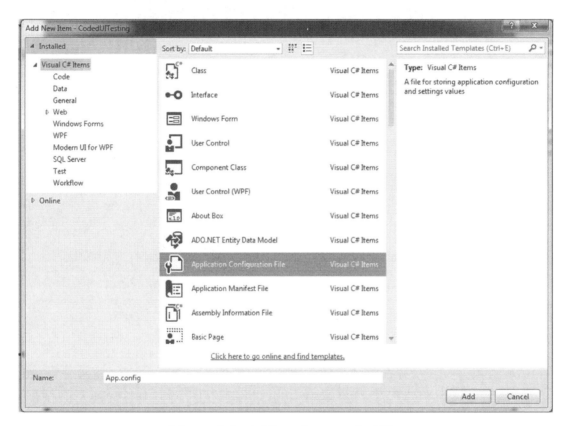

Figure 3.9: Adding App.config File

Add Listing 3.10 code to it.

Listing 3.10: 'App.config' - Set EqtTraceLevel value

```
1  <?xml version="1.0" encoding="utf-8" ?>
2  <configuration>
3    <system.diagnostics>
4      <switches>
5        <add name="EqtTraceLevel" value="4" />
6      </switches>
```

```
7    </system.diagnostics>
8  </configuration>
```

Let's re-execute the test with the changes above. In the *Test Explorer* window, right click on `WebUITesterLogin` and select *Run Selected Tests*.

☞ If the *Test Explorer* window is not visible, you can display it by selecting Visual Studio's menu item *Test ⇒ Windows ⇒ Test Explorer*, as shown in Figure 3.10.

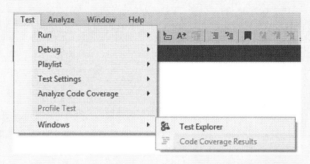

Figure 3.10: Test Explorer Window

Now, you should be able to follow the steps as shown in Figure 3.7 and view the Html log file as shown in Figure 3.8.

3.3 Adding More Tests

Let's perform the following Test Scenario for our next automated test:

- Launch the demo website.

- Click on the *Login* link.

- Login with the user 'Admin'.

- Close the demo website.

Open the 'WebUITests.cs' file by double clicking it in the *Solution Explorer*. Add Listing 3.11 code to it.

☞ To save time, just copy-paste the existing `WebUITesterLogin` test and make the required changes. Please ensure to precede it with the `[TestMethod]` *Attribute*.

```
1  [TestMethod]
2  public void WebUIAdminLogin()
3  {
4      Utility.LaunchWebApp();
5
6      pageUIHome Home = new pageUIHome();
7      Home.ClickLogin();
8
9      pageUILogin Login = new pageUILogin();
10     Login.LoginUser("Admin", "Admin123");
11
12     Utility.CloseWebApp();
13 }
```

◈ Line 10: Invokes the `LoginUser` function with the Admin user's credentials.

In order to execute this test, as we did before, right click anywhere in the `[TestMethod]` `WebUIAdminLogin()` and click *Run Tests*. Visual Studio® will then compile the Coded UI Tests and begin the test execution.

☞ Note that this new test won't appear in the *Test Explorer* window just after writing the code as the code hasn't been compiled yet. However, if the test has been run once (which automatically compiles the code), it will start appearing in the *Test Explorer* window. If you want the newly created test to appear in the *Test Explorer* window without executing it then in the *Solution Explorer*, right click on the *CodedUITesting* project and select *Rebuild* as shown in Figure 3.11. The test will now appear in the *Test Explorer* window.

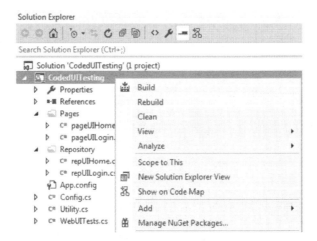

Figure 3.11: Rebuild Coded UI Project

3.4 Executing Multiple Tests

Usually during automated testing, you wouldn't execute tests one by one but as a set of tests together. You can select and execute multiple tests just by holding down the Ctrl key and clicking on the individual tests that you want to execute in the *Test Explorer* window. Alternatively, you can right click the grouping at the top level and select *Run Selected Tests* as shown in Figure 3.12. This will execute all the tests in the group i.e. `WebUIAdminLogin` and `WebUITesterLogin` in our case. Once the test execution is complete, you can click on individual tests followed by clicking on the *Output* link and then on the *UITestActionLog.html* link to view the html log. Note that each test will have its own html log file.

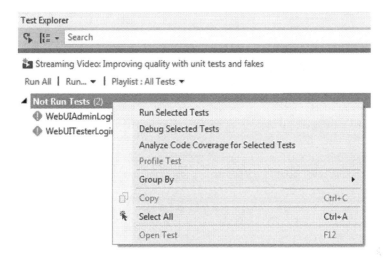

Figure 3.12: Executing Multiple Tests

Chapter 4

Web Based Application - HtmlControls

Web Based Application - HtmlControls

In this chapter, we will learn about how to:

- *Write automated Coded UI tests using HtmlControls*

- *Log useful information to the Standard Output window and CSV files during the test execution*

- *Save screenshots during the test execution*

- *Perform Negative automated testing*

- *Perform data entry and verification tasks on various types of HtmlControls controls on a web page*

- *Create a Test Result Summary file*

So let's get on with it...

I<small>N</small> the previous chapter we learnt about how to automate our login tests using the generic test controls only i.e. `UITestControls`. In this chapter, we will learn how to automate various tests using `HtmlControls` which are used to test the User Interface (UI) of Web pages.

4.1   Automate Using HtmlControls

We will perform the following Test Scenarios to demonstrate the use of `HtmlControls`:

Test Scenario 1

- Launch the demo website.

- Click on the *Login* link.

- Login with the user 'Tester'.

- Close the demo website.

Test Scenario 2

- Launch the demo website.

- Click on the *Login* link.

- Login with the user 'Admin'.

- Close the demo website.

4.1.1 Configuration Parameters

First of all, let's add some configuration variables which we will need throughout our Automation Framework. Double click the 'Config.cs' file in *Solution Explorer* and add Listing 4.1 code to it.

Listing 4.1: 'Config.cs' - Parameters for HtmlControls

```
1 public const string HTML_EDIT = ↵
    ↪ "Microsoft.VisualStudio.TestTools.UITesting. ↵
    ↪ HtmlControls.HtmlEdit";
2
3 public const string HTML_INPUT_BUTTON = ↵
    ↪ "Microsoft.VisualStudio.TestTools.UITesting. ↵
    ↪ HtmlControls.HtmlInputButton";
4
5 public const string HTML_HYPERLINK = ↵
    ↪ "Microsoft.VisualStudio.TestTools.UITesting. ↵
    ↪ HtmlControls.HtmlHyperlink";
```

◈ Line 1: Defines a string constant for the `HtmlEdit` control.
◈ Line 3: Defines a string constant for the `HtmlInputButton` control.
◈ Line 5: Defines a string constant for the `HtmlHyperlink` control.

4.1.2 Object Repository

Using *UI Spy*, please note down the following controls on the demo website's *Home* page:

Home Page Controls			
Control	***Type***	***Property***	***Value***
Home	Hyperlink	TechnologyName	Web
		ControlType	Hyperlink
		InnerText	Home
Login	Hyperlink	TechnologyName	Web
		ControlType	Hyperlink
		InnerText	Login
Help	Hyperlink	TechnologyName	Web
		ControlType	Hyperlink
		InnerText	Help

Similarly, note down the following controls on the *Login* page:

Login Page Controls			
Control	***Type***	***Property***	***Value***
User ID	EditBox	TechnologyName	Web
		ControlType	Edit
		Name	TxtUserId
Password	EditBox	TechnologyName	Web
		ControlType	Edit
		Name	TxtPassword
Login	Button	TechnologyName	Web
		ControlType	Button
		Display Text	Login

Let's start writing the repository code.

- In the *Solution Explorer*, right click on the *Repository* folder.

- Click *Add ⇒ Class...*

- Type the *Name:* as 'repHtmlHome.cs'.

- Add Listing 4.2 code to the 'repHtmlHome.cs' file.

Listing 4.2: 'repHtmlHome.cs' - Home page repository

```
1  /************************************************************
2   * All rights reserved. Copyright 2017 Arkenstone-ltd.com *
3   ************************************************************/
4
5  using ↵
       ↪ Microsoft.VisualStudio.TestTools.UITesting.HtmlControls;
6
7  namespace CodedUITesting
8  {
9      public static class repHtmlHome
10     {
11         private static HtmlHyperlink mLink_Home;
12         private static HtmlHyperlink mLink_Login;
13         private static HtmlHyperlink mLink_Help;
14
15         public static HtmlHyperlink Link_Home
16         {
17             get
18             {
19                 if (mLink_Home == null || ↵
                    ↪ !mLink_Home.Exists)
20                 {
21                     mLink_Home = new ↵
                        ↪ HtmlHyperlink(Utility.Browser);
22                     mLink_Home.SearchProperties.Add( ↵
                        ↪ HtmlHyperlink.PropertyNames. ↵
                        ↪ InnerText, "Home");
23                 }
24                 return mLink_Home;
25             }
26         }
27
28         public static HtmlHyperlink Link_Login
29         {
30             get
31             {
32                 if (mLink_Login == null || ↵
                    ↪ !mLink_Login.Exists)
33                 {
34                     mLink_Login = new ↵
                        ↪ HtmlHyperlink(Utility.Browser);
35                     mLink_Login.SearchProperties.Add( ↵
                        ↪ HtmlHyperlink.PropertyNames. ↵
                        ↪ InnerText, "Login");
36                 }
```

```
37                    return mLink_Login;
38                }
39            }
40
41        public static HtmlHyperlink Link_Help
42        {
43            get
44            {
45                if (mLink_Help == null || ←
                    ↪ !mLink_Help.Exists)
46                {
47                    mLink_Help = new ←
                        ↪ HtmlHyperlink(Utility.Browser);
48                    mLink_Help.FilterProperties.Add( ←
                        ↪ HtmlHyperlink.PropertyNames. ←
                        ↪ InnerText, "Help");
49                }
50                return mLink_Help;
51            }
52        }
53    }
54 }
```

◈ Note that all the controls are of type **HtmlControls** i.e. **HtmlHyperlink**.

Similarly add a new class 'repHtmlLogin.cs' to the *Repository* folder and add Listing 4.3 code to it.

Listing 4.3: 'repHtmlLogin.cs' - Login page repository

```
1  /**********************************************************
2   * All rights reserved. Copyright 2017 Arkenstone-ltd.com *
3   **********************************************************/
4
5  using ←
      ↪ Microsoft.VisualStudio.TestTools.UITesting.HtmlControls;
6
7  namespace CodedUITesting
8  {
9      public static class repHtmlLogin
10     {
11         private static HtmlEdit mEditBox_Username;
12         private static HtmlEdit mEditBox_Password;
13         private static HtmlInputButton mButton_Login;
```

```
14
15      public static HtmlEdit EditBox_Username
16      {
17          get
18          {
19              if (mEditBox_Username == null || ←
                    ↪ !mEditBox_Username.Exists)
20              {
21                  mEditBox_Username = new ←
                        ↪ HtmlEdit(Utility.Browser);
22                  mEditBox_Username.SearchProperties. ←
                        ↪ Add(HtmlEdit.PropertyNames. ←
                        ↪ Name, "TxtUserId");
23              }
24              return mEditBox_Username;
25          }
26      }
27
28      public static HtmlEdit EditBox_Password
29      {
30          get
31          {
32              if (mEditBox_Password == null || ←
                    ↪ !mEditBox_Password.Exists)
33              {
34                  mEditBox_Password = new ←
                        ↪ HtmlEdit(Utility.Browser);
35                  mEditBox_Password.SearchProperties. ←
                        ↪ Add(HtmlEdit.PropertyNames. ←
                        ↪ Name, "TxtPassword");
36              }
37              return mEditBox_Password;
38          }
39      }
40
41      public static HtmlInputButton Button_Login
42      {
43          get
44          {
45              if (mButton_Login == null || ←
                    ↪ !mButton_Login.Exists)
46              {
47                  mButton_Login = new ←
                        ↪ HtmlInputButton(Utility.Browser);
48                  mButton_Login.SearchProperties. ←
```

```
                                ↪ Add(HtmlInputButton.PropertyNames. ↩
                                ↪ DisplayText, "Login");
49                      }
50                      return mButton_Login;
51                  }
52              }
53          }
54  }
```

☞ In the above repositories, we have defined the member variables and properties of type `HtmlControls` instead of the generic type `UITestControls`. For example, we have defined the username edit box (member variable `mEditBox_Username`) as type `HtmlEdit`. Also for the control of type `HtmlEdit`, `TechnologyName = "Web"` and `ControlType = "Edit"` is implicit so there is no need to specify these properties while defining the repository. The same is true for other `HtmlControls`.

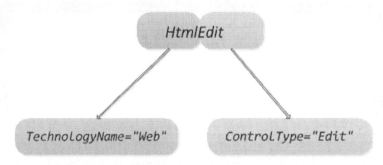

Figure 4.1: HtmlEdit Control

4.1.3 Utility Functions

We need to update our existing `Click()` function as per Listing 4.4 to take care of clicking the `HtmlInputButton` and `HtmlHyperlink` controls.

Listing 4.4: 'Utility.cs' - Updates to the Click() function

```
1  using ↩
     ↪ Microsoft.VisualStudio.TestTools.UITesting.HtmlControls;
2
3  case Config.HTML_INPUT_BUTTON:
4      ((HtmlInputButton)obj).WaitForControlExist( ↩
         ↪ Config.TIMEOUT_MILLISEC);
```

```
5     ((HtmlInputButton)obj).WaitForControlReady( ↵
          ↪ Config.TIMEOUT_MILLISEC);
6     Console.WriteLine("Click HtmlInputButton: Id - " + ↵
          ↪ ((HtmlInputButton)obj).Id + " (DisplayText - " ↵
          ↪ + ((HtmlInputButton)obj).DisplayText + ")");
7
8     Mouse.Click((HtmlInputButton)obj);
9     break;
10
11 case Config.HTML_HYPERLINK:
12     ((HtmlHyperlink)obj).WaitForControlExist( ↵
          ↪ Config.TIMEOUT_MILLISEC);
13     ((HtmlHyperlink)obj).WaitForControlReady( ↵
          ↪ Config.TIMEOUT_MILLISEC);
14     Console.WriteLine("Click HtmlHyperlink: Id - " + ↵
          ↪ ((HtmlHyperlink)obj).Id + " (DisplayText - " + ↵
          ↪ ((HtmlHyperlink)obj).InnerText + ")");
15
16     Mouse.Click((HtmlHyperlink)obj);
17     break;
```

◇ Line 1: Additional import required to support the functionality.

◇ Line 3: Additional **case** statement in the **Click()** function to handle **HtmlInputButton**.

◇ Line 11: Additional **case** statement in the **Click()** function to handle **HtmlHyperlink**.

Similarly we need to update our existing **SetValue()** function as per Listing 4.5 to take care of setting the text in **HtmlEdit** control.

Listing 4.5: 'Utility.cs' - Updates to the SetValue() function

```
1 case Config.HTML_EDIT:
2     ((HtmlEdit)obj).WaitForControlExist( ↵
          ↪ Config.TIMEOUT_MILLISEC);
3     ((HtmlEdit)obj).WaitForControlReady( ↵
          ↪ Config.TIMEOUT_MILLISEC);
4     Console.WriteLine("SetValue HtmlEdit: Id - " + ↵
          ↪ ((HtmlEdit)obj).Id + " (Name - " + ↵
          ↪ ((HtmlEdit)obj).Name + ")" + " Value: " + val);
5
6     ((HtmlEdit)obj).Text = val;
7     break;
```

◇ Line 1: Additional **case** statement in the **SetValue()** function to handle **HtmlEdit**.

4.1.4 Page Logic

The *Home* page of our demo website will have the following actions:

Action	Description
ClickHome()	This action will navigate to the *Home* page.
ClickLogin()	This action will navigate to the *Login* page.
ClickHelp()	This action will navigate to the *Help* page.

Add a new class 'pageHtmlHome.cs' to the *Pages* folder and add Listing 4.6 code to it.

Listing 4.6: 'pageHtmlHome.cs' - Page logic for the Home page

```
1   /************************************************************
2    * All rights reserved. Copyright 2017 Arkenstone-ltd.com *
3    ************************************************************/
4
5   namespace CodedUITesting
6   {
7       class pageHtmlHome
8       {
9           public void ClickHome()
10          {
11              Utility.Click(repHtmlHome.Link_Home);
12          }
13
14          public void ClickLogin()
15          {
16              Utility.Click(repHtmlHome.Link_Login);
17          }
18
19          public void ClickHelp()
20          {
21              Utility.Click(repHtmlHome.Link_Help);
22          }
23      }
24  }
```

◈ Lines 11, 16 and 21: Please ensure to use the correct html repository for the *Home* page i.e. **repHtmlHome**.

Let's define the business logic for the *Login* page of our demo website which will have the following action:

Action	Description
LoginUser()	Action for the user login with given credentials.

Add a new class 'pageHtmlLogin.cs' to the *Pages* folder and add Listing 4.7 code to it.

Listing 4.7: 'pageHtmlLogin.cs' - Page logic for the Login page

```
1  /****************************************************
2   * All rights reserved. Copyright 2017 Arkenstone-ltd.com *
3   ****************************************************/
4
5  namespace CodedUITesting
6  {
7      class pageHtmlLogin
8      {
9          public void LoginUser(string uid, string pwd)
10         {
11             Utility.SetValue(repHtmlLogin.EditBox_Username, ↵
                 ↪ uid);
12             Utility.SetValue(repHtmlLogin.EditBox_Password, ↵
                 ↪ pwd);
13             Utility.Click(repHtmlLogin.Button_Login);
14         }
15     }
16 }
```

◈ Lines 11, 12 and 13: Please ensure to use the correct html repository for the *Login* page i.e. `repHtmlLogin`.

4.1.5 Creating Tests

Let's start writing the code for the Test Scenarios that we defined in the beginning.

- In the *Solution Explorer*, right click on the *CodedUITesting* project.
- Click *Add* ⇒ *Class...*
- Type the *Name:* as 'WebHtmlTests.cs'.
- Add Listing 4.8 code to it.

```
1   /*******************************************************
2    * All rights reserved. Copyright 2017 Arkenstone-ltd.com *
3    *******************************************************/
4
5   using Microsoft.VisualStudio.TestTools.UITesting;
6   using Microsoft.VisualStudio.TestTools.UnitTesting;
7
8   namespace CodedUITesting
9   {
10      [CodedUITest]
11      public class WebHtmlTests
12      {
13          public WebHtmlTests()
14          {
15          }
16
17          [TestInitialize()]
18          public void Initialize()
19          {
20          }
21
22          [TestMethod]
23          public void WebHtmlTesterLogin()
24          {
25              Utility.LaunchWebApp();
26
27              pageHtmlHome Home = new pageHtmlHome();
28              Home.ClickLogin();
29
30              pageHtmlLogin Login = new pageHtmlLogin();
31              Login.LoginUser("Tester", "Tester123");
32
33              Utility.CloseWebApp();
34          }
35
36          [TestMethod]
37          public void WebHtmlAdminLogin()
38          {
39              Utility.LaunchWebApp();
40
41              pageHtmlHome Home = new pageHtmlHome();
42              Home.ClickLogin();
```

```
43
44              pageHtmlLogin Login = new pageHtmlLogin();
45              Login.LoginUser("Admin", "Admin123");
46
47              Utility.CloseWebApp();
48
49          }
50
51          public TestContext TestContext
52          {
53              get
54              {
55                  return testContextInstance;
56              }
57              set
58              {
59                  testContextInstance = value;
60              }
61          }
62          private TestContext testContextInstance;
63      }
64 }
```

4.1.6 Executing Tests

In the *Solution Explorer* right click on the *CodedUITesting* project and select *Rebuild* to compile all the tests.

In the *Test Explorer* window, right click on WebHtmlTests and select *Run Selected Tests* to execute WebHtmlTesterLogin and WebHtmlAdminLogin.

If the *Test Explorer* window is not visible, you can display it by selecting Visual Studio's menu item *Test ⇒ Windows ⇒ Test Explorer*.

☞ Note that I've used the *Group By Class* option for the *Test Explorer* as shown in Figure 4.2. If you have a different setting, you can multi-select tests WebHtmlTesterLogin and WebHtmlAdminLogin while holding down the Ctrl key. Now right click and select *Run Selected Tests*.

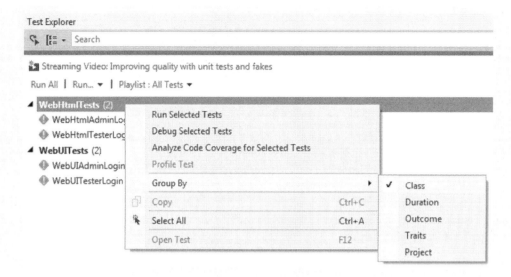

Figure 4.2: Coded UI Test Grouping

4.2 Logging Information

So far we have developed a simple Automation Framework which we have seen in action. Log generation is an important part of the test execution. It is very important to generate debug information at various points in a test. This information can help you identify problematic areas quickly and also reduce bug fixing time for developers.

In all the examples so far, the framework has used the 'Console.WriteLine' function for logging information. However, we need our framework to provide a robust logging mechanism so that we can log different types of messages e.g.

- Info i.e. informational messages

- Error i.e. error messages

- Debug i.e. debug messages

Logging different types of messages provides better control over the flow of the test script. We will use 'Apache log4net' as the mechanism for logging different types of messages since it is very easy to use. So let's see how to extend the Automation Framework to include logging. Please download 'Apache log4net' - a logging library for Microsoft® .NET from https://logging.apache.org/log4net/download_log4net.cgi

The book assumes that you have extracted the contents to the 'C:\log4net' folder.

4.2.1 Adding Necessary Reference

First of all let's add a required reference to our Automation Framework.

- In the *Solution Explorer* window, right click on the *References* folder and select *Add Reference...*

- Click on the *Browse...* button.

- Navigate to the 'C:\log4net\log4net-1.2.13\bin\net\4.0\release' folder. You may need to navigate to a different folder depending on the version you downloaded.

- Select the file 'log4net.dll' as shown in Figure 4.3.

- Click the *Add* button and then press *OK*.

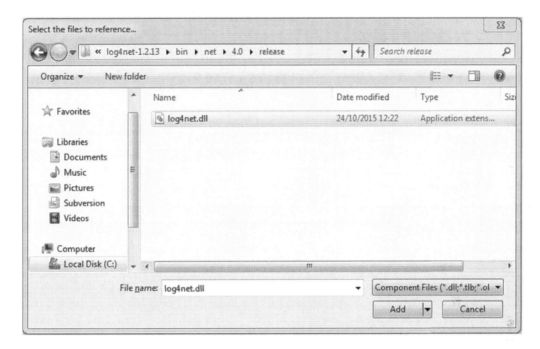

Figure 4.3: Add Log4net Reference

4.2.2 Configuration Parameters

Let's define a configuration parameter in the 'Config.cs' file as per Listing 4.9 which we will need later on.

Listing 4.9: 'Config.cs' - Configuration parameters for logging

```
1  public const string PROJECT_FOLDER = ↵
       ↪ @"C:\CodedUITesting\CodedUITesting\";
```

◈ Line 1: Defines a string constant for the project folder.

4.2.3 Logging to Standard Output Window

Firstly, let's use *log4net* to log our messages to the *Standard Output* window in Visual Studio®.

4.2.3.1   Updating Utility Functions

While we are there to update the 'Utility.cs' file for logging, there are two other important tasks our Automation Framework should be able to perform:

- Compare the Expected and Actual Result of a *Test Step* and report the outcome - either Pass or Fail.

- Report the final outcome of the *Test* - again either Pass or Fail.

Let us also add these two new features to the framework as well. We need to define two new functions in the Utility file as follows:

ReportExpectedVsActual - Reports the outcome of expected versus actual result comparison		
Input Parameters	*expResult*	Expected result
	actResult	Actual result
Return Value	*void*	Returns nothing

ReportResult - Reports the final outcome of the test		
Input Parameters	*void*	No parameters
Return Value	*void*	Returns nothing

Open the 'Utility.cs' file and make the changes as shown in Listing 4.10.

 Note that the listing shows the complete code of 'Utility.cs' file created so far along with the changes.

Listing 4.10: 'Utility.cs' - Changes for logging to the Standard Output Window

```
1  /************************************************************
2   * All rights reserved. Copyright 2017 Arkenstone-ltd.com *
3   ************************************************************/
4
5  using Microsoft.VisualStudio.TestTools.UITesting;
6  using ↵
      ↳ Microsoft.VisualStudio.TestTools.UITesting.HtmlControls;
7  using System;
8  using log4net;
9  using Microsoft.VisualStudio.TestTools.UnitTesting;
10
11 namespace CodedUITesting
12 {
13     public static class Utility
```

```
14      {
15          public static BrowserWindow Browser;
16          public static readonly ILog Log = ←
                ↪ LogManager.GetLogger(System.Reflection. ←
                ↪ MethodBase.GetCurrentMethod().DeclaringType);
17          public static string TestResult;
18          public static string TestName;
19
20          public static void Click(Object obj)
21          {
22              switch (obj.GetType().ToString())
23              {
24                  case Config.UI_TESTCONTROL:
25                      ((UITestControl)obj).WaitForControlExist( ←
                            ↪ Config.TIMEOUT_MILLISEC);
26                      ((UITestControl)obj).WaitForControlReady( ←
                            ↪ Config.TIMEOUT_MILLISEC);
27                      Log.Info("Click UITestControl: ←
                            ↪ FriendlyName - " + ←
                            ↪ ((UITestControl)obj).FriendlyName ←
                            ↪ + " (Name - " + ←
                            ↪ ((UITestControl)obj).Name + ←
                            ↪ ")");
28                      Mouse.Click((UITestControl)obj);
29                      break;
30
31                  case Config.HTML_INPUT_BUTTON:
32                      ((HtmlInputButton)obj).WaitForControlExist( ←
                            ↪ Config.TIMEOUT_MILLISEC);
33                      ((HtmlInputButton)obj).WaitForControlReady( ←
                            ↪ Config.TIMEOUT_MILLISEC);
34                      Log.Info("Click HtmlInputButton: Id - ←
                            ↪ " + ((HtmlInputButton)obj).Id + ←
                            ↪ " (DisplayText - " + ←
                            ↪ ((HtmlInputButton)obj).DisplayText ←
                            ↪ + ")");
35                      Mouse.Click((HtmlInputButton)obj);
36                      break;
37
38                  case Config.HTML_HYPERLINK:
39                      ((HtmlHyperlink)obj).WaitForControlExist( ←
                            ↪ Config.TIMEOUT_MILLISEC);
40                      ((HtmlHyperlink)obj).WaitForControlReady( ←
                            ↪ Config.TIMEOUT_MILLISEC);
```

```
41              Log.Info("Click HtmlHyperlink: Id - " ↵
                    ↪ + ((HtmlHyperlink)obj).Id + " ↵
                    ↪ (DisplayText - " + ↵
                    ↪ ((HtmlHyperlink)obj).InnerText + ↵
                    ↪ ")");
42              Mouse.Click((HtmlHyperlink)obj);
43              break;
44
45          default:
46              Log.Error("Error, Unknown object ↵
                    ↪ type: " + ↵
                    ↪ obj.GetType().ToString());
47              ReportExpectedVsActual("Error", "Not ↵
                    ↪ Implemented");
48              break;
49          }
50      }
51
52      public static void SetValue(Object obj, String val)
53      {
54          switch (obj.GetType().ToString())
55          {
56              case Config.UI_TESTCONTROL:
57                  ((UITestControl)obj).WaitForControlExist( ↵
                        ↪ Config.TIMEOUT_MILLISEC);
58                  ((UITestControl)obj).WaitForControlReady( ↵
                        ↪ Config.TIMEOUT_MILLISEC);
59                  Log.Info("SetValue UITestControl: ↵
                        ↪ FriendlyName - " + ↵
                        ↪ ((UITestControl)obj).FriendlyName ↵
                        ↪ + " (Name - " + ↵
                        ↪ ((UITestControl)obj).Name + ")" ↵
                        ↪ + " Value: " + val);
60                  Keyboard.SendKeys((UITestControl)obj, ↵
                        ↪ val);
61                  break;
62
63              case Config.HTML_EDIT:
64                  ((HtmlEdit)obj).WaitForControlExist( ↵
                        ↪ Config.TIMEOUT_MILLISEC);
65                  ((HtmlEdit)obj).WaitForControlReady( ↵
                        ↪ Config.TIMEOUT_MILLISEC);
66                  Log.Info("SetValue HtmlEdit: Id - " + ↵
                        ↪ ((HtmlEdit)obj).Id + " (Name - ↵
                        ↪ " + ((HtmlEdit)obj).Name + ")" + ↵
```

```
                                ↪ "  Value: " + val);
67                    ((HtmlEdit)obj).Text = val;
68                    break;
69
70                default:
71                    Log.Error("Error, Unknown object ↩
                          ↪ type: " + ↩
                          ↪ obj.GetType().ToString());
72                    ReportExpectedVsActual("Error", "Not ↩
                          ↪ Implemented");
73                    break;
74            }
75        }
76
77        public static void LaunchWebApp()
78        {
79            Browser = BrowserWindow.Launch(Config.WEB_URL);
80            Browser.Maximized = true;
81        }
82
83        public static void CloseWebApp()
84        {
85            if (Browser != null)
86                if (Browser.Exists)
87                {
88                    Playback.Wait(2000);
89                    Browser.Close();
90                }
91        }
92
93        public static void ReportExpectedVsActual(string ↩
              ↪ expected, string actual)
94        {
95            if (expected.Trim() == actual.Trim())
96            {
97                Log.Info("[Expected:] " + expected + " ↩
                      ↪       [Actual:] " + actual + "       ↩
                      ↪ [Step Passed]");
98            }
99            else
100            {
101                Log.Error("[Expected:] " + expected + " ↩
                      ↪       [Actual:] " + actual + "       ↩
                      ↪ [Step Failed]");
102                TestResult = Config.FAIL;
```

```
103                }
104            }
105
106        public static void ReportResult()
107        {
108            Log.Info("Reporting Result...... ");
109
110            if (TestResult.Equals(Config.FAIL))
111            {
112                Log.Error("Test Failed");
113                Assert.Fail("Test failed, please check ←
                    ↪ error log.");
114            }
115            else
116                Log.Info("Test Passed");
117        }
118    }
119 }
```

◈ Lines 8 and 9: Additional imports required to support the functionality.

◈ Line 16: Logger declaration which is used throughout the Automation Framework.

◈ Line 17: Test outcome declaration which is used throughout the Automation Framework.

◈ Line 18: Test name declaration which is used throughout the Automation Framework.

◈ Lines 27, 34, 41, 59 and 66: Change the `Console.WriteLine` calls to the new logger function `Log.Info` to display an **informational** message.

◈ Lines 46 and 71: Change the `Console.WriteLine` calls to the new logger function `Log.Error` to log an **error** message.

◈ Lines 47 and 72: Call to the generic function to report the outcome of comparison.

◈ Line 93: New function `ReportExpectedVsActual`.

◈ Line 95: Compares the expected result with the actual result which are passed as parameters to this function. Note the removal of leading and trailing spaces before the comparison is performed by using the `Trim()` function.

◈ Line 97: If the expected value matches the actual value, logs a `Step Pass` message along with the matching values.

◈ Line 101: If the expected value doesn't match the actual value, logs a `Step Fail` message along with the mismatched values.

◈ Line 102: Sets the `TestResult` configuration parameter's value to `Config.FAIL`.

◈ Line 106: New function `ReportResult`.

◈ Line 110: If the configuration parameter `TestResult` was set to fail in any of the *Test Step* comparisons then reports the final outcome of the *Test* as fail.

◈ Line 112: Logs a test fail error message.

◈ Line 113: Fails the assertion with a message.

◈ Line 116: Logs a test pass info message.

4.2.3.2 Creating The Configuration File

We now need to create a configuration file for the logger. Open the Notepad application (or any other text editor of your choice) and create a 'log4net.config' file in the 'C:\CodedUITesting\CodedUITesting' folder as shown in Listing 4.11.

Listing 4.11: 'log4net.config' - Code for the configuration file

```
1  <?xml version="1.0" encoding="utf-8" ?>
2  <log4net>
3    <appender name="Console" ↵
         ↪ type="log4net.Appender.ConsoleAppender">
4      <layout type="log4net.Layout.PatternLayout">
5        <conversionPattern value="%date{yyyy-MM-dd ↵
             ↪ HH:mm:ss.fff} %-5level %logger - ↵
             ↪ %message%newline" />
6      </layout>
7    </appender>
8    <root>
9      <level value="DEBUG" />
10     <appender-ref ref="Console" />
11   </root>
12 </log4net>
```

The 'log4net.config' file has three main components:

- **Appender** - is responsible for publishing the logging information to the preferred destination. We define the `appender` first with a name, which in our case is 'Console'. This is the name used to refer to the appender in the rest of the configuration file. The `type` method is used to choose which console stream to print messages to, which in our case is 'ConsoleAppender'.

- **Layout** - is responsible for formatting the logging information in the preferred style. The format of the result depends on the conversion pattern. For example, in our case we have used `%message%newline` which outputs the message followed by a new line character.

- **Logger** - is responsible for capturing the logging information to the desired appender. We have a 'root' logger that is configured to `level` 'DEBUG'. The appender 'Console' is attached to it. Since all loggers inherit from the 'root', all debug or higher messages from all the loggers will be printed to the 'Console' appender.

4.2.3.3 Adding Configuration File

We now need to add the 'log4net.config' file to the project as follows:

- In the *Solution Explorer* window, right click on the *CodedUITesting* project and select *Add ⇒ Existing Item...*

- Navigate to 'C:\CodedUITesting\CodedUITesting' folder.

- Ensure to select the filter *All Files (*.*)* as shown in Figure 4.4.

- Select the 'log4net.config' file.

- Click the *Add* button.

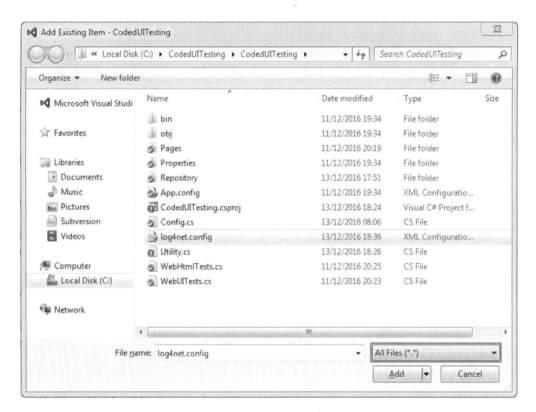

Figure 4.4: Add Log4net.config File

4.2.3.4   Updating Tests

Update the 'WebHtmlTests.cs' file as per Listing 4.12.

 Note that the listing shows the complete code of 'WebHtmlTests.cs' file along with the changes.

Listing 4.12: 'WebHtmlTests.cs' - Changes to support logging and error handling

```
1  /****************************************************************
2   * All rights reserved. Copyright 2017 Arkenstone-ltd.com *
3   ****************************************************************/
```

```
 4
 5  using Microsoft.VisualStudio.TestTools.UITesting;
 6  using Microsoft.VisualStudio.TestTools.UnitTesting;
 7  using System;
 8  using System.IO;
 9
10  namespace CodedUITesting
11  {
12      [CodedUITest]
13      public class WebHtmlTests
14      {
15          public WebHtmlTests()
16          {
17          }
18
19          [TestInitialize()]
20          public void Initialize()
21          {
22              Utility.TestResult = Config.PASS;
23              Utility.TestName = TestContext.TestName;
24              log4net.Config.XmlConfigurator. ↵
                  ↪ ConfigureAndWatch(new ↵
                  ↪ FileInfo(Config.PROJECT_FOLDER + ↵
                  ↪ "log4net.config"));
25          }
26
27          [TestMethod]
28          public void WebHtmlTesterLogin()
29          {
30           Utility.Log.Info("Starting Test ***** " + ↵
                  ↪ Utility.TestName + " *****");
31
32           try
33           {
34              Utility.LaunchWebApp();
35
36              pageHtmlHome Home = new pageHtmlHome();
37              Home.ClickLogin();
38
39              pageHtmlLogin Login = new pageHtmlLogin();
40              Login.LoginUser("Tester", "Tester123");
41
42              Utility.CloseWebApp();
43
44              Utility.ReportResult();
```

```
45          }
46          catch (Exception exception)
47          {
48              Utility.ReportExpectedVsActual(Utility.TestName, ↵
                    ↪ "Exception occurred");
49              Utility.Log.Error("Exception: " + ↵
                    ↪ exception.ToString());
50              throw exception;
51          }
52      }
53
54      [TestMethod]
55      public void WebHtmlAdminLogin()
56      {
57        Utility.Log.Info("Starting Test ***** " + ↵
              ↪ Utility.TestName + " *****");
58
59        try
60        {
61            Utility.LaunchWebApp();
62
63            pageHtmlHome Home = new pageHtmlHome();
64            Home.ClickLogin();
65
66            pageHtmlLogin Login = new pageHtmlLogin();
67            Login.LoginUser("Admin", "Admin123");
68
69            Utility.CloseWebApp();
70
71            Utility.ReportResult();
72        }
73        catch (Exception exception)
74        {
75            Utility.ReportExpectedVsActual(Utility.TestName, ↵
                  ↪ "Exception occurred");
76            Utility.Log.Error("Exception: " + ↵
                  ↪ exception.ToString());
77            throw exception;
78        }
79      }
80
81      public TestContext TestContext
82      {
83          get
84          {
```

```
85              return testContextInstance;
86          }
87          set
88          {
89              testContextInstance = value;
90          }
91      }
92      private TestContext testContextInstance;
93  }
94 }
```

◈ Lines 7 and 8: Additional imports required to support the functionality.

◈ Line 22: Sets the initial value of `Utility.TestResult` to *Pass* in the beginning of each test.

◈ Line 23: Sets the value of `Utility.TestName` from the `TestContext`.

◈ Line 24: Specifies the configuration file to be used for *log4net*.

◈ Lines 30 and 57: Log the starting of each test.

◈ Lines 32, 46, 59 and 73: Try-catch statements to handle any exception thrown during the test execution. Also log the exception string.

◈ Lines 44 and 71: Report the result at the end of each test.

4.2.3.5 Executing Tests

Rebuild and execute the tests. You will see an output as shown in Figure 4.5. The *Standard Output* window shows a date and timestamp for each test step. The test steps that were logged as `Log.Info` are displayed as INFO. The final outcome of the test is shown as Passed.

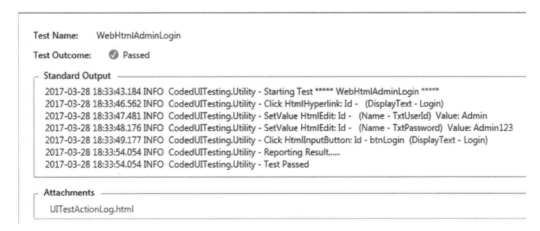

Figure 4.5: Standard Output Logging

4.2.4 Logging To A File

So far we have extended the Automation Framework to use our own logger to log additional information in the *Standard Output* window. However, it lacks one important feature which is the ability to save the test results to an output file (because the *Standard Output* window is overwritten as soon as you run the next set of tests and all of the information is lost).

We need all the test results to be saved automatically so that we can refer to them at a later stage for investigation purposes. Also, these results are your proof that the tests have been executed and can be used as evidence or for audit purposes. I personally log a lot of information for each test execution as it often proves to be very handy when you need to refer back to logs at a later stage. So, how do we extend our Automation Framework to automatically save logs at the end of the test execution? Here is how to save the *Standard Output* window information in a log file.

4.2.4.1 Updating Configuration File

Modify the 'log4net.config' file as shown in Listing 4.13.

Listing 4.13: 'log4net.config' - Updated code

```
1  <?xml version="1.0" encoding="utf-8" ?>
2  <log4net>
3    <appender name="Console" ↵
       ↳ type="log4net.Appender.ConsoleAppender" >
4      <layout type="log4net.Layout.PatternLayout">
5        <conversionPattern value="%date{yyyy-MM-dd ↵
           ↳ HH:mm:ss.fff} %-5level %logger - ↵
           ↳ %message%newline" />
6      </layout>
7    </appender>
8    <appender name="CsvFileAppender" ↵
       ↳ type="log4net.Appender.FileAppender">
9      <file value="C:\\CodedUITesting\\CodedUITesting\\ ↵
         ↳ DetailLog.csv" />
10     <appendToFile value="false" />
11     <lockingModel ↵
         ↳ type="log4net.Appender.FileAppender+MinimalLock" />
12     <layout type="log4net.Layout.PatternLayout">
13       <header value="DateTime, Level, Logger, ↵
           ↳ Message&#13;&#10;" />
14       <conversionPattern value="%date{yyyy-MM-dd ↵
           ↳ HH:mm:ss.fff}, %-5level, %logger, ↵
           ↳ %message%newline" />
15     </layout>
```

```
16   </appender>
17   <root>
18     <level value="DEBUG" />
19     <appender-ref ref="Console" />
20     <appender-ref ref="CsvFileAppender" />
21   </root>
22 </log4net>
```

Let's see what changes have been made to the 'log4net.config' file.

- We have defined a new `Appender` called `CsvFileAppender` that writes to a CSV file named 'DetailLog.csv'.

- We have set the append mode to `false` so that the file will be cleared before new records are written to it.

- We have created a header row for the log file.

- We are using a similar layout pattern as the *Standard Output* but with commas inserted after each field to facilitate the CSV file creation.

- Under 'Loggers', we have attached `CsvFileAppender` appender to the `root`.

- Since all the loggers inherit from the `root`, all trace or higher messages from our logger will be logged to the file.

4.2.4.2 The Log File

Rebuild and re-execute the tests. Navigate to the 'C:\CodedUITesting\CodedUITesting' folder. You will see a 'DetailLog.csv' file as shown in Figure 4.6.

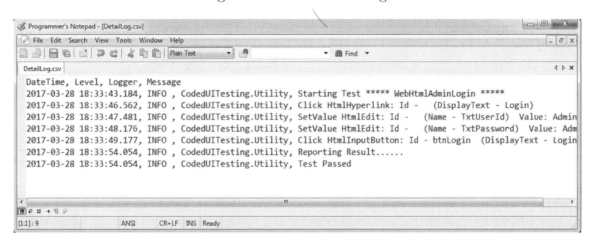

Figure 4.6: Log File - DetailLog.csv

If you are using Excel® to open the CSV file, you may have to format the first column i.e. DateTime as **'dd-mmm-yyyy hh:mm:ss.000'** to display it properly. Here are the steps to format this column:

- Select the *DateTime* column in Excel®.

- Right click and select *Format Cells...*

- In the *Number* Tab select *Custom* under *Category*.

- Specify the format under *Type* as 'dd-mmm-yyyy hh:mm:ss.00' as shown in Figure 4.7

- Click the *OK* button. The log entries should display properly in Excel® now!

Figure 4.7: Excel - Format DateTime

Now all of the runtime *Standard Output* information is also available in the 'DetailLog.csv' file. However, we still have the problem of this log file being overwritten every time a test is run. Therefore, we need to save a copy of this file after each test is executed. Let's see how to achieve this.

4.2.4.3 Configuration Parameters

First of all, add a new declaration to the 'Config.cs' file as shown in Listing 4.14.

Listing 4.14: 'Config.cs' - Add new declaration

```
1  public const string LOG_FILENAME = "DetailLog.csv";
```

◈ Line 1: Defines a string constant for the log file name. Note that its value is the same as what we have set in the 'log4net.config' file.

4.2.4.4 Utility Functions

Now we need to define a new generic function in the Utility file as follows:

SaveLogFile - Saves the log file		
Input Parameters	*none*	No parameter
Return Value	*filePathName*	Returns file pathname of the log file

Add Listing 4.15 code to the 'Utility.cs' file.

Listing 4.15: 'Utility.cs' - Code for SaveLogFile

```
1  public static class Utility
2  {
3      public static string TestResultFolder;
4
5      public static string SaveLogFile()
6      {
7          string sourceFile = Config.PROJECT_FOLDER + ↵
                ↪ Config.LOG_FILENAME;
8          string destFile = TestResultFolder + @"\" + ↵
                ↪ TestName + "(" + TestResult + ")" + ".csv";
9
10         System.IO.File.Copy(sourceFile, destFile, true);
11         System.IO.File.Delete(sourceFile);
12
13         return destFile;
14     }
15 }
```

◈ Line 3: Test Result Folder declaration which is used throughout the Automation Framework.

◈ Line 7: Constructs the source file pathname by combining the folder name with the log filename.

◈ Line 8: Constructs the destination file pathname by combining the Test Result Folder name, Test Name and Test Result with a 'CSV' file extension.

◈ Line 10: Copies the source file to the destination file where overwriting is allowed.

◈ Line 11: Deletes the source file.

◈ Line 13: Returns the destination file pathname string.

4.2.4.5 Updating Tests

Let's make some further modifications to the 'WebHtmlTests.cs' file as shown in Listing 4.16.

Listing 4.16: 'WebHtmlTests.cs' - changes for saving to a log file

```
1  [TestInitialize()]
2  public void Initialize()
3  {
4      Utility.TestResult = Config.PASS;
5      Utility.TestName = TestContext.TestName;
6      Utility.TestResultFolder = ↵
           ↪ TestContext.TestResultsDirectory;
7
8      log4net.Config.XmlConfigurator.ConfigureAndWatch(new ↵
           ↪ FileInfo(Config.PROJECT_FOLDER + ↵
           ↪ "log4net.config"));
9  }
10
11 [TestCleanup()]
12 public void Cleanup()
13 {
14     Utility.SaveLogFile();
15     Utility.CloseWebApp();
16     Playback.Cleanup();
17 }
```

◈ Line 6: Sets the value of `Utility.TestResultFolder` from the `TestContext`.

◈ Line 11: The *Attribute* `[TestCleanup()]` lists the method to be executed after each test has finished execution.

◈ Line 14: Saves the log file.

◈ Line 15: Note that although we have called the `CloseWebApp` function at the end of each test, we are also calling this function again in the `[TestCleanup()]`. This is to handle the case when there is an exception in the test run and the function is not executed, therefore ensuring to close the browser at the end of each test. Otherwise you may end up having too many open browser windows at the end of a test run.

◈ Line 16: Performs the clean-up operation after Coded UI test execution is complete.

4.2.4.6 Executing Tests

Rebuild and re-execute the tests. You will see a *Standard Output* window as shown in Figure 4.8 for the `WebHtmlAdminLogin` test. Under *Attachments*, in addition to the Html log file link, you will also see another link for the CSV log file. The name of the CSV file will be the test's name along with its result status - either Pass or Fail. Separate CSV log files are generated for each Coded UI test.

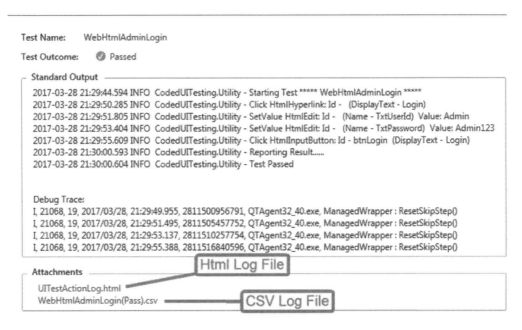

Figure 4.8: CSV Log File

4.3 Saving Screenshots

Sometimes you may not want to save screenshots for all the test steps but only for the errors. You can set the `EqtTraceLevel="1"` to achieve this. However, you may want to save a screenshot at an important event occurring in the frontend e.g. take a screenshot when a new order number is displayed. Let's enhance our Automation Framework to save a screenshot of the web page being displayed.

4.3.1 Configuration Parameters

First of all, add a new declaration to the 'Config.cs' file as shown in Listing 4.17.

Listing 4.17: 'Config.cs' - Changes for screenshot capture

```
1  public const string TEMP_FOLDER = ↵
       ↪ @"C:\CodedUITesting\temp";
```

◈ Line 1: Defines a string constant for the temporary folder location to store the screenshot(s).

4.3.2 Utility Functions

Let's now define two new functions in the Utility file as follows:

SaveScreenshot - Saves a screenshot of the current screen		
Input Parameters	*stg*	String to be used in the screenshot filename
Return Value	*void*	Returns nothing.

MoveScreenshots - Moves screenshots from the temporary location to the TestResultFolder		
Input Parameters	*none*	No parameter
Return Value	*void*	Returns nothing.

Let's make modifications in the 'Utility.cs' file to include the new functions as shown in Listing 4.18.

Listing 4.18: 'Utility.cs' - Changes to support the screenshot functionality

```
1  using System.IO;
2
3  public static void SaveScreenshot(string stg)
4  {
5      if (!Directory.Exists(Config.TEMP_FOLDER))
6      {
7          Directory.CreateDirectory(Config.TEMP_FOLDER);
8      }
9
10     System.Drawing.Image myImage = ↵
           ↪ UITestControl.Desktop.CaptureImage();
11     string scrshotFile = Config.TEMP_FOLDER + @"\" + ↵
           ↪ TestName + "_" + stg.Trim() + "_"+ ↵
           ↪ DateTime.Now.ToString("yyyy-MM-dd_HH_mm_ss") + ↵
           ↪ ".png";
12     myImage.Save(scrshotFile);
13     Log.Info("Screenshot saved at: " + scrshotFile);
14 }
15
16 public static void MoveScreenshots()
17 {
18     Log.Info("Source: " + Config.TEMP_FOLDER);
19     Log.Info("Destination: " + TestResultFolder);
20
21     string filePath = Config.TEMP_FOLDER;
22
23     DirectoryInfo myDir = new DirectoryInfo(filePath);
24     foreach (var file in myDir.GetFiles("*.png"))
25     {
```

```
26          Log.Info("Moving file: " + file);
27          System.IO.File.Move(Config.TEMP_FOLDER + @"\" + ↵
              ↪ file, TestResultFolder + @"\" + file);
28       }
29 }
```

◈ Line 1: Additional import required to support the functionality.

◈ Line 5: If the temporary folder doesn't exist then creates it.

◈ Line 10: Captures the desktop image.

◈ Line 11: Constructs the screenshot path filename with the Test Name including the string provided and current date and timestamp.

◈ Line 12: Saves the image with the path filename constructed above.

◈ Line 13: Logs the information about where the screenshot has been saved.

◈ Line 23: Initialises a new instance of the `DirectoryInfo` class on the temporary folder path.

◈ Line 24: Iterates through each image file in the temporary folder path.

◈ Line 27: Moves the image file from the temporary folder path to the `TestResultFolder`.

Ok, just one more change is needed in the 'Utility.cs' file as shown in Listing 4.19 before we are ready!

Listing 4.19: 'Utility.cs' - Changes to support the screenshot functionality

```
1 public static void ReportExpectedVsActual(string ↵
     ↪ expected, string actual)
2 {
3    if (expected.Trim() == actual.Trim())
4    {
5       Log.Info("[Expected:] " + expected + "          ↵
          ↪ [Actual:] " + actual + "        [Step Passed]");
6    }
7    else
8    {
9       Log.Error("[Expected:] " + expected + "          ↵
          ↪ [Actual:] " + actual + "        [Step Failed]");
10      TestResult = Config.FAIL;
11      SaveScreenshot(Config.FAIL);
12   }
13 }
```

◈ Line 11: For a failed test step, saves a screenshot with the string "Fail" included in the filename.

4.3.3 Updating Tests

Since the test result folder is not finalised until clean-up is performed, let's move the screenshots to the test result folder before the clean-up operation. Update the `Cleanup` function in the 'WebHtmlTests.cs' file as shown in Listing 4.20.

Listing 4.20: 'WebHtmlTests.cs' - Move screenshots to the test result folder

```
1  [TestCleanup()]
2  public void Cleanup()
3  {
4      Utility.MoveScreenshots();
5      Utility.SaveLogFile();
6      Utility.CloseWebApp();
7      Playback.Cleanup();
8  }
```

◈ Line 4: Calls the generic function to move screenshots to the test result folder.

4.3.4 Capturing An Event

Let's take a screenshot of an event taking place during the test execution e.g. take a screenshot of the *Home* page before you click the *Login* link so that you get an audit point of the website's version number. Let's modify the `ClickLogin` function in the 'pageHtmlHome.cs' file to implement this as shown in Listing 4.21.

Listing 4.21: 'pageHtmlHome.cs' - Take a screenshot of the Home page

```
1  public void ClickLogin()
2  {
3      Utility.SaveScreenshot("Home");
4      Utility.Click(repHtmlHome.Link_Login);
5  }
```

◈ Line 3: Takes a screenshot of the *Home* page before clicking the *Login* link. Note the string "Home" passed as a parameter which will be used when constructing the screenshot filename.

Rebuild and execute the test `WebHtmlTesterLogin` and you will see an output as shown in Figure 4.9. This time along with the Html and CSV log files, we also get a link to the screenshot of the *Home* page.

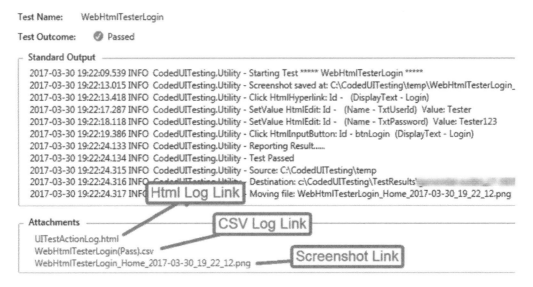

Figure 4.9: Capturing An Event

4.3.5 Capturing A Test Step Failure

A test step can fail when the *expected* value doesn't match the *actual* value during a call to the generic function `ReportExpectedVsActual`. In order to demonstrate a test step failure, let us perform the following Test Scenario:

- Launch the demo website.

- Verify that the browser window's `Uri` is `http://testing.arkenstone-ltd.com/`. However, in order to fail this test step we will compare it with a wrong `Uri` i.e. `http://arkenstone-ltd.com/` and see our test step failing. Ensure that a screenshot is automatically saved to capture the step failure.

- Click on the *Login* link.

- Login with the user 'Tester'.

- Close the demo website.

Update the `LaunchWebApp` function in the 'Utility.cs' file as shown in Listing 4.22

Listing 4.22: 'Utility.cs' - LaunchWebApp with a wrong Uri check

```
1 public static void LaunchWebApp()
2 {
3     Browser = BrowserWindow.Launch(Config.WEB_URL);
4     Browser.Maximized = true;
5
```

```
6   ReportExpectedVsActual("http://arkenstone-ltd.com/", ↵
        ↪ Browser.Uri.ToString());
7   }
```

◈ Line 6: Compares browser window's `Uri` with `http://arkenstone-ltd.com/` i.e. the wrong Uri. This step will fail resulting in overall test failure.

Rebuild and execute the test `WebHtmlTesterLogin` and you will see an output as shown in Figure 4.10. As expected, the test step fails and saves a desktop screenshot at the time of failure.

Test Name: WebHtmlTesterLogin

Test Outcome: ⊗ Failed

Message: Assert.Fail failed. Test failed, please check error log.

```
┌─ Standard Output ─────────────────────────────────────────────────────────────────
  2017-03-29 22:07:06.290 INFO  CodedUITesting.Utility - Starting Test **** WebHtmlTesterLogin ****
  2017-03-29 22:07:10.408 ERROR CodedUITesting.Utility - [Expected:] http://arkenstone-ltd.com/    [Actual:] http://testing.arkenstone-ltd.com/    [Step Failed]
  2017-03-29 22:07:10.558 INFO  CodedUITesting.Utility - Screenshot saved at: C:\CodedUITesting\temp\WebHtmlTesterLogin_Fail_2017-03-29_22_07_10.png
  2017-03-29 22:07:11.407 INFO  CodedUITesting.Utility - Click HtmlHyperlink: Id -  (DisplayText - Login)
  2017-03-29 22:07:16.486 INFO  CodedUITesting.Utility - SetValue HtmlEdit: Id -  (Name - TxtUserId)  Value: Tester
  2017-03-29 22:07:17.901 INFO  CodedUITesting.Utility - SetValue HtmlEdit: Id -  (Name - TxtPassword)  Value: Tester123
  2017-03-29 22:07:19.906 INFO  CodedUITesting.Utility - Click HtmlInputButton: Id - btnLogin  (DisplayText - Login)
  2017-03-29 22:07:24.984 INFO  CodedUITesting.Utility - Reporting Result.....
  2017-03-29 22:07:25.001 ERROR CodedUITesting.Utility - Test Failed
  2017-03-29 22:07:25.053 ERROR CodedUITesting.Utility - [Expected:] WebHtmlTesterLogin    [Actual:] Exception occurred    [Step Failed]
  2017-03-29 22:07:25.178 INFO  CodedUITesting.Utility - Screenshot saved at: C:\CodedUITesting\temp\WebHtmlTesterLogin_Fail_2017-03-29_22_07_25.png
  2017-03-29 22:07:25.199 ERROR CodedUITesting.Utility - Exception: Microsoft.VisualStudio.TestTools.UnitTesting.AssertFailedException: Assert.Fail failed. Test fa
    at Microsoft.VisualStudio.TestTools.UnitTesting.Assert.HandleFailure(String assertionName, String message)
    at Microsoft.VisualStudio.TestTools.UnitTesting.Assert.Fail(String message)
    at CodedUITesting.Utility.ReportResult() in c:\CodedUITesting\CodedUITesting\Utility.cs:line 118
    at CodedUITesting.WebHtmlTests.WebHtmlTesterLogin() in c:\CodedUITesting\CodedUITesting\WebHtmlTests.cs:line 52
```

Figure 4.10: Capturing A Test Step Failure

Now modify the `LaunchWebApp` function in 'Utility.cs' file as shown in Listing 4.23.

Listing 4.23: 'Utility.cs' - LaunchWebApp with a correct Uri check

```
1   public static void LaunchWebApp()
2   {
3       Browser = BrowserWindow.Launch(Config.WEB_URL);
4       Browser.Maximized = true;
5
6       ReportExpectedVsActual( ↵
            ↪ "http://testing.arkenstone-ltd.com/", ↵
            ↪ Browser.Uri.ToString());
7   }
```

◈ Line 6: Compares browser window's `Uri` with `"http://testing.arkenstone-ltd.com/` i.e. the correct Uri.

Rebuild and execute the test `WebHtmlTesterLogin` and this time the test should pass successfully.

4.3.6   Capturing A Test Failure

A test can fail when Coded UI encounters a problem during its execution e.g. an exception occurred. We already have covered this via the `try-catch` block in each test. Figure 4.11 shows a sample output when an exception was raised due to no internet connection and the test failed. The log file also records the exception string with a screenshot at the time of exception.

Figure 4.11: Capturing A Test Failure

4.4   Negative Tests - Login

So far we have considered only a positive scenario for the user login i.e. logging in with a valid user id and a valid password. There could be a number of negative scenarios like entering:

- Nothing in the User ID and the Password data entry fields and pressing the Login button.

- A valid User ID but no Password in the data entry fields and pressing the Login button.

- An invalid User ID but no Password in the data entry fields and pressing the Login button.

- Nothing in the User ID and a valid Password in the data entry fields and pressing the Login button.

- Nothing in the User ID and an invalid Password in the data entry fields and pressing the Login button.

- An invalid User ID and Password in the data entry fields and pressing the Login button.

- And so on...

In all these scenarios, the demo website displays appropriate error messages. Let's see how to perform these negative tests using Coded UI.

4.4.1   Configuration Parameters

Let's add some configuration variables which we will need throughout our Automation Framework. Double click on the 'Config.cs' file in the *Solution Explorer* and add Listing 4.24 code to it.

Listing 4.24: 'Config.cs' - Parameters for Error Messages

```
1  public const string HTML_SPAN = ↵
       ↪ "Microsoft.VisualStudio.TestTools.UITesting. ↵
       ↪ HtmlControls.HtmlSpan";
2
3  public const string USERID_MANDATORY_ERROR = "Error: User ↵
       ↪ ID is mandatory";
4
5  public const string PASSWORD_MANDATORY_ERROR = "Error: ↵
       ↪ Password is mandatory";
6
7  public const string INVALID_USERID_PASSWORD_ERROR = ↵
       ↪ "Error: Invalid User ID or Password";
```

◈ Line 1: Defines a string constant for the `HtmlSpan` control.
◈ Line 3: Defines a string constant to hold the value of User ID error message.
◈ Line 5: Defines a string constant to hold the value of Password error message.
◈ Line 7: Defines a string constant to hold the value of User ID or Password error message.

4.4.2   Object Repository

Let us identify additional error message controls on the *Login* page as shown in the table below:

Login Page Controls			
Control	*Type*	*Property*	*Value*
User ID	EditBox	TechnologyName	Web
		ControlType	Edit
		Name	TxtUserId
Password	EditBox	TechnologyName	Web
		ControlType	Edit
		Name	TxtPassword
Login	Button	TechnologyName	Web
		ControlType	Button
		Display Text	Login
User ID Err Msg[†]	Label/Span	TechnologyName	Web
		ControlType	Pane
		Id	LblUserIdError
Password Err Msg[†]	Label/Span	TechnologyName	Web
		ControlType	Pane
		Id	LblPasswordError

[†]New entries in the table.

Now double click the 'repHtmlLogin.cs' file in the *Solution Explorer* and add the additional code as shown in Listing 4.25.

Listing 4.25: 'repHtmlLogin.cs' - Additional repository controls for the Login page

```
1  private static HtmlSpan mSpan_UserIdError;
2  private static HtmlSpan mSpan_PasswordError;
3
4  public static HtmlSpan Span_UserIdError
5  {
6      get
7      {
8          if (mSpan_UserIdError == null || ←
              ↪ !mSpan_UserIdError.Exists)
9          {
10             mSpan_UserIdError = new ←
                 ↪ HtmlSpan(Utility.Browser);
11             mSpan_UserIdError.SearchProperties.Add( ←
                 ↪ HtmlSpan.PropertyNames.Id, ←
                 ↪ "LblUserIdError");
12         }
13         return mSpan_UserIdError;
14     }
```

```
15  }
16
17  public static HtmlSpan Span_PasswordError
18  {
19      get
20      {
21          if (mSpan_PasswordError == null || ←
                 ↪ !mSpan_PasswordError.Exists)
22          {
23              mSpan_PasswordError = new ←
                    ↪ HtmlSpan(Utility.Browser);
24              mSpan_PasswordError.SearchProperties.Add( ←
                    ↪ HtmlSpan.PropertyNames.Id, ←
                    ↪ "LblPasswordError");
25          }
26          return mSpan_PasswordError;
27      }
28  }
```

4.4.3   Utility Functions

Let's define a new generic function as follows:

GetValue - Gets the value of an object on the screen		
Input Parameters	*object*	Object whose value to get
Return Value	*string*	Returns object's value as a string

Add Listing 4.26 code to the 'Utility.cs' file.

Listing 4.26: 'Utility.cs' - Additional function GetValue

```
1  public static string GetValue(Object obj)
2  {
3      string retValue = null;
4
5      switch (obj.GetType().ToString())
6      {
7          case Config.HTML_SPAN:
8              ((HtmlSpan)obj).WaitForControlExist( ←
                    ↪ Config.TIMEOUT_MILLISEC);
9              ((HtmlSpan)obj).WaitForControlReady( ←
                    ↪ Config.TIMEOUT_MILLISEC);
```

```
10                Log.Info("GetValue HtmlSpan: Id - " + ↵
                      ↪ ((HtmlSpan)obj).Id + "  (Name - " + ↵
                      ↪ ((HtmlSpan)obj).Name + ")");
11                retValue = ((HtmlSpan)obj).InnerText;
12                break;
13
14          default:
15                Log.Error("Error, Unknown object type: " + ↵
                      ↪ obj.GetType().ToString());
16                ReportExpectedVsActual("Error", "Not ↵
                      ↪ Implemented");
17                break;
18      }
19
20      return retValue;
21 }
```

◈ Line 11: Returns `InnerText` of the `HtmlSpan` control.

4.4.4 Page Logic

In order to carry out the negative tests, the following actions will be affected:

Action	Description
`LoginUser()`	Action for the user login with given credentials.
`LoginWithInvalidDetails()`	Action for the user login with invalid credentials.

Update 'pageHtmlLogin.cs' code as shown in Listing 4.27.

Listing 4.27: 'pageHtmlLogin.cs' - Updated code

```
1  /*****************************************************
2   * All rights reserved. Copyright 2017 Arkenstone-ltd.com *
3   *****************************************************/
4
5  namespace CodedUITesting
6  {
7      class pageHtmlLogin
8      {
9          public void LoginUser(string uid, string pwd)
10         {
```

```
11        Utility.SetValue(repHtmlLogin.EditBox_Username, ↵
              ↪ uid);
12        Utility.SetValue(repHtmlLogin.EditBox_Password, ↵
              ↪ pwd);
13        Utility.Click(repHtmlLogin.Button_Login);
14
15        if (uid.Equals("") && pwd.Equals(""))
16        {
17            Utility.ReportExpectedVsActual( ↵
                  ↪ Config.USERID_MANDATORY_ERROR, ↵
                  ↪ Utility.GetValue(repHtmlLogin. ↵
                  ↪ Span_UserIdError));
18            Utility.ReportExpectedVsActual( ↵
                  ↪ Config.PASSWORD_MANDATORY_ERROR, ↵
                  ↪ Utility.GetValue(repHtmlLogin. ↵
                  ↪ Span_PasswordError));
19        }
20        else if (uid.Equals(""))
21        {
22            Utility.ReportExpectedVsActual( ↵
                  ↪ Config.USERID_MANDATORY_ERROR, ↵
                  ↪ Utility.GetValue(repHtmlLogin. ↵
                  ↪ Span_UserIdError));
23        }
24        else if (pwd.Equals(""))
25        {
26            Utility.ReportExpectedVsActual( ↵
                  ↪ Config.PASSWORD_MANDATORY_ERROR, ↵
                  ↪ Utility.GetValue(repHtmlLogin. ↵
                  ↪ Span_PasswordError));
27        }
28    }
29
30    public void LoginWithInvalidDetails(string uid, ↵
          ↪ string pwd)
31    {
32        Utility.SetValue(repHtmlLogin.EditBox_Username, ↵
              ↪ uid);
33        Utility.SetValue(repHtmlLogin.EditBox_Password, ↵
              ↪ pwd);
34        Utility.Click(repHtmlLogin.Button_Login);
35
36        Utility.ReportExpectedVsActual( ↵
              ↪ Config.INVALID_USERID_PASSWORD_ERROR, ↵
              ↪ Utility.GetValue(repHtmlLogin. ↵
```

```
                    ↪ Span_UserIdError));
37            }
38        }
39 }
```

◈ Line 15: If the User ID and Password are not entered then ensures that both the messages are displayed i.e. "Error: User ID is mandatory" and "Error: Password is mandatory".

◈ Line 20: Otherwise if the User ID is not entered then ensures that "Error: User ID is mandatory" message is displayed.

◈ Line 24: Otherwise if the Password is not entered then ensures that "Error: Password is mandatory" message is displayed.

◈ Line 30: New function to check login with invalid credentials.

◈ Line 36: Ensures that "Error: Invalid User ID or Password" message is displayed.

4.4.5 Creating Tests

Add new tests to the 'WebHtmlTests.cs' file as shown in Listing 4.28.

Listing 4.28: 'WebHtmlTests.cs' - Negative login tests

```
1  [TestMethod]
2  public void LoginWithBlankDetails()
3  {
4      Utility.Log.Info("Starting Test ***** " + ↵
           ↪ Utility.TestName + " *****");
5
6      try
7      {
8          Utility.LaunchWebApp();
9
10         pageHtmlHome Home = new pageHtmlHome();
11         Home.ClickLogin();
12
13         pageHtmlLogin Login = new pageHtmlLogin();
14         Login.LoginUser("", "");
15
16         Utility.CloseWebApp();
17
18         Utility.ReportResult();
19     }
20     catch (Exception exception)
21     {
```

```
22          Utility.ReportExpectedVsActual(Utility.TestName, ←
                ↪ "Exception occurred");
23          Utility.Log.Error("Exception: " + ←
                ↪ exception.ToString());
24          throw exception;
25      }
26  }
27
28  [TestMethod]
29  public void LoginWithValidUserOnly()
30  {
31      Utility.Log.Info("Starting Test ***** " + ←
            ↪ Utility.TestName + " *****");
32
33      try
34      {
35          Utility.LaunchWebApp();
36
37          pageHtmlHome Home = new pageHtmlHome();
38          Home.ClickLogin();
39
40          pageHtmlLogin Login = new pageHtmlLogin();
41          Login.LoginUser("Admin", "");
42
43          Utility.CloseWebApp();
44
45          Utility.ReportResult();
46      }
47      catch (Exception exception)
48      {
49          Utility.ReportExpectedVsActual(Utility.TestName, ←
                ↪ "Exception occurred");
50          Utility.Log.Error("Exception: " + ←
                ↪ exception.ToString());
51          throw exception;
52      }
53  }
54
55  [TestMethod]
56  public void LoginWithInvalidUserOnly()
57  {
58      Utility.Log.Info("Starting Test ***** " + ←
            ↪ Utility.TestName + " *****");
59
60      try
```

```
61          {
62              Utility.LaunchWebApp();
63
64              pageHtmlHome Home = new pageHtmlHome();
65              Home.ClickLogin();
66
67              pageHtmlLogin Login = new pageHtmlLogin();
68              Login.LoginUser("Administrator", "");
69
70              Utility.CloseWebApp();
71
72              Utility.ReportResult();
73          }
74          catch (Exception exception)
75          {
76              Utility.ReportExpectedVsActual(Utility.TestName, ↵
                    ↪ "Exception occurred");
77              Utility.Log.Error("Exception: " + ↵
                    ↪ exception.ToString());
78              throw exception;
79          }
80      }
81
82      [TestMethod]
83      public void LoginWithValidPasswordOnly()
84      {
85          Utility.Log.Info("Starting Test ***** " + ↵
                ↪ Utility.TestName + " *****");
86
87          try
88          {
89              Utility.LaunchWebApp();
90
91              pageHtmlHome Home = new pageHtmlHome();
92              Home.ClickLogin();
93
94              pageHtmlLogin Login = new pageHtmlLogin();
95              Login.LoginUser("", "Admin123");
96
97              Utility.CloseWebApp();
98
99              Utility.ReportResult();
100         }
101         catch (Exception exception)
102         {
```

```
103        Utility.ReportExpectedVsActual(Utility.TestName, ↵
            ↪ "Exception occurred");
104        Utility.Log.Error("Exception: " + ↵
            ↪ exception.ToString());
105        throw exception;
106    }
107 }
108
109 [TestMethod]
110 public void LoginWithInvalidPasswordOnly()
111 {
112    Utility.Log.Info("Starting Test ***** " + ↵
        ↪ Utility.TestName + " *****");
113
114    try
115    {
116        Utility.LaunchWebApp();
117
118        pageHtmlHome Home = new pageHtmlHome();
119        Home.ClickLogin();
120
121        pageHtmlLogin Login = new pageHtmlLogin();
122        Login.LoginUser("", "ggggg");
123
124        Utility.CloseWebApp();
125
126        Utility.ReportResult();
127    }
128    catch (Exception exception)
129    {
130        Utility.ReportExpectedVsActual(Utility.TestName, ↵
            ↪ "Exception occurred");
131        Utility.Log.Error("Exception: " + ↵
            ↪ exception.ToString());
132        throw exception;
133    }
134 }
135
136 [TestMethod]
137 public void LoginWithInvalidUserIdPassword()
138 {
139    Utility.Log.Info("Starting Test ***** " + ↵
        ↪ Utility.TestName + " *****");
140
141    try
```

```
142        {
143            Utility.LaunchWebApp();
144
145            pageHtmlHome Home = new pageHtmlHome();
146            Home.ClickLogin();
147
148            pageHtmlLogin Login = new pageHtmlLogin();
149            Login.LoginWithInvalidDetails("InvalidUser", ↵
                 ↪ "InvalidPwd");
150
151            Utility.CloseWebApp();
152
153            Utility.ReportResult();
154        }
155        catch (Exception exception)
156        {
157            Utility.ReportExpectedVsActual(Utility.TestName, ↵
                 ↪ "Exception occurred");
158            Utility.Log.Error("Exception: " + ↵
                 ↪ exception.ToString());
159            throw exception;
160        }
161 }
```

◇ Line 2: New test `LoginWithBlankDetails`.

◇ Line 14: Calls the Login function with no values.

◇ Line 29: New test `LoginWithValidUserOnly`.

◇ Line 41: Calls the Login function with a valid user id and no password.

◇ Line 56: New test `LoginWithInvalidUserOnly`.

◇ Line 68: Calls the Login function with an invalid user id and no password.

◇ Line 83: New test `LoginWithValidPasswordOnly`.

◇ Line 95: Calls the Login function with a valid password and no user id.

◇ Line 110: New test `LoginWithInvalidPasswordOnly`.

◇ Line 122: Calls the Login function with an invalid password and no user id.

◇ Line 137: New test `LoginWithInvalidUserIdPassword`.

◇ Line 149: Calls the Login function with an invalid user id and an invalid password.

4.4.6 Executing Tests

Rebuild and execute the tests in class `WebHtmlTests` and you will see a *Test Explorer* outcome as shown in Figure 4.12. The negative login tests written above are not an exhaustive list. You may want to write more negative tests based on the requirements that you are testing.

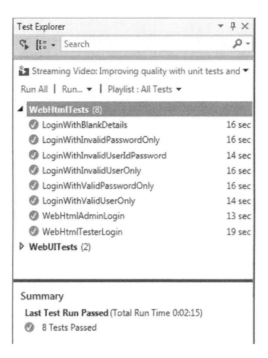

Figure 4.12: Negative Test Results Output

4.5   Data Entry - More HtmlControls

A web page usually contains different types of controls for user interaction. So far we have seen examples on how to interact with Edit Boxes, Command Buttons, Links and Labels (static text). In this section we will learn how to perform data entry tasks on three special types of controls:

- Drop-down ListBox - allows a user to select one item from a predefined list.

- RadioButton - represents a single choice within a limited set of mutually exclusive choices.

- CheckBox - allows a user to pick a combination of options (in contrast, a RadioButton control allows a user to choose from mutually exclusive options.)

We will perform the following Test Scenario to demonstrate the use of above `HtmlControls`:

- Launch the demo website.

- Click on the *Login* link.

- Login with the user 'Tester'.

- Click on the *Add Employee* link.

- Add a new employee.

- Take a screenshot after data entry.

- Log the user out.

4.5.1 Configuration Parameters

Let's define some new configuration parameters as shown in Listing 4.29 which we are going to need.

Listing 4.29: 'Config.cs' - Additional parameters

```
1 public const string HTML_COMBOBOX = ↵
      ↪ "Microsoft.VisualStudio.TestTools.UITesting. ↵
      ↪ HtmlControls.HtmlComboBox";
2 public const string HTML_RADIOBUTTON = ↵
      ↪ "Microsoft.VisualStudio.TestTools.UITesting. ↵
      ↪ HtmlControls.HtmlRadioButton";
3 public const string HTML_CHECKBOX = ↵
      ↪ "Microsoft.VisualStudio.TestTools.UITesting. ↵
      ↪ HtmlControls.HtmlCheckBox";
4
5 public const string TRUE = "True";
6 public const string FALSE = "False";
```

◈ Line 5: Defines a string constant to hold the value **"True"**.
◈ Line 6: Defines a string constant to hold the value **"False"**.

4.5.2 Object Repository

When you login as a Tester user, on successful login, the Tester's *Home* page is displayed with the following elements:

Tester's Home Page Controls			
Control	*Type*	*Property*	*Value*
Home	Hyperlink	TechnologyName ControlType InnerText	Web Hyperlink Home
Add Employee	Hyperlink	TechnologyName ControlType InnerText	Web Hyperlink Add Employee
View Employee	Hyperlink	TechnologyName ControlType InnerText	Web Hyperlink View Employee
Other	Hyperlink	TechnologyName ControlType InnerText	Web Hyperlink Other

Tester's Home Page Controls Contd...			
Control	**Type**	**Property**	**Value**
Drag-n-Drop	Hyperlink	TechnologyName ControlType InnerText	Web Hyperlink Drag-n-Drop
Logout	Hyperlink	TechnologyName ControlType InnerText	Web Hyperlink Logout

Add a new class 'repHtmlTesterHome.cs' to the *Repository* folder and insert the code as shown in Listing 4.30.

Listing 4.30: 'repHtmlTesterHome.cs' - Repository for the Tester's Home page

```
1  /***********************************************************
2   * All rights reserved. Copyright 2017 Arkenstone-ltd.com *
3   ***********************************************************/
4
5  using
       ↪ Microsoft.VisualStudio.TestTools.UITesting.HtmlControls;
6
7  namespace CodedUITesting
8  {
9      public static class repHtmlTesterHome
10     {
11         private static HtmlHyperlink mLink_Home;
12         private static HtmlHyperlink mLink_AddEmployee;
13         private static HtmlHyperlink mLink_ViewEmployee;
14         private static HtmlHyperlink mLink_Other;
15         private static HtmlHyperlink mLink_DragnDrop;
16         private static HtmlHyperlink mLink_Logout;
17
18         public static HtmlHyperlink Link_Home
19         {
20             get
21             {
22                 if (mLink_Home == null ||
                       ↪ !mLink_Home.Exists)
23                 {
24                     mLink_Home = new
                           ↪ HtmlHyperlink(Utility.Browser);
25                     mLink_Home.SearchProperties.Add(
                           ↪ HtmlHyperlink.PropertyNames.
```

```
                            ↪ InnerText, "Home");
26                  }
27                  return mLink_Home;
28              }
29          }
30
31          public static HtmlHyperlink Link_AddEmployee
32          {
33              get
34              {
35                  if (mLink_AddEmployee == null || ↵
                        ↪ !mLink_AddEmployee.Exists)
36                  {
37                      mLink_AddEmployee = new ↵
                            ↪ HtmlHyperlink(Utility.Browser);
38                      mLink_AddEmployee.SearchProperties.Add( ↵
                            ↪ HtmlHyperlink.PropertyNames. ↵
                            ↪ InnerText, "Add Employee");
39                  }
40                  return mLink_AddEmployee;
41              }
42          }
43
44          public static HtmlHyperlink Link_ViewEmployee
45          {
46              get
47              {
48                  if (mLink_ViewEmployee == null || ↵
                        ↪ !mLink_ViewEmployee.Exists)
49                  {
50                      mLink_ViewEmployee = new ↵
                            ↪ HtmlHyperlink(Utility.Browser);
51                      mLink_ViewEmployee.SearchProperties.Add( ↵
                            ↪ HtmlHyperlink.PropertyNames. ↵
                            ↪ InnerText, "View Employee");
52                  }
53                  return mLink_ViewEmployee;
54              }
55          }
56
57          public static HtmlHyperlink Link_Other
58          {
59              get
60              {
61                  if (mLink_Other == null || ↵
```

```
                    ↪ !mLink_Other.Exists)
62                  {
63                      mLink_Other = new ↵
                            ↪ HtmlHyperlink(Utility.Browser);
64                      mLink_Other.SearchProperties.Add( ↵
                            ↪ HtmlHyperlink.PropertyNames. ↵
                            ↪ InnerText, "Other");
65                  }
66                  return mLink_Other;
67              }
68          }
69
70          public static HtmlHyperlink Link_DragnDrop
71          {
72              get
73              {
74                  if (mLink_DragnDrop == null || ↵
                        ↪ !mLink_DragnDrop.Exists)
75                  {
76                      mLink_DragnDrop = new ↵
                            ↪ HtmlHyperlink(Utility.Browser);
77                      mLink_DragnDrop.SearchProperties.Add( ↵
                            ↪ HtmlHyperlink.PropertyNames. ↵
                            ↪ InnerText, "Drag-n-Drop");
78                  }
79                  return mLink_DragnDrop;
80              }
81          }
82
83          public static HtmlHyperlink Link_Logout
84          {
85              get
86              {
87                  if (mLink_Logout == null || ↵
                        ↪ !mLink_Logout.Exists)
88                  {
89                      mLink_Logout = new ↵
                            ↪ HtmlHyperlink(Utility.Browser);
90                      mLink_Logout.FilterProperties.Add( ↵
                            ↪ HtmlHyperlink.PropertyNames. ↵
                            ↪ InnerText, "Logout");
91                  }
92                  return mLink_Logout;
93              }
94          }
```

```
95        }
96 }
```

When you click on the *Add Employee* link, the *Add Employee* page is displayed with the following elements:

Add Employee Page Controls			
Control	*Type*	*Property*	*Value*
Title	ListBox	TechnologyName ControlType Name	Web ComboBox LbTitle
Name	EditBox	TechnologyName ControlType Id	Web Edit TxtName
Gender	RadioButton	TechnologyName ControlType Id Value	Web RadioButton RbGender male/female
Date of Birth	EditBox	TechnologyName ControlType Name	Web Edit TxtDOB
Email Address	EditBox	TechnologyName ControlType Name	Web Edit TxtEmail
Contract Job	CheckBox	TechnologyName ControlType Name	Web CheckBox CbContract
Postcode	EditBox	TechnologyName ControlType Id	Web Edit TxtPostcode
Add	Button	TechnologyName ControlType Id	Web Button btnAdd
Cancel	Button	TechnologyName ControlType DisplayText	Web Button Cancel

Add a new class 'repHtmlEmployeeDetail.cs' to the *Repository* folder and insert the code as shown in Listing 4.31.

```
1   /***************************************************
2    * All rights reserved. Copyright 2017 Arkenstone-ltd.com *
3    ***************************************************/
4
5   using ↵
        ↪ Microsoft.VisualStudio.TestTools.UITesting.HtmlControls;
6
7   namespace CodedUITesting
8   {
9       public static class repHtmlEmployeeDetail
10      {
11          private static HtmlComboBox mComboBox_Title;
12          private static HtmlEdit mEditBox_Name;
13          private static HtmlRadioButton ↵
                ↪ mRadioButton_GenderFemale;
14          private static HtmlRadioButton ↵
                ↪ mRadioButton_GenderMale;
15          private static HtmlEdit mEditBox_DateOfBirth;
16          private static HtmlEdit mEditBox_Email;
17          private static HtmlCheckBox mCheckBox_Contract;
18          private static HtmlEdit mEditBox_Postcode;
19          private static HtmlInputButton mButton_Add;
20          private static HtmlButton mButton_Cancel;
21
22          public static HtmlComboBox ComboBox_Title
23          {
24              get
25              {
26                  if (mComboBox_Title == null || ↵
                        ↪ !mComboBox_Title.Exists)
27                  {
28                      mComboBox_Title = new ↵
                            ↪ HtmlComboBox(Utility.Browser);
29                      mComboBox_Title.SearchProperties.Add( ↵
                            ↪ HtmlComboBox.PropertyNames. ↵
                            ↪ Name, "LbTitle");
30                  }
31                  return mComboBox_Title;
32              }
33          }
34
35          public static HtmlEdit EditBox_Name
```

```
36          {
37              get
38              {
39                  if (mEditBox_Name == null || ↵
                        ↪ !mEditBox_Name.Exists)
40                  {
41                      mEditBox_Name = new ↵
                            ↪ HtmlEdit(Utility.Browser);
42                      mEditBox_Name.SearchProperties.Add( ↵
                            ↪ HtmlEdit.PropertyNames.Id, ↵
                            ↪ "TxtName");
43                  }
44                  return mEditBox_Name;
45              }
46          }
47
48          public static HtmlRadioButton ↵
                ↪ RadioButton_GenderFemale
49          {
50              get
51              {
52                  if (mRadioButton_GenderFemale == null || ↵
                        ↪ !mRadioButton_GenderFemale.Exists)
53                  {
54                      mRadioButton_GenderFemale = new ↵
                            ↪ HtmlRadioButton(Utility.Browser);
55                      mRadioButton_GenderFemale. ↵
                            ↪ SearchProperties.Add( ↵
                            ↪ HtmlRadioButton.PropertyNames.Id, ↵
                            ↪ "RbGender");
56                      mRadioButton_GenderFemale. ↵
                            ↪ SearchProperties[ ↵
                            ↪ HtmlRadioButton.PropertyNames. ↵
                            ↪ Value] = "female";
57                  }
58                  return mRadioButton_GenderFemale;
59              }
60          }
61
62          public static HtmlRadioButton RadioButton_GenderMale
63          {
64              get
65              {
66                  if (mRadioButton_GenderMale == null || ↵
                        ↪ !mRadioButton_GenderMale.Exists)
```

```
67                        {
68                                mRadioButton_GenderMale = new ↵
                                    ↪ HtmlRadioButton(Utility.Browser);
69                                mRadioButton_GenderMale. ↵
                                    ↪ SearchProperties.Add( ↵
                                    ↪ HtmlRadioButton.PropertyNames.Id, ↵
                                    ↪ "RbGender");
70                                mRadioButton_GenderMale. ↵
                                    ↪ SearchProperties[ ↵
                                    ↪ HtmlRadioButton.PropertyNames. ↵
                                    ↪ Value] = "male";
71                        }
72                        return mRadioButton_GenderMale;
73                }
74        }
75
76        public static HtmlEdit EditBox_DateOfBirth
77        {
78            get
79            {
80                if (mEditBox_DateOfBirth == null || ↵
                        ↪ !mEditBox_DateOfBirth.Exists)
81                {
82                        mEditBox_DateOfBirth = new ↵
                            ↪ HtmlEdit(Utility.Browser);
83                        mEditBox_DateOfBirth.SearchProperties. ↵
                            ↪ Add(HtmlEdit.PropertyNames.Name, ↵
                            ↪ "TxtDOB");
84                }
85                return mEditBox_DateOfBirth;
86            }
87        }
88
89        public static HtmlEdit EditBox_Email
90        {
91            get
92            {
93                if (mEditBox_Email == null || ↵
                        ↪ !mEditBox_Email.Exists)
94                {
95                        mEditBox_Email = new ↵
                            ↪ HtmlEdit(Utility.Browser);
96                        mEditBox_Email.SearchProperties.Add( ↵
                            ↪ HtmlEdit.PropertyNames.Name, ↵
                            ↪ "TxtEmail");
```

```
 97                  }
 98                      return mEditBox_Email;
 99              }
100          }
101
102      public static HtmlCheckBox CheckBox_Contract
103      {
104          get
105          {
106              if (mCheckBox_Contract == null || ↵
                     ↪ !mCheckBox_Contract.Exists)
107              {
108                  mCheckBox_Contract = new ↵
                         ↪ HtmlCheckBox(Utility.Browser);
109                  mCheckBox_Contract.SearchProperties.Add( ↵
                         ↪ HtmlCheckBox.PropertyNames.Name, ↵
                         ↪ "CbContract");
110              }
111              return mCheckBox_Contract;
112          }
113      }
114
115      public static HtmlEdit EditBox_Postcode
116      {
117          get
118          {
119              if (mEditBox_Postcode == null || ↵
                     ↪ !mEditBox_Postcode.Exists)
120              {
121                  mEditBox_Postcode = new ↵
                         ↪ HtmlEdit(Utility.Browser);
122                  mEditBox_Postcode.SearchProperties.Add( ↵
                         ↪ HtmlEdit.PropertyNames.Id, ↵
                         ↪ "TxtPostcode");
123              }
124              return mEditBox_Postcode;
125          }
126      }
127
128      public static HtmlInputButton Button_Add
129      {
130          get
131          {
132              if (mButton_Add == null || ↵
                     ↪ !mButton_Add.Exists)
```

```
133                     {
134                         mButton_Add = new ↵
                              ↪ HtmlInputButton(Utility.Browser);
135                         mButton_Add.SearchProperties.Add( ↵
                              ↪ HtmlInputButton.PropertyNames.Id, ↵
                              ↪ "btnAdd");
136                     }
137                     return mButton_Add;
138                 }
139             }
140
141         public static HtmlButton Button_Cancel
142         {
143             get
144             {
145                 if (mButton_Cancel == null || ↵
                      ↪ !mButton_Cancel.Exists)
146                 {
147                     mButton_Cancel = new ↵
                          ↪ HtmlButton(Utility.Browser);
148                     mButton_Cancel.SearchProperties.Add( ↵
                          ↪ HtmlButton.PropertyNames.DisplayText, ↵
                          ↪ "Cancel");
149                 }
150                 return mButton_Cancel;
151             }
152         }
153     }
154 }
```

4.5.3 Utility Functions

We need to update our existing `Click()` function as per Listing 4.32 to take care of clicking the `HtmlRadioButton` control.

Listing 4.32: 'Utility.cs' - Extra case statement in the Click function

```
1 case Config.HTML_RADIOBUTTON:
2     ((HtmlRadioButton)obj).WaitForControlExist( ↵
          ↪ Config.TIMEOUT_MILLISEC);
3     ((HtmlRadioButton)obj).WaitForControlReady( ↵
          ↪ Config.TIMEOUT_MILLISEC);
4     Log.Info("Click HtmlRadioButton: Id - " + ↵
```

```
               ↪ ((HtmlRadioButton)obj).Id + "  (LabeledBy - " + ↵
               ↪ ((HtmlRadioButton)obj).LabeledBy + ")");
5      Mouse.Click((HtmlRadioButton)obj);
6      ((HtmlRadioButton)obj).Selected = true;
7      break;
```

◈ Line 6: Sets the **Selected** property to **true**.

Similarly, we need to update our existing **SetValue()** function as per Listing 4.33 to take care of setting the value of **HtmlComboBox** and **HtmlCheckBox** controls.

Listing 4.33: 'Utility.cs' - Extra case statements in the SetValue function

```
1  case Config.HTML_COMBOBOX:
2      ((HtmlComboBox)obj).WaitForControlExist( ↵
           ↪ Config.TIMEOUT_MILLISEC);
3      ((HtmlComboBox)obj).WaitForControlReady( ↵
           ↪ Config.TIMEOUT_MILLISEC);
4      Log.Info("SetValue HtmlComboBox: Id - " + ↵
           ↪ ((HtmlComboBox)obj).Id + "  (Name - " + ↵
           ↪ ((HtmlComboBox)obj).Name + ")" + "  Value: " + ↵
           ↪ val);
5      ((HtmlComboBox)obj).SelectedItem = val;
6      break;
7
8  case Config.HTML_CHECKBOX:
9      ((HtmlCheckBox)obj).WaitForControlExist( ↵
           ↪ Config.TIMEOUT_MILLISEC);
10     ((HtmlCheckBox)obj).WaitForControlReady( ↵
           ↪ Config.TIMEOUT_MILLISEC);
11     Log.Info("SetValue HtmlCheckBox: Id - " + ↵
           ↪ ((HtmlCheckBox)obj).Id + "  (Name - " + ↵
           ↪ ((HtmlCheckBox)obj).Name + ")" + "  Value: " + ↵
           ↪ val);
12     if (val.Equals(Config.TRUE))
13         ((HtmlCheckBox)obj).Checked = true;
14     else if (val.Equals(Config.FALSE))
15         ((HtmlCheckBox)obj).Checked = false;
16     else
17         ReportExpectedVsActual("HtmlCheckBox Error", ↵
               ↪ "Unknown value");
18     break;
```

◈ Line 12: Checks or Unchecks the control based on the parameter supplied.

◈ Line 17: Handles invalid values and fails the test step.

Now let's define a new generic function in the Utility file as follows:

HandleBrowserDialog - Handles the dialog message box on the browser window		
Input Parameters	*none*	No parameter
Return Value	*void*	Returns nothing

Add Listing 4.34 code to the 'Utility.cs' file.

Listing 4.34: 'Utility.cs' - Code for HandleBrowserDialog

```
1  using Microsoft.VisualStudio.TestTools.UITest.Extension;
2
3  public static void HandleBrowserDialog()
4  {
5      Browser.PerformDialogAction(BrowserDialogAction.Ok);
6  }
```

◈ Line 5: Clicks the *Ok* button on the dialog window.

4.5.4 Page Logic

4.5.4.1 Tester's Home Page

The Tester's *Home* page of our demo website will have the following actions:

Action	Description
ClickHome()	This action will navigate to the Tester's *Home* page.
ClickAddEmployee()	This action will navigate to the *Add Employee* page.
ClickViewEmployee()	This action will navigate to the *View Employee* page.
ClickOther()	This action will navigate to the *Other* page.
ClickDragnDrop()	This action will navigate to the *Drag-n-Drop* page.
ClickLogout()	This action will log the user out and navigate to the generic *Home* page.

Add a new class 'pageHtmlTesterHome.cs' to the *Pages* folder and insert the code as shown in Listing 4.35.

```
1  /*************************************************************
2   * All rights reserved. Copyright 2017 Arkenstone-ltd.com *
3   *************************************************************/
4
5  namespace CodedUITesting
6  {
7      class pageHtmlTesterHome
8      {
9          public void ClickHome()
10         {
11             Utility.Click(repHtmlTesterHome.Link_Home);
12         }
13
14         public void ClickAddEmployee()
15         {
16             Utility.Click(repHtmlTesterHome.Link_AddEmployee);
17         }
18
19         public void ClickViewEmployee()
20         {
21             Utility.Click(repHtmlTesterHome.Link_ViewEmployee);
22         }
23
24         public void ClickOther()
25         {
26             Utility.Click(repHtmlTesterHome.Link_Other);
27         }
28
29         public void ClickDragnDrop()
30         {
31             Utility.Click(repHtmlTesterHome.Link_DragnDrop);
32         }
33
34         public void ClickLogout()
35         {
36             Utility.Click(repHtmlTesterHome.Link_Logout);
37         }
38     }
39 }
```

4.5.4.2 Add Employee Page

The *Add Employee* page of our demo website will have the following action:

Action	Description
AddEmployee()	This action will add a new employee.

Add a new class 'pageHtmlTesterAddEmployee.cs' to the *Pages* folder and insert the code as shown in Listing 4.36.

Listing 4.36: 'pageHtmlTesterAddEmployee.cs' - Add an employee

```
1  /**********************************************************
2   * All rights reserved. Copyright 2017 Arkenstone-ltd.com *
3   **********************************************************/
4
5  namespace CodedUITesting
6  {
7      class pageHtmlTesterAddEmployee
8      {
9          public void AddEmployee()
10         {
11             Utility.SetValue( ↵
                   ↪ repHtmlEmployeeDetail.ComboBox_Title, ↵
                   ↪ "Miss");
12             Utility.SetValue( ↵
                   ↪ repHtmlEmployeeDetail.EditBox_Name, ↵
                   ↪ "Nicola");
13             Utility.Click(repHtmlEmployeeDetail. ↵
                   ↪ RadioButton_GenderFemale);
14             Utility.SetValue( ↵
                   ↪ repHtmlEmployeeDetail.EditBox_DateOfBirth, ↵
                   ↪ "01/02/1977");
15             Utility.SetValue( ↵
                   ↪ repHtmlEmployeeDetail.EditBox_Email, ↵
                   ↪ "Nicola@arkenstone-ltd.com");
16             Utility.SetValue( ↵
                   ↪ repHtmlEmployeeDetail.CheckBox_Contract, ↵
                   ↪ Config.TRUE);
17             Utility.SetValue( ↵
                   ↪ repHtmlEmployeeDetail.EditBox_Postcode, ↵
                   ↪ "SN1 5GS");
18
```

```
19          Utility.SaveScreenshot("AddEmployee");
20
21          Utility.Click(repHtmlEmployeeDetail.Button_Add);
22
23          Utility.HandleBrowserDialog();
24       }
25    }
26 }
```

◈ Line 11: Selects ListBox option "Miss".
◈ Line 13: Selects RadioButton option "Female".
◈ Line 16: Selects CheckBox "Contract Job".
◈ Line 19: Saves an image of the screen with string "AddEmployee" added to the filename.
◈ Line 23: Handles the dialog message box.

4.5.5 Updating Tests

Add a new test to the 'WebHtmlTests.cs' file as shown in Listing 4.37.

Listing 4.37: 'WebHtmlTests.cs' - Code for WebHtmlTesterAddEmployee

```
1  [TestMethod]
2  public void WebHtmlTesterAddEmployee()
3  {
4     Utility.Log.Info("Starting Test ***** " + ↵
           ↳ Utility.TestName + " *****");
5
6     try
7     {
8        Utility.LaunchWebApp();
9
10       pageHtmlHome Home = new pageHtmlHome();
11       Home.ClickLogin();
12
13       pageHtmlLogin Login = new pageHtmlLogin();
14       Login.LoginUser("Tester", "Tester123");
15
16       pageHtmlTesterHome homeTester = new ↵
              ↳ pageHtmlTesterHome();
17       homeTester.ClickAddEmployee();
18
19       pageHtmlTesterAddEmployee emp = new ↵
              ↳ pageHtmlTesterAddEmployee();
20       emp.AddEmployee();
```

```
21
22          homeTester.ClickLogout();
23
24          Utility.CloseWebApp();
25
26          Utility.ReportResult();
27      }
28    catch (Exception exception)
29    {
30        Utility.ReportExpectedVsActual(Utility.TestName, ↵
            ↪ "Exception occurred");
31        Utility.Log.Error("Exception: " + ↵
            ↪ exception.ToString());
32        throw exception;
33    }
34 }
```

◈ Line 2: New test `WebHtmlTesterAddEmployee`.

◈ Line 17: Clicks the *Add Employee* link on the Tester's *Home* page.

◈ Line 20: Calls the `AddEmployee` function in the page logic.

◈ Line 22: Logs the user out.

4.5.6   Executing Test

Execute the test `WebHtmlTesterAddEmployee` and you will see an output as shown in Figure 4.13. The test should execute successfully.

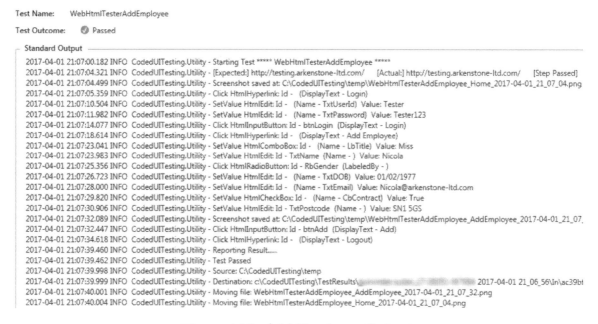

Figure 4.13: Add Employee Output

☞ Please note that the demo website has no database attached to it. It only mimics the record addition and just gives a success message to facilitate our automated testing.

4.6 Data Verification - HtmlControls

In this section we will learn about how to perform verification tasks on different types of controls that we have used so far. We will perform the following Test Scenario to demonstrate the use of these controls:

- Launch the demo website.

- Click on the *Login* link.

- Login with the user 'Tester'.

- Click on the *View Employee* link.

- Verify the employee's detail displayed on the web page.

- Log the user out.

4.6.1 Configuration Parameters

First of all, add a new declaration to the 'Config.cs' file as shown in Listing 4.38.

Listing 4.38: 'Config.cs' - New parameter

```
1  public const string HTML_BUTTON = ↵
       ↪ "Microsoft.VisualStudio.TestTools.UITesting. ↵
       ↪ HtmlControls.HtmlButton";
```

4.6.2 Object Repository

The *View Employee* page has the following controls:

View Employee Page Controls			
Control	*Type*	*Property*	*Value*
Employee Id	EditBox	TechnologyName	Web
		ControlType	Edit
		Name	TxtEmpId
Title	ListBox	TechnologyName	Web
		ControlType	ComboBox
		Name	LbTitle
Name	EditBox	TechnologyName	Web
		ControlType	Edit
		Id	TxtName
Gender	RadioButton	TechnologyName	Web
		ControlType	RadioButton
		Id	RbGender
		Value	male/female
Date of Birth	EditBox	TechnologyName	Web
		ControlType	Edit
		Name	TxtDOB
Email Address	EditBox	TechnologyName	Web
		ControlType	Edit
		Name	TxtEmail
Contract Job	CheckBox	TechnologyName	Web
		ControlType	CheckBox
		Name	CbContract
Postcode	EditBox	TechnologyName	Web
		ControlType	Edit
		Id	TxtPostcode
Close	Button	TechnologyName	Web
		ControlType	Button
		DisplayText	Close
		TagName	INPUT

You will have noticed that all of these screen elements have the same attribute values as the *Add Employee* screen (except *Employee Id* and the *Close* button which weren't present in the *Add Employee* page). These elements are displayed in this screen as read-only as it is just for viewing purposes. So what we will do is, reuse the repository we already have i.e. reuse the `repHtmlEmployeeDetail` repository and add the additional elements to it as shown in Listing 4.39.

Listing 4.39: 'repHtmlEmployeeDetail.cs' - Additional controls for View Employee page

```
1  private static HtmlEdit mEditBox_EmployeeId;
2  private static HtmlButton mButton_Close;
3
4  public static HtmlEdit EditBox_EmployeeId
5  {
6      get
7      {
8          if (mEditBox_EmployeeId == null || ↵
               ↪ !mEditBox_EmployeeId.Exists)
9          {
10             mEditBox_EmployeeId = new ↵
                  ↪ HtmlEdit(Utility.Browser);
11             mEditBox_EmployeeId.SearchProperties.Add( ↵
                  ↪ HtmlEdit.PropertyNames.Name, "TxtEmpId");
12         }
13         return mEditBox_EmployeeId;
14     }
15 }
16
17 public static HtmlButton Button_Close
18 {
19     get
20     {
21         if (mButton_Close == null || !mButton_Close.Exists)
22         {
23             mButton_Close = new HtmlButton(Utility.Browser);
24             mButton_Close.SearchProperties.Add( ↵
                  ↪ HtmlButton.PropertyNames.DisplayText, ↵
                  ↪ "Close");
25             mButton_Close.SearchProperties.Add( ↵
                  ↪ HtmlButton.PropertyNames.TagName, ↵
                  ↪ "INPUT");
26         }
27         return mButton_Close;
28     }
29 }
```

◈ Line 25: Note the additional search property `TagName` is required to find the control on the page.

4.6.3 Utility Functions

We need to update our existing `Click()` function as per Listing 4.40 to take care of clicking the `HtmlButton` control.

Listing 4.40: 'Utility.cs' - Code to click HtmlButton

```
1  case Config.HTML_BUTTON:
2      ((HtmlButton)obj).WaitForControlExist( ↵
          ↪ Config.TIMEOUT_MILLISEC);
3      ((HtmlButton)obj).WaitForControlReady( ↵
          ↪ Config.TIMEOUT_MILLISEC);
4      Log.Info("Click HtmlButton: Id - " + ↵
          ↪ ((HtmlButton)obj).Id + "  (DisplayText - " + ↵
          ↪ ((HtmlButton)obj).DisplayText + ")");
5      Mouse.Click((HtmlButton)obj);
6      break;
```

Also, we need to update our existing `GetValue()` function as per Listing 4.41 to take care of additional controls.

Listing 4.41: 'Utility.cs' - Additional case statements in the GetValue function

```
1  case Config.HTML_EDIT:
2      ((HtmlEdit)obj).WaitForControlExist( ↵
          ↪ Config.TIMEOUT_MILLISEC);
3      ((HtmlEdit)obj).WaitForControlReady( ↵
          ↪ Config.TIMEOUT_MILLISEC);
4      Log.Info("GetValue HtmlEdit: Id - " + ↵
          ↪ ((HtmlEdit)obj).Id + "  (Name - " + ↵
          ↪ ((HtmlEdit)obj).Name + ")");
5      retValue = ((HtmlEdit)obj).Text;
6      break;
7
8  case Config.HTML_COMBOBOX:
9      ((HtmlComboBox)obj).WaitForControlExist( ↵
          ↪ Config.TIMEOUT_MILLISEC);
10     ((HtmlComboBox)obj).WaitForControlReady( ↵
          ↪ Config.TIMEOUT_MILLISEC);
11     Log.Info("GetValue HtmlComboBox: Id - " + ↵
          ↪ ((HtmlComboBox)obj).Id + "  (Name - " + ↵
          ↪ ((HtmlComboBox)obj).Name + ")");
12     retValue = ((HtmlComboBox)obj).SelectedItem;
```

```
13      break;
14
15 case Config.HTML_CHECKBOX:
16      ((HtmlCheckBox)obj).WaitForControlExist( ↵
            ↪ Config.TIMEOUT_MILLISEC);
17      ((HtmlCheckBox)obj).WaitForControlReady( ↵
            ↪ Config.TIMEOUT_MILLISEC);
18      Log.Info("GetValue HtmlCheckBox: Id - " + ↵
            ↪ ((HtmlCheckBox)obj).Id + " (Name - " + ↵
            ↪ ((HtmlCheckBox)obj).Name + ")");
19
20      if (((HtmlCheckBox)obj).Checked.ToString() == ↵
            ↪ Config.TRUE)
21          retValue = Config.TRUE;
22      else if (((HtmlCheckBox)obj).Checked.ToString() == ↵
            ↪ Config.FALSE)
23          retValue = Config.FALSE;
24      else
25          ReportExpectedVsActual("HtmlCheckBox Error", ↵
                ↪ "Unknown value");
26
27      break;
28
29 case Config.HTML_RADIOBUTTON:
30      ((HtmlRadioButton)obj).WaitForControlExist( ↵
            ↪ Config.TIMEOUT_MILLISEC);
31      ((HtmlRadioButton)obj).WaitForControlReady( ↵
            ↪ Config.TIMEOUT_MILLISEC);
32      Log.Info("GetValue HtmlRadioButton: Id - " + ↵
            ↪ ((HtmlRadioButton)obj).Id + " (LabeledBy - " + ↵
            ↪ ((HtmlRadioButton)obj).LabeledBy + ")");
33      retValue = ↵
            ↪ ((HtmlRadioButton)obj).Selected.ToString();
34      break;
```

◈ Line 21: Returns `Config.TRUE` if the `CheckBox` is ticked.

◈ Line 23: Returns `Config.FALSE` if the `CheckBox` is unticked.

◈ Line 25: Handles invalid values and fails the test step.

◈ Line 33: Gets and returns its value that indicates whether this `RadioButton` has been selected.

4.6.4 Page Logic

The *View Employee* page of our demo website will have the following action:

Action	Description
VerifyEmployee()	This action will verify the employee's detail displayed on the web page.

Add a new class 'pageHtmlTesterViewEmployee.cs' to the *Pages* folder and insert the code as shown in Listing 4.42.

Listing 4.42: 'pageHtmlTesterViewEmployee.cs' - Page logic for View Employee page

```
1    /********************************************************
2     * All rights reserved. Copyright 2017 Arkenstone-ltd.com *
3     ********************************************************/
4
5    namespace CodedUITesting
6    {
7        class pageHtmlTesterViewEmployee
8        {
9            public void VerifyEmployee()
10           {
11               Utility.ReportExpectedVsActual("10004", ↵
                     ↪ Utility.GetValue(repHtmlEmployeeDetail. ↵
                     ↪ EditBox_EmployeeId));
12               Utility.ReportExpectedVsActual("Miss", ↵
                     ↪ Utility.GetValue(repHtmlEmployeeDetail. ↵
                     ↪ ComboBox_Title));
13               Utility.ReportExpectedVsActual("Sarah Smith", ↵
                     ↪ Utility.GetValue(repHtmlEmployeeDetail. ↵
                     ↪ EditBox_Name));
14               Utility.ReportExpectedVsActual(Config.TRUE, ↵
                     ↪ Utility.GetValue(repHtmlEmployeeDetail. ↵
                     ↪ RadioButton_GenderFemale));
15               Utility.ReportExpectedVsActual("25/12/1982", ↵
                     ↪ Utility.GetValue(repHtmlEmployeeDetail. ↵
                     ↪ EditBox_DateOfBirth));
16               Utility.ReportExpectedVsActual( ↵
                     ↪ "sarah.smith@arkenstone-ltd.com", ↵
                     ↪ Utility.GetValue(repHtmlEmployeeDetail. ↵
                     ↪ EditBox_Email));
17               Utility.ReportExpectedVsActual(Config.FALSE, ↵
                     ↪ Utility.GetValue(repHtmlEmployeeDetail. ↵
                     ↪ CheckBox_Contract));
18               Utility.ReportExpectedVsActual("SN1 5GS", ↵
                     ↪ Utility.GetValue(repHtmlEmployeeDetail. ↵
```

```
19                         ↪ EditBox_Postcode));
20              Utility.Click(repHtmlEmployeeDetail.Button_Close);
21          }
22      }
23  }
```

◈ Line 9: Business logic to verify employee's detail where we have specified the *expected* values but the *actual* values are taken from the controls on the web page. In later chapters, we will learn how to use the *expected* values from an Excel® file or a database table instead of using the hard-coded values.

4.6.5 Updating Tests

Add a new test to the 'WebHtmlTests.cs' file as shown in Listing 4.43.

Listing 4.43: 'WebHtmlTests.cs' - WebHtmlTesterVerifyEmployee

```
1  [TestMethod]
2  public void WebHtmlTesterVerifyEmployee()
3  {
4      Utility.Log.Info("Starting Test ***** " + ↵
           ↪ Utility.TestName + " *****");
5
6      try
7      {
8          Utility.LaunchWebApp();
9
10         pageHtmlHome Home = new pageHtmlHome();
11         Home.ClickLogin();
12
13         pageHtmlLogin Login = new pageHtmlLogin();
14         Login.LoginUser("Tester", "Tester123");
15
16         pageHtmlTesterHome homeTester = new ↵
              ↪ pageHtmlTesterHome();
17         homeTester.ClickViewEmployee();
18
19         pageHtmlTesterViewEmployee emp = new ↵
              ↪ pageHtmlTesterViewEmployee();
20         emp.VerifyEmployee();
21
22         Playback.Wait(2000);
23         homeTester.ClickLogout();
24
```

```
25        Utility.CloseWebApp();
26        Utility.ReportResult();
27    }
28  catch (Exception exception)
29  {
30        Utility.ReportExpectedVsActual(Utility.TestName, ↵
          ↪ "Exception occurred");
31        Utility.Log.Error("Exception: " + ↵
          ↪ exception.ToString());
32        throw exception;
33  }
34 }
```

◈ Line 22: Allows some breathing time before logging out (handling synchronisation issue).

4.6.6   Executing Tests

Execute the test `WebHtmlTesterVerifyEmployee` and you will see an output as shown in Figure 4.14. The test should execute successfully.

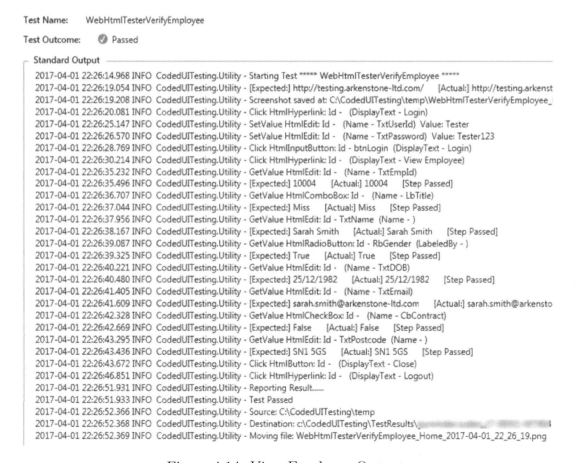

Figure 4.14: View Employee Output

4.7   Creating Test Results Summary

The *Test Explorer* window gives us a summary of all the tests executed along with their test result - either Passed or Failed. However, the *Test Explorer* window is refreshed as soon as next set of tests are executed and it would be really helpful if this summary is saved in a file that can be viewed at a later stage. So let's enhance our Automation Framework to generate a test result summary file.

4.7.1   Add Necessary References

First of all, let's add the necessary references to our Coded UI project which are needed to support the functionality.

- In the *Solution Explorer*, right click on the *References* folder.

- Select *Add Reference...*

- In the left hand pane, click on *COM* as shown for (Step ①).

- In the right hand pane, type *script* in the search area as shown for (Step ②).

- Select the *Windows Script Host Object Model* as shown in Figure 4.15.

- Click the *OK* button.

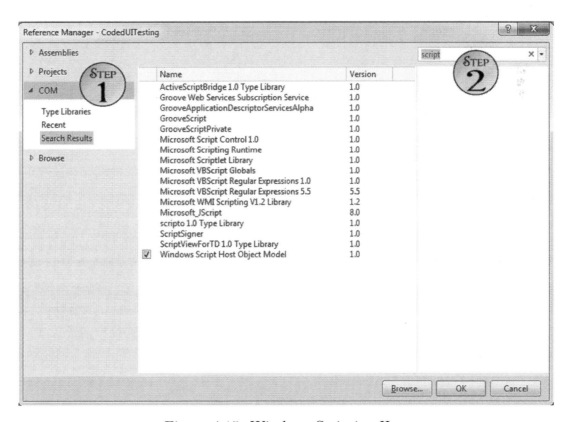

Figure 4.15: Windows Scripting Host

- Again in the *Solution Explorer*, right click on the *References* folder.

- Select *Add Reference...*

- In the left hand pane, click on *Assemblies*.

- In the right hand pane, type *CSharp* in the search area.

- Select *Microsoft.CSharp* as shown in Figure 4.16.

- Click the *OK* button.

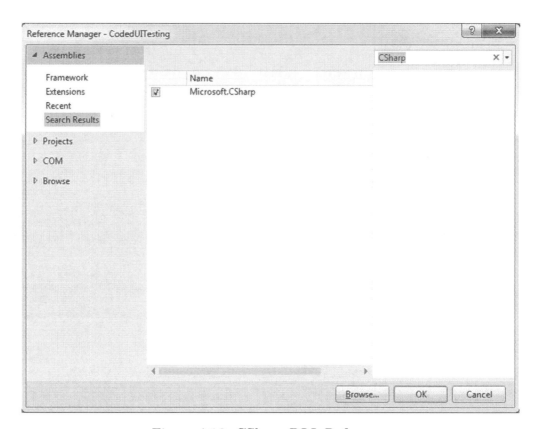

Figure 4.16: CSharp DLL Reference

4.7.2   Configuration Parameters

Let's define a configuration parameter as per Listing 4.44.

Listing 4.44: 'Config.cs' - Parameters for the Test Results Summary

```
1 using System;
2 public static string SUMMARY_PATHFILENAME = ↵
     ↪ Utility.TestRunFolder + @"\Summary" + ↵
     ↪ DateTime.Now.ToString("_dd_MMM_yyyy HH_mm_ss", ↵
     ↪ System.Globalization.CultureInfo. ↵
     ↪ GetCultureInfo("en-GB")) + ".csv";
```

◈ Line 1: Additional import required to support the functionality.
◈ Line 2: Defines a configuration variable to hold the summary file name with the current date and timestamp.

 At this stage you will see an error on the `TestRunFolder` variable but don't worry, we will define it in the next section.

4.7.3   Utility Functions

We will now define three new generic functions as follows:

SetupSummaryFile - Sets up the Test Summary File		
Input Parameters	*none*	No parameters
Return Value	*void*	Returns nothing

CreateSummaryFileEntry - Creates an entry into the Test Summary File		
Input Parameters	*strData*	Data to be written to the test summary file
Return Value	*void*	Returns nothing

CreateShortcut - Creates a shortcut of the Test Summary File		
Input Parameters	*linkName*	Name of the shortcut
	linkPath	Path of the shortcut
	sourceLocation	Location of the source
Return Value	*void*	Returns nothing

Update the 'Utility.cs' file as shown in Listing 4.45.

Listing 4.45: 'Utility.cs' - Changes for the Test Summary File

```
1  using IWshRuntimeLibrary;
2
3  public static string TestRunFolder;
4
5  public static void SetupSummaryFile()
6  {
7      Log.Info("SetupSummaryFile");
8
```

```
 9        if (!System.IO.File.Exists( ↵
              ↪ Config.SUMMARY_PATHFILENAME))
10        {
11            FileStream fs1 = new ↵
                  ↪ FileStream(Config.SUMMARY_PATHFILENAME, ↵
                  ↪ FileMode.Create, FileAccess.Write);
12            StreamWriter writer = new StreamWriter(fs1);
13            writer.Write("Date Time, Test Name, Test Result, ↵
                  ↪ Log File" + Environment.NewLine);
14            writer.Close();
15        }
16    }
17
18 public static void CreateSummaryFileEntry(String ↵
       ↪ strData)
19 {
20     Log.Info("CreateSummaryFileEntry");
21     FileStream fs1 = new ↵
           ↪ FileStream(Config.SUMMARY_PATHFILENAME, ↵
           ↪ FileMode.Append, FileAccess.Write);
22     StreamWriter writer = new StreamWriter(fs1);
23     writer.Write(strData + Environment.NewLine);
24     writer.Close();
25 }
26
27 public static void CreateShortcut(string linkName, string ↵
       ↪ linkPath, string sourceLocation)
28 {
29     string shortcutLocation = ↵
           ↪ System.IO.Path.Combine(linkPath, linkName + ↵
           ↪ ".lnk");
30     WshShell shell = new WshShell();
31     IWshShortcut shortcut = (IWshShortcut) ↵
           ↪ shell.CreateShortcut(shortcutLocation);
32
33     shortcut.TargetPath = sourceLocation;
34     shortcut.Save();
35 }
```

◈ Line 1: Additional import required to support the functionality.

◈ Line 3: Defines a public variable to hold the name of the **TestRunFolder**.

◈ Line 5: New function to setup the test summary file.

◈ Line 9: Creates the test summary file if it doesn't exist. Note that we want to create it once only for the first test in a run. Later tests should use the same file to add the summary info.

◈ Line 11: Initialises a new instance of the `FileStream` class with the specified file pathname, creation mode and access permission.

- FileName - the summary file is created with the name that is stored in the `Config.SUMMARY_PATHFILENAME` configuration parameter.

- FileMode `Create` - the operating system should create a new file. If the file already exists, it will be overwritten.

- FileAccess `Write` - provide a write access to the file. Data can be written to the file.

◈ Line 12: Initialises a new instance of the `StreamWriter` class for the specified stream.
◈ Line 13: Writes the header record followed by a new line character.
◈ Line 14: Closes the stream.
◈ Line 18: New function to create a summary file entry for a test.
◈ Line 21: Opens the summary file in `Append` mode i.e. open the file and seek to the end of the file.
◈ Line 22: Initialises the `StreamWriter` class.
◈ Line 23: Writes the string of data followed by a new line character.
◈ Line 24: Closes the stream.
◈ Line 27: New function to create a shortcut of the summary file.
◈ Line 29: Combines two strings into a path.
◈ Line 30: Initialises a new instance of the `WshShell` class.
◈ Line 31: Creates a shortcut at the location.
◈ Line 33: Specifies the path of the source location.
◈ Line 34: Saves the shortcut.

4.7.4 Updating Scripts

Update the 'WebHtmlTests.cs' file as shown in Listing 4.46.

Listing 4.46: 'WebHtmlTests.cs' - Updates for the Test Summary File

```
1  [TestInitialize()]
2  public void Initialize()
3  {
4      Utility.TestResult = Config.PASS;
5      Utility.TestName = TestContext.TestName;
6      Utility.TestResultFolder = ↵
           ↪ TestContext.TestResultsDirectory;
7      Utility.TestRunFolder = ↵
           ↪ TestContext.TestRunDirectory;
8
9      log4net.Config.XmlConfigurator.ConfigureAndWatch(new ↵
           ↪ FileInfo(Config.PROJECT_FOLDER + ↵
           ↪ "log4net.config"));
```

```
10        Utility.SetupSummaryFile();
11  }
12
13  [TestCleanup()]
14  public void Cleanup()
15  {
16      Utility.MoveScreenshots();
17
18      string logFile = Utility.SaveLogFile();
19      Utility.CreateSummaryFileEntry(DateTime.Now.ToString() ↵
          ↪ + "," + TestContext.TestName + "," + ↵
          ↪ Utility.TestResult + "," + logFile);
20
21      Utility.CreateShortcut("TestSummary", ↵
          ↪ Utility.TestResultFolder, ↵
          ↪ Config.SUMMARY_PATHFILENAME);
22
23      Utility.CloseWebApp();
24
25      Playback.Cleanup();
26  }
```

◈ Line 7: Assigns a value to the public variable `Utility.TestRunFolder` from the `TestContext`.
◈ Line 10: Sets up the test summary file.
◈ Line 18: Retrieves the log filename for later use.
◈ Line 19: Creates an entry into the test summary file with relevant information.
◈ Line 21: Creates a shortcut of the test summary file.

4.7.5 Executing Tests

Rebuild and execute all the tests in the *WebHtmlTests* class. After the execution is complete, when you click on the *Output* link of any test, you will see an *Attachments* window as shown in Figure 4.17. This time you will also see a link to the test summary file.

Figure 4.17: Test Execution Attachments

When you click on the *TestSummary.lnk* shortcut, you will see a test execution summary as shown in Figure 4.18.

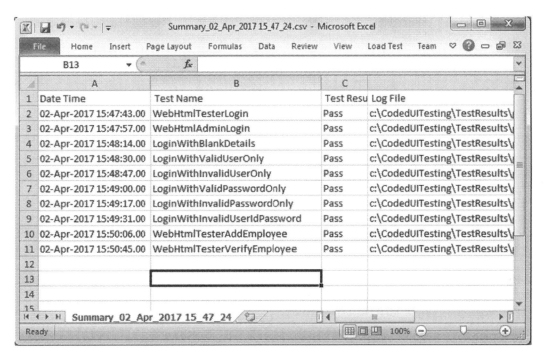

Figure 4.18: Test Summary File

Chapter 5

Automate with Databases

Automate with Databases

In this chapter, we will learn about how to:

- *Setup a testing database*

- *Perform verification tasks using data fetched from the testing database tables*

- *Perform verification tasks using random data fetched from the database tables*

So let's get on with it...

U SUALLY every website is connected to a database which stores information related to it. Various pages in a website provide the means to:

- create new data e.g. add a new employee

- edit existing data e.g. change employees' details

- view existing data e.g. view an employee's details

- delete data e.g. delete an employee's record

- display reports in various formats e.g. show an employee's details in a tabular form

When performing the testing of a website, a tester has to refer to the database tables to verify that the information displayed in the web page is the same as stored in the database tables e.g. if you login as an Admin user in our demo website and click the *Reports* link, an *Employee Report by Gender* page is displayed. As a tester, you must ensure that the *counts by gender* displayed in the web page report match the counts retrieved by the SQL Query executed on the database table. This is a very simple example but in real life testing, you may have to deal with more complex reports with database verifications. In this chapter we will cover how we can perform these verification tasks via automated testing i.e. retrieve data from the database table and compare it with the contents on the web page.

The demo website has no database attached to it but to demonstrate this kind of automated testing, we will set up a test database on our local workstation and mimic that the demo website is fetching data from your local database. We will essentially create the same data in your local database as is displayed in the static demo website e.g. record level data for the *Employee Report by Gender* report. The data will then be fetched from your local database via SQL Query and compared with the demo website.

5.1 Setting up Testing Database

You can use *SQL Server Management Studio*, as I have done, to execute the SQL scripts provided in this section. I have used the `sa` login to execute the scripts but you can use any login that has the database create/update permissions. The script creates the required database 'CUITesting' in the 'C:\CodedUITesting\CUITestingDB' folder. However, you can change the destination folder in the script to your preferred location. Make sure the folder 'C:\CodedUITesting\CUITestingDB' exists before you execute the first SQL script.

> ☞ As a tester in a real environment, you probably wouldn't need to create this database as it should already exist but here we need to create this database as we need something to automate our tests against. If you don't understand any of the code here, don't worry. You are not a database administrator! Just execute these SQL scripts to create the environment you need to be able to start writing your automated tests.

5.1.1 Creating The Database

Use Listing 5.1 SQL to create the 'CUITesting' database.

Listing 5.1: Creating the 'CUITesting' Database

```
1  /******************************************************
2   * All rights reserved. Copyright 2017 Arkenstone-ltd.com *
3   ******************************************************/
4  USE [master]
5  GO
6
```

```
 7  CREATE DATABASE [CUITesting] ON  PRIMARY
 8    ( NAME = N'CUITesting', FILENAME = ↵
          ↪ N'C:\CodedUITesting\CUITestingDB\CUITesting.mdf' ↵
          ↪ , SIZE = 5504KB , MAXSIZE = UNLIMITED, FILEGROWTH ↵
          ↪ = 10%)
 9     LOG ON
10    ( NAME = N'CUITesting_log', FILENAME = ↵
          ↪ N'C:\CodedUITesting\CUITestingDB\CUITesting.ldf' ↵
          ↪ , SIZE = 3456KB , MAXSIZE = UNLIMITED, FILEGROWTH ↵
          ↪ = 10%)
11     GO
12
13  ALTER DATABASE [CUITesting] SET COMPATIBILITY_LEVEL = 90
14
15  IF (1 = FULLTEXTSERVICEPROPERTY('IsFullTextInstalled'))
16  begin
17     EXEC [CUITesting].[dbo].[sp_fulltext_database] @action ↵
          ↪ = 'disable'
18  end
19
20  ALTER DATABASE [CUITesting] SET ANSI_NULL_DEFAULT OFF
21  ALTER DATABASE [CUITesting] SET ANSI_NULLS OFF
22  ALTER DATABASE [CUITesting] SET ANSI_PADDING OFF
23  ALTER DATABASE [CUITesting] SET ANSI_WARNINGS OFF
24  ALTER DATABASE [CUITesting] SET ARITHABORT OFF
25  ALTER DATABASE [CUITesting] SET AUTO_CLOSE ON
26  ALTER DATABASE [CUITesting] SET AUTO_CREATE_STATISTICS ON
27  ALTER DATABASE [CUITesting] SET AUTO_SHRINK OFF
28  ALTER DATABASE [CUITesting] SET AUTO_UPDATE_STATISTICS ON
29  ALTER DATABASE [CUITesting] SET CURSOR_CLOSE_ON_COMMIT OFF
30  ALTER DATABASE [CUITesting] SET CURSOR_DEFAULT  GLOBAL
31  ALTER DATABASE [CUITesting] SET CONCAT_NULL_YIELDS_NULL OFF
32  ALTER DATABASE [CUITesting] SET NUMERIC_ROUNDABORT OFF
33  ALTER DATABASE [CUITesting] SET QUOTED_IDENTIFIER OFF
34  ALTER DATABASE [CUITesting] SET RECURSIVE_TRIGGERS OFF
35  ALTER DATABASE [CUITesting] SET ENABLE_BROKER
36  ALTER DATABASE [CUITesting] SET ↵
        ↪ AUTO_UPDATE_STATISTICS_ASYNC OFF
37  ALTER DATABASE [CUITesting] SET ↵
        ↪ DATE_CORRELATION_OPTIMIZATION OFF
38  ALTER DATABASE [CUITesting] SET TRUSTWORTHY OFF
39  ALTER DATABASE [CUITesting] SET ALLOW_SNAPSHOT_ISOLATION OFF
40  ALTER DATABASE [CUITesting] SET PARAMETERIZATION SIMPLE
41  ALTER DATABASE [CUITesting] SET READ_COMMITTED_SNAPSHOT OFF
42  ALTER DATABASE [CUITesting] SET HONOR_BROKER_PRIORITY OFF
```

```
43  ALTER DATABASE [CUITesting] SET READ_WRITE
44  ALTER DATABASE [CUITesting] SET RECOVERY SIMPLE
45  ALTER DATABASE [CUITesting] SET MULTI_USER
46  ALTER DATABASE [CUITesting] SET PAGE_VERIFY ↵
        ↪ TORN_PAGE_DETECTION
47  ALTER DATABASE [CUITesting] SET DB_CHAINING OFF
48  GO
```

5.1.2 Creating Employees Table

Our database will have a single table that stores details of all the employees. Use Listing 5.2 SQL to create the *Employees* table.

Listing 5.2: Creating the Employees Table

```
1  /*****************************************************
2   * All rights reserved. Copyright 2017 Arkenstone-ltd.com *
3   *****************************************************/
4  USE [CUITesting]
5  GO
6
7  SET ANSI_NULLS ON
8  SET QUOTED_IDENTIFIER ON
9  CREATE TABLE [dbo].[Employees](
10    [EmployeeID] [nvarchar](10) NOT NULL,
11    [Title] [nvarchar](20) NOT NULL,
12    [Name] [nvarchar](40) NOT NULL,
13    [Gender] [nvarchar](1) NULL,
14    [DateOfBirth] [datetime] NULL,
15    [Email] [nvarchar](75) NULL,
16    [ContractJob] [nvarchar](3) NULL,
17    [Postcode] [nvarchar](10) NULL,
18   CONSTRAINT [PK_Employees] PRIMARY KEY CLUSTERED
19  (
20    [EmployeeID] ASC
21  )WITH (PAD_INDEX  = OFF, STATISTICS_NORECOMPUTE  = OFF, ↵
        ↪ IGNORE_DUP_KEY = OFF, ALLOW_ROW_LOCKS  = ON, ↵
        ↪ ALLOW_PAGE_LOCKS  = ON) ON [PRIMARY]
22  ) ON [PRIMARY]
23  GO
```

5.1.3 Creating The Test Data

Now using Notepad, Excel® or any other suitable editor, create an 'Employees.csv' file in the 'C:\CodedUITesting\CUITestingDB' folder with the data as shown below:

```
EmployeeID,Title,Name,Gender,DateOfBirth,Email,ContractJob,PostalCode
10001,Mrs,Carla Brown,2,02/05/1965,carla.brown@arkenstone-ltd.com,Yes,SN1 5GS
10002,Mr,James Jones,1,03/12/1978,James.Jones@arkenstone-ltd.com,Yes,MK17 5TY
10003,Miss,D Mellons,2,10/10/1970,D.Mellons@arkenstone-ltd.com,No,HP11 8YZ
10004,Miss,Sarah Smith,2,25/12/1982,sarah.smith@arkenstone-ltd.com,No,SN1 5GS
10005,Mrs,Nicola,2,31/12/1978,Nicola@arkenstone-ltd.com,Yes,BR7 4TY
```

This is the same data as used by our demo website.

5.1.4 Loading The Test Data

Use Listing 5.3 SQL Query to load the 'Employees.csv' test data into the *Employees* table.

Listing 5.3: Loading the 'Employees.csv' Test Data

```
1   /****************************************************************
2    * All rights reserved. Copyright 2017 Arkenstone-ltd.com *
3    ****************************************************************/
4   USE [CUITesting]
5   GO
6
7   SET DATEFORMAT dmy;
8   GO
9
10  Truncate table dbo.[Employees]
11  BULK INSERT dbo.[Employees] FROM ↵
       ↪ 'C:\CodedUITesting\CUITestingDB\Employees.csv'  WITH ↵
       ↪ (FIRSTROW = 2, FIELDTERMINATOR = ',', ROWTERMINATOR ↵
       ↪ = '\n')
12  GO
```

Now we are ready with a local database which we will use to compare with the data displayed in our demo website.

5.2 Table Handling - Summary Reports

A tabular report is the most common type of report displayed on a web page. The report's output is organised in a row-column format, with each column usually corresponding to a field in the database table. A summary report is similar to a tabular report, but displays rows of data in a grouped form with subtotals and totals instead. In this section, we will learn how to automate the testing of a typical summary report, *Employee Report by Gender*. In doing so, we will also learn how to perform automated verification tasks on a Table *HtmlControl*. We will perform the following Test Scenario for the purposes of demonstration:

- Launch the demo website.

- Click on the *Login* link.

- Login with the user 'Admin'.

- Click on the *Reports* link.

- Verify the summary report displayed on the web page with the counts in database.

5.2.1 Configuration Parameters

Let's define some configuration parameters as per Listing 5.4.

Listing 5.4: 'Config.cs' - Additional parameters

```
1 public const string HTML_TABLE = ↵
     ↪ "Microsoft.VisualStudio.TestTools.UITesting. ↵
     ↪ HtmlControls.HtmlTable";
2
3 public const string MALE_TEXT = "Male";
4 public const string FEMALE_TEXT = "Female";
5
6 public const string MALE = "1";
7 public const string FEMALE = "2";
8
9 public const string connectionString = ↵
     ↪ "Server=localhost;Database=CUITesting; ↵
     ↪ Uid=sa;Pwd=sa;connect timeout=180;";
```

◈ Line 3: Defines a string constant for the Male text value.
◈ Line 4: Defines a string constant for the Female text value.
◈ Line 6: Defines a string constant for the Male numeric value.
◈ Line 7: Defines a string constant for the Female numeric value.
◈ Line 9: Defines a string constant for the database connection. The connection string's parameters are:

- Server - identifies the server. This could be a local machine (localhost), a machine domain name or an IP Address. In our case, we have specified a `localhost`.

- Database - identifies the database on the server for connection. In our case, we are connecting to the `CUITesting` database. If you gave a different name while creating the database, please change this parameter to the name you have used.

- Uid - name of the user configured in the SQL Server. I've used the `sa` user, change it if you are connecting to the database with a different user id.

- Pwd - password matching the SQL Server Uid.

- Connect Timeout - the length of time (in seconds) to wait for a connection to the server before terminating the attempt and generating an error.

5.2.2 Object Repository

When you login as an Admin user, on successful login, the Admin's *Home* page is displayed with the following elements:

Admin's Home Page Controls			
Control	*Type*	*Property*	*Value*
Home	Hyperlink	TechnologyName ControlType InnerText	Web Hyperlink Home
Reports	Hyperlink	TechnologyName ControlType InnerText	Web Hyperlink Reports
Employee List	Hyperlink	TechnologyName ControlType InnerText	Web Hyperlink Employee List
Logout	Hyperlink	TechnologyName ControlType InnerText	Web Hyperlink Logout

Add a new class 'repHtmlAdminHome.cs' to the *Repository* folder and insert the code as shown in Listing 5.5.

Listing 5.5: 'repHtmlAdminHome.cs' - Repository for the Admin's Home page

```
1  /*********************************************************
2   * All rights reserved. Copyright 2017 Arkenstone-ltd.com *
3   *********************************************************/
4
5  using ↵
       ↳ Microsoft.VisualStudio.TestTools.UITesting.HtmlControls;
6
```

```
 7  namespace CodedUITesting
 8  {
 9      public static class repHtmlAdminHome
10      {
11          private static HtmlHyperlink mLink_Home;
12          private static HtmlHyperlink mLink_Reports;
13          private static HtmlHyperlink mLink_EmployeeList;
14          private static HtmlHyperlink mLink_Logout;
15
16          public static HtmlHyperlink Link_Home
17          {
18              get
19              {
20                  if (mLink_Home == null || ↵
                        ↪ !mLink_Home.Exists)
21                  {
22                      mLink_Home = new ↵
                            ↪ HtmlHyperlink(Utility.Browser);
23                      mLink_Home.SearchProperties.Add( ↵
                            ↪ HtmlHyperlink.PropertyNames. ↵
                            ↪ InnerText, "Home");
24                  }
25
26                  return mLink_Home;
27              }
28          }
29
30          public static HtmlHyperlink Link_Reports
31          {
32              get
33              {
34                  if (mLink_Reports == null || ↵
                        ↪ !mLink_Reports.Exists)
35                  {
36                      mLink_Reports = new ↵
                            ↪ HtmlHyperlink(Utility.Browser);
37                      mLink_Reports.SearchProperties.Add( ↵
                            ↪ HtmlHyperlink.PropertyNames. ↵
                            ↪ InnerText, "Reports");
38                  }
39
40                  return mLink_Reports;
41              }
42          }
43
```

```
44      public static HtmlHyperlink Link_EmployeeList
45      {
46          get
47          {
48              if (mLink_EmployeeList == null || ↵
                    ↪ !mLink_EmployeeList.Exists)
49              {
50                  mLink_EmployeeList = new ↵
                        ↪ HtmlHyperlink(Utility.Browser);
51                  mLink_EmployeeList.SearchProperties.Add( ↵
                        ↪ HtmlHyperlink.PropertyNames. ↵
                        ↪ InnerText, "Employee List");
52              }
53
54              return mLink_EmployeeList;
55          }
56      }
57
58      public static HtmlHyperlink Link_Logout
59      {
60          get
61          {
62              if (mLink_Logout == null || ↵
                    ↪ !mLink_Logout.Exists)
63              {
64                  mLink_Logout = new ↵
                        ↪ HtmlHyperlink(Utility.Browser);
65                  mLink_Logout.SearchProperties.Add( ↵
                        ↪ HtmlHyperlink.PropertyNames. ↵
                        ↪ InnerText, "Logout");
66              }
67
68              return mLink_Logout;
69          }
70      }
71   }
72 }
```

When you click on the *Reports* link, the *Employee Report by Gender* page is displayed with the following elements:

Admin's Reports Page Controls			
Control	*Type*	*Property*	*Value*
Gender Counts	Table	TechnologyName	Web
		ControlType	Table
		Id	tblCounts
Total Employees	Label/Span	TechnologyName	Web
		ControlType	Pane
		Id	TotalEmployees

Add a new class 'repHtmlAdminReports.cs' to the *Repository* folder and insert the code as shown in Listing 5.6.

Listing 5.6: 'repHtmlAdminReports.cs' - Repository for the Admin's Reports page

```
1  /************************************************************
2   * All rights reserved. Copyright 2017 Arkenstone-ltd.com *
3   ************************************************************/
4
5  using ↵
       ↪ Microsoft.VisualStudio.TestTools.UITesting.HtmlControls;
6
7  namespace CodedUITesting
8  {
9      public static class repHtmlAdminReports
10     {
11         private static HtmlTable mTable_ReportByGender;
12         private static HtmlSpan mSpan_TotalEmployees;
13
14         public static HtmlTable Table_ReportByGender
15         {
16             get
17             {
18                 if (mTable_ReportByGender == null || ↵
                    ↪ !mTable_ReportByGender.Exists)
19                 {
20                     mTable_ReportByGender = new ↵
                        ↪ HtmlTable(Utility.Browser);
21                     mTable_ReportByGender.SearchProperties. ↵
                        ↪ Add(HtmlTable.PropertyNames.Id, ↵
                        ↪ "tblCounts");
22                 }
23                 return mTable_ReportByGender;
24             }
25         }
```

```
26
27          public static HtmlSpan Span_TotalEmployees
28          {
29              get
30              {
31                  if (mSpan_TotalEmployees == null || ↵
                        ↪ !mSpan_TotalEmployees.Exists)
32                  {
33                      mSpan_TotalEmployees = new ↵
                            ↪ HtmlSpan(Utility.Browser);
34                      mSpan_TotalEmployees.SearchProperties. ↵
                            ↪ Add(HtmlSpan.PropertyNames.Id, ↵
                            ↪ "TotalEmployees");
35                  }
36                  return mSpan_TotalEmployees;
37              }
38          }
39      }
40  }
```

5.2.3   Utility Functions

Let's now define some new functions in the Utility file as follows:

GetCountOfRecs - Gets count of records via the provided SQL Query		
Input Parameters	*stringSQL*	SQL Query to be used to get count of records.
Return Value	*count*	Returns count of records.

CompareDetails - Compares the count of expected and actual value of gender type and reports the outcome		
Input Parameters	*stgGenderType*	Gender type either Config.MALE or Config.FEMALE
	actValue	Actual value of count to compare with
Return Value	*void*	Returns nothing.

GetTableData - Gets the values from all the cells in a table object		
Input Parameters	*object*	Object table whose cell values to get
Return Value	*jaggedArray*	Returns table values as an array-of-arrays

Add Listing 5.7 code to the 'Utility.cs' file.

Listing 5.7: 'Utility.cs' - Additional functions

```
1  using System.Data.SqlClient;
2
3  public static Int32 GetCountOfRecs(string stringSQL)
4  {
5      Log.Info("SQL is: " + stringSQL);
6      using (SqlConnection con = new ↵
           ↪ SqlConnection(Config.connectionString))
7      {
8          con.Open();
9
10         using (SqlCommand command = new ↵
               ↪ SqlCommand(stringSQL, con))
11         using (SqlDataReader reader = ↵
               ↪ command.ExecuteReader())
12         {
13             while (reader.Read())
14             {
15                 Int32 cnt = reader.GetInt32(0);
16                 Log.Info("Record count: " + cnt);
17                 return cnt;
18             }
19
20             return -1;
21         }
22     }
23 }
24
25 public static void CompareDetails(string stgGenderType, ↵
       ↪ string actValue)
26 {
27     String stringSQL = "Select Count(*) from ↵
           ↪ [dbo].[Employees] where [Gender] = '" + ↵
           ↪ stgGenderType + "'";
28     ReportExpectedVsActual(GetCountOfRecs(stringSQL). ↵
           ↪ ToString(), actValue);
29 }
30
31 public static String[][] GetTableData(Object obj)
32 {
33     String[][] tblData = { };
34     int rowCount = 0;
35
```

```
36      try
37      {
38          switch (obj.GetType().ToString())
39          {
40              case Config.HTML_TABLE:
41                  ((HtmlTable)obj).WaitForControlExist( ↵
                      ↪ Config.TIMEOUT_MILLISEC);
42                  ((HtmlTable)obj).WaitForControlReady( ↵
                      ↪ Config.TIMEOUT_MILLISEC);
43                  Log.Info("GetTableData HtmlTable: Id - " ↵
                      ↪ + ((HtmlTable)obj).Id + " (Name - " ↵
                      ↪ + ((HtmlTable)obj).Name + ")");
44
45                  rowCount = ((HtmlTable)obj).RowCount;
46
47                  Array.Resize(ref tblData, rowCount);
48
49                  for (int i = 0; i < rowCount; i++)
50                  {
51                      int colCount = ↵
                          ↪ ((HtmlTable)obj).ColumnCount;
52                      Array.Resize(ref tblData[i], ↵
                          ↪ colCount);
53
54                      for (int j = 0; j < colCount; j++)
55                      {
56                          tblData[i][j] = ↵
                              ↪ ((HtmlTable)obj).GetCell(i, ↵
                              ↪ j).InnerText;
57                          Log.Info("Row: " + i + "  Col: " ↵
                              ↪ + j + "   Value: " + ↵
                              ↪ tblData[i][j]);
58                      }
59                  }
60                  break;
61
62              default:
63                  Log.Error("Error, Unknown object type: " ↵
                      ↪ + obj.GetType().ToString());
64                  ReportExpectedVsActual("Error", "Not ↵
                      ↪ Implemented");
65                  break;
66          }
67
68      return tblData;
```

```
69      }
70      catch (Exception exception)
71      {
72          Log.Error("GetTableData Exception: " + ↵
               ↪ exception.ToString());
73          throw exception;
74      }
75 }
```

◈ Line 1: Additional import needed to support database connectivity.

◈ Line 6: Initialises a new instance of the `SqlConnection` class with a given connection string.

◈ Line 8: Opens the database connection.

◈ Line 10: Initialises a new instance of the `SqlCommand` class.

◈ Line 11: Sends the command text to the connection and builds the `SqlDataReader`.

◈ Line 13: While there is data, advances the `SqlDataReader`.

◈ Line 15: Gets the value of first column as a 32-bit signed integer.

◈ Line 16: Logs some useful information (it is a good practice to do so).

◈ Line 17: Returns the count.

◈ Line 20: Returns -1 if there was nothing in the `SqlDataReader`.

◈ Line 27: Constructs the SQL string with the gender type.

◈ Line 28: Compares the expected and the actual value and reports the outcome.

◈ Line 33: Initialises an array-of-arrays to store table data.

◈ Line 34: Initialises a row counter.

◈ Line 40: Ensures that the object is of type `HtmlTable` as we will be adding cases for another table types later on.

◈ Line 45: Gets the number of rows in this table.

◈ Line 47: Changes the number of elements of the array to the specified new size i.e. number of rows in the web table.

◈ Line 49: Loops through each row of the table.

◈ Line 51: Gets the number of columns in this table.

◈ Line 52: Changes the number of elements of the specified row array to the new size i.e. number of columns in the web table for that particular row.

◈ Line 54: Loops through each column in that row of the table.

◈ Line 54: Returns the table data in the form of an array-of-arrays.

5.2.4   Page Logic

5.2.4.1   Admin's Home Page

The Admin's *Home* page of our demo website will have the following actions:

Action	Description
ClickHome()	This action will navigate to the Admin user's *Home* page.
ClickReports()	This action will navigate to the *Employee Report by Gender* page.
ClickEmployeeList()	This action will navigate to the *Employee List* page.
ClickLogout()	This action will log the Admin user out and navigate to the generic *Home* page.

Add a new class 'pageHtmlAdminHome.cs' to the *Pages* folder and insert the code as shown in Listing 5.8.

Listing 5.8: 'pageHtmlAdminHome.cs' - Page logic for Admin's Home page

```
1  /*************************************************************
2   * All rights reserved. Copyright 2017 Arkenstone-ltd.com *
3   *************************************************************/
4
5  namespace CodedUITesting
6  {
7      class pageHtmlAdminHome
8      {
9          public void ClickHome()
10         {
11             Utility.Click(repHtmlAdminHome.Link_Home);
12         }
13
14         public void ClickReports()
15         {
16             Utility.Click(repHtmlAdminHome.Link_Reports);
17         }
18
19         public void ClickEmployeeList()
20         {
21             Utility.Click(repHtmlAdminHome.Link_EmployeeList);
22         }
23
24         public void ClickLogout()
25         {
26             Utility.Click(repHtmlAdminHome.Link_Logout);
```

```
27            }
28
29        }
30 }
```

5.2.4.2 Admin's Reports Page

The Admin's *Reports* page of our demo website will have the following action:

Action	Description
VerifyReportDetails()	This action will verify the details of the *Employee Report by Gender* with the values in the database.

Add a new class 'pageHtmlAdminReports.cs' to the *Pages* folder and insert the code as shown in Listing 5.9.

Listing 5.9: 'pageHtmlAdminReports.cs' - Page logic for the Admin's Reports page

```
1  /*****************************************************************
2   * All rights reserved. Copyright 2017 Arkenstone-ltd.com *
3   *****************************************************************/
4
5  using System;
6
7  namespace CodedUITesting
8  {
9      class pageHtmlAdminReports
10     {
11         public void VerifyReportDetails()
12         {
13             String[][] rptTable = Utility.GetTableData( ↵
                   ↪ repHtmlAdminReports.Table_ReportByGender);
14
15             for (int ii = 1; ii < rptTable.Length; ii++)
16             {
17                 switch (rptTable[ii][0])
18                 {
19                     case Config.FEMALE_TEXT:
20                         Utility.CompareDetails( ↵
                             ↪ Config.FEMALE, ↵
                             ↪ rptTable[ii][1]);
21                         break;
```

```
22
23                          case Config.MALE_TEXT:
24                              Utility.CompareDetails(Config.MALE, ↵
                                 ↪ rptTable[ii][1]);
25                          break;
26                      }
27                  }
28              Utility.ReportExpectedVsActual(Utility. ↵
                   ↪ GetValue(repHtmlAdminReports. ↵
                   ↪ Span_TotalEmployees), ↵
                   ↪ Utility.GetCountOfRecs("Select Count(*) ↵
                   ↪ from [dbo].[Employees]").ToString());
29          }
30      }
31 }
```

◈ Line 13: Gets the values of report table into an array-of-arrays by calling our Utility function `GetTableData`.

◈ Line 15: Iterates through the array-of-arrays from row 1 onwards. We are skipping row 0 which is the header row of the table. Note that `C#` arrays are zero indexed i.e. the array indexes start at zero.

◈ Line 17: Array items `rptTable[ii][0]` denote the first column of the table which store employee's gender.

◈ Lines 19 - 20: If it is a *"Female"* then call function `CompareDetails` with the expected value as *"Female"* and the actual value as `rptTable[ii][1]`.

◈ Lines 23 - 24: If it is a *"Male"* then call function `CompareDetails` with the expected value as *"Male"* and the actual value as `rptTable[ii][1]`.

◈ Line 28: Compares the expected value of the total displayed on the web page with the actual count received via SQL Query and reports the outcome.

5.2.5 Writing Tests

Add a new test to the 'WebHtmlTests.cs' file as shown in Listing 5.10.

Listing 5.10: 'WebHtmlTests.cs' - WebHtmlAdminVerifyReportByGender

```
1 [TestMethod]
2 public void WebHtmlAdminVerifyReportByGender()
3 {
4     Utility.Log.Info("Starting Test ***** " + ↵
          ↪ Utility.TestName + " *****");
5
6     try
7     {
8         Utility.LaunchWebApp();
```

```
 9
10        pageHtmlHome Home = new pageHtmlHome();
11        Home.ClickLogin();
12
13        pageHtmlLogin Login = new pageHtmlLogin();
14        Login.LoginUser("Admin", "Admin123");
15
16        pageHtmlAdminHome homeAdmin = new ↵
               ↪ pageHtmlAdminHome();
17        homeAdmin.ClickReports();
18
19        pageHtmlAdminReports rep = new ↵
               ↪ pageHtmlAdminReports();
20        rep.VerifyReportDetails();
21        homeAdmin.ClickLogout();
22        Utility.CloseWebApp();
23        Utility.ReportResult();
24    }
25    catch (Exception exception)
26    {
27        Utility.ReportExpectedVsActual(Utility.TestName, ↵
               ↪ "Exception occurred");
28        Utility.Log.Error("Exception: " + ↵
               ↪ exception.ToString());
29        throw exception;
30    }
31 }
```

◇ Line 17: Clicks the *Reports* link in the Admin user's *Home* Page.
◇ Line 20: Calls the `VerifyReportDetails` function in the page logic.

5.2.6 Executing Tests

Rebuild and execute the test `WebHtmlAdminVerifyReportByGender` and you will see an output as shown in Figure 5.1.

Test Name: WebHtmlAdminVerifyReportByGender

Test Outcome: Passed

Standard Output

```
2017-04-04 18:35:53.966 INFO  CodedUITesting.Utility - SetupSummaryFile
2017-04-04 18:35:54.068 INFO  CodedUITesting.Utility - Starting Test ***** WebHtmlAdminVerifyReportByGender *****
2017-04-04 18:36:00.421 INFO  CodedUITesting.Utility - [Expected:] http://testing.arkenstone-ltd.com/    [Actual:] http://testing.arkenstone-ltd.com/
2017-04-04 18:36:00.585 INFO  CodedUITesting.Utility - Screenshot saved at: C:\CodedUITesting\temp\WebHtmlAdminVerifyReportByGender_Home_
2017-04-04 18:36:01.315 INFO  CodedUITesting.Utility - Click HtmlHyperlink: Id -   (DisplayText - Login)
2017-04-04 18:36:06.154 INFO  CodedUITesting.Utility - SetValue HtmlEdit: Id -   (Name - TxtUserId)  Value: Admin
2017-04-04 18:36:07.483 INFO  CodedUITesting.Utility - SetValue HtmlEdit: Id -   (Name - TxtPassword)  Value: Admin123
2017-04-04 18:36:09.391 INFO  CodedUITesting.Utility - Click HtmlInputButton: Id - btnLogin  (DisplayText - Login)
2017-04-04 18:36:13.395 INFO  CodedUITesting.Utility - Click HtmlHyperlink: Id -   (DisplayText - Reports)
2017-04-04 18:36:17.456 INFO  CodedUITesting.Utility - GetTableData HtmlTable: Id - tblCounts  (Name - )
2017-04-04 18:36:18.306 INFO  CodedUITesting.Utility - Row: 0  Col: 0   Value: EmployeeGender
2017-04-04 18:36:18.696 INFO  CodedUITesting.Utility - Row: 0  Col: 1   Value: Count
2017-04-04 18:36:19.123 INFO  CodedUITesting.Utility - Row: 1  Col: 0   Value: Female
2017-04-04 18:36:19.496 INFO  CodedUITesting.Utility - Row: 1  Col: 1   Value: 4
2017-04-04 18:36:19.951 INFO  CodedUITesting.Utility - Row: 2  Col: 0   Value: Male
2017-04-04 18:36:20.421 INFO  CodedUITesting.Utility - Row: 2  Col: 1   Value: 1
2017-04-04 18:36:20.422 INFO  CodedUITesting.Utility - SQL is: Select Count(*) from [dbo].[Employees] where [Gender] = '2'
2017-04-04 18:36:20.655 INFO  CodedUITesting.Utility - Record count: 4
2017-04-04 18:36:20.656 INFO  CodedUITesting.Utility - [Expected:] 4    [Actual:] 4    [Step Passed]
2017-04-04 18:36:20.657 INFO  CodedUITesting.Utility - SQL is: Select Count(*) from [dbo].[Employees] where [Gender] = '1'
2017-04-04 18:36:20.659 INFO  CodedUITesting.Utility - Record count: 1
2017-04-04 18:36:20.660 INFO  CodedUITesting.Utility - [Expected:] 1    [Actual:] 1    [Step Passed]
2017-04-04 18:36:20.928 INFO  CodedUITesting.Utility - GetValue HtmlSpan: Id - TotalEmployees  (Name - )
2017-04-04 18:36:20.962 INFO  CodedUITesting.Utility - SQL is: Select Count(*) from [dbo].[Employees]
2017-04-04 18:36:20.965 INFO  CodedUITesting.Utility - Record count: 5
2017-04-04 18:36:20.966 INFO  CodedUITesting.Utility - [Expected:] 5    [Actual:] 5    [Step Passed]
2017-04-04 18:36:21.257 INFO  CodedUITesting.Utility - Click HtmlHyperlink: Id -   (DisplayText - Logout)
2017-04-04 18:36:25.961 INFO  CodedUITesting.Utility - Reporting Result......
2017-04-04 18:36:25.962 INFO  CodedUITesting.Utility - Test Passed
2017-04-04 18:36:26.241 INFO  CodedUITesting.Utility - Source: C:\CodedUITesting\temp
2017-04-04 18:36:26.243 INFO  CodedUITesting.Utility - Destination: c:\CodedUITesting\TestResults\                          2017-04-04 1
2017-04-04 18:36:26.244 INFO  CodedUITesting.Utility - Moving file: WebHtmlAdminVerifyReportByGender_Home_2017-04-04_18_36_00.png
2017-04-04 18:36:26.252 INFO  CodedUITesting.Utility - CreateSummaryFileEntry
```

Figure 5.1: Report By Gender Output

5.3   Table Handling - Tabular Reports

In this section we will learn about how to automate a typical tabular report i.e. *Employee List*. In doing so, we will also learn how to perform automated verification tasks on a Table control which has CheckBoxes displayed in its columns.

We will cover three scenarios in this section:

Test Scenario 1

- Launch the demo website.

- Click on the *Login* link.

- Login with the user 'Admin'.

- Click on the *Employee List* link.

- Verify employees' list displayed on web page with the values in the database.

Test Scenario 2

- Launch the demo website.
- Click on the *Login* link.
- Login with the user 'Admin'.
- Click on the *Employee List* link.
- Click on the Employee Id "10003" in the employee list table.
- Verify employee's detail displayed on web page with the corresponding values in the database.

Test Scenario 3

- Launch the demo website.
- Click on the *Login* link.
- Login with the user 'Admin'.
- Click on the *Employee List* link.
- Randomly select a row from the *Employees* table in our database.
- Click on the corresponding Employee Id in the web page.
- Verify employee's detail displayed on web page with the random row fetched above from the database.

5.3.1 Configuration Parameters

Let's define some configuration parameters as per Listing 5.11.

Listing 5.11: 'Config.cs' - Parameters to support tabular reports

```
1  public const string UNKNOWN_TEXT = "Unknown";
2
3  public const string YES = "Yes";
4  public const string NO = "No";
```

◈ Line 1: Defines a string constant for the **"Unknown"** text.
◈ Line 3: Defines a string constant for the **"Yes"** text.
◈ Line 4: Defines a string constant for the **"No"** text.

5.3.2 Object Repository

When you click on the *Employee List* link, the *Employee List* page is displayed with the following elements:

Admin's Employee List Page Controls			
Control	*Type*	*Property*	*Value*
Employees	Table	TechnologyName	Web
		ControlType	Table
		Id	TblEmployees
Total Employees	Label/Span	TechnologyName	Web
		ControlType	Pane
		Id	TotalEmployees

Add a new class 'repHtmlAdminEmpList.cs' to the *Repository* folder and insert the code as shown in Listing 5.12.

Listing 5.12: 'repHtmlAdminEmpList.cs' - Repository for Admin's Employee List page

```
1   /*****************************************************
2    * All rights reserved. Copyright 2017 Arkenstone-ltd.com *
3    ****************************************************/
4
5   using ↵
        ↪ Microsoft.VisualStudio.TestTools.UITesting.HtmlControls;
6
7   namespace CodedUITesting
8   {
9       public static class repHtmlAdminEmpList
10      {
11          private static HtmlTable mTable_EmployeesList;
12          private static HtmlSpan mSpan_TotalEmployees;
13
14          public static HtmlTable Table_EmployeesList
15          {
16              get
17              {
18                  if (mTable_EmployeesList == null || ↵
                        ↪ !mTable_EmployeesList.Exists)
19                  {
20                      mTable_EmployeesList = new ↵
                            ↪ HtmlTable(Utility.Browser);
21                      mTable_EmployeesList.SearchProperties. ↵
```

```
                          ↪ Add(HtmlTable.PropertyNames.Id, ↵
                          ↪ "TblEmployees");
22                }
23                return mTable_EmployeesList;
24            }
25        }
26
27        public static HtmlSpan Span_TotalEmployees
28        {
29            get
30            {
31                if (mSpan_TotalEmployees == null || ↵
                      ↪ !mSpan_TotalEmployees.Exists)
32                {
33                    mSpan_TotalEmployees = new ↵
                          ↪ HtmlSpan(Utility.Browser);
34                    mSpan_TotalEmployees.SearchProperties. ↵
                          ↪ Add(HtmlSpan.PropertyNames.Id, ↵
                          ↪ "TotalEmployees");
35                }
36                return mSpan_TotalEmployees;
37            }
38        }
39    }
40 }
```

5.3.3 Utility Functions

Let's now define some new functions in the Utility file as follows:

DecodeGender - Decodes the gender code and returns its text value		
Input Parameters	*genderCode*	Gender code to be decoded
Return Value	*genderText*	Returns the gender text.

DecodeContract - Decodes the contract type from a Yes/No value		
Input Parameters	*contCode*	Contract code to be decoded.
Return Value	*string*	Returns True, False or Unknown.

ClickCellWithValue - Clicks the cell in a table with the specified value		
Input Parameters	*object*	Object of type table.
	val	Click the cell whose value is *val*.
Return Value	*void*	Returns nothing.

Add Listing 5.13 code to the 'Utility.cs' file.

Listing 5.13: 'Utility.cs' - Additional functions

```
 1  public static String DecodeGender(string genderCode)
 2  {
 3      if (genderCode.Trim() == Config.MALE)
 4          return Config.MALE_TEXT;
 5      else if (genderCode.Trim() == Config.FEMALE)
 6          return Config.FEMALE_TEXT;
 7      else
 8          return Config.UNKNOWN_TEXT;
 9  }
10
11  public static String DecodeContract(string contCode)
12  {
13      if (contCode.Trim() == Config.YES)
14          return Config.TRUE;
15      else if (contCode.Trim() == Config.NO)
16          return Config.FALSE;
17      else
18          return Config.UNKNOWN_TEXT;
19  }
20
21  public static void ClickCellWithValue(Object obj, string ↵
      ↪ val)
22  {
23      try
24      {
25          switch (obj.GetType().ToString())
26          {
27              case Config.HTML_TABLE:
28                  ((HtmlTable)obj).WaitForControlExist( ↵
                      ↪ Config.TIMEOUT_MILLISEC);
29                  ((HtmlTable)obj).WaitForControlReady( ↵
                      ↪ Config.TIMEOUT_MILLISEC);
30
31                  HtmlCell myCell = ((HtmlTable)obj). ↵
                      ↪ FindFirstCellWithValue(val);
32                  Mouse.Click(myCell);
33                  break;
34
35              default:
36                  Log.Error("Error, Unknown object type: " ↵
                      ↪ + obj.GetType().ToString());
```

```
37            ReportExpectedVsActual("Error", "Not ←
                 ↪ Implemented");
38            break;
39        }
40    }
41    catch (Exception exception)
42    {
43        Log.Error("ClickCellWithValue Exception: " + ←
              ↪ exception.ToString());
44        throw exception;
45    }
46 }
```

◈ Line 3: If the gender code is *male* then returns its text's equivalent.

◈ Line 5: If the gender code is *female* then returns its text's equivalent.

◈ Line 7: Otherwise returns an unknown text.

◈ Line 13: If the contract code is *yes* then returns a true value.

◈ Line 15: If the contract code is *no* then returns a false value.

◈ Line 17: Otherwise returns an unknown text.

◈ Line 31: Finds the first cell with the specified value.

◈ Line 32: Clicks the cell.

5.3.4 Page Logic

The *Employee List* page of our demo website will have the following actions:

Action	Description
VerifyEmployeeList()	This action will verify the details of the complete employees list with the values in the database.
VerifyEmployeeById()	This action will verify the details of an individual employee with the values in the database.
VerifyEmployeeWithDBRandom()	This action will verify a randomly selected employee from the database with its corresponding details in the web page.

Add a new class 'pageHtmlAdminEmpList.cs' to the *Pages* folder and insert the code as shown in Listing 5.14.

```
1   /*************************************************************
2    * All rights reserved. Copyright 2017 Arkenstone-ltd.com *
3    *************************************************************/
4   using ↵
        ↪ Microsoft.VisualStudio.TestTools.UITesting.HtmlControls;
5   using System;
6   using System.Data.SqlClient;
7
8   namespace CodedUITesting
9   {
10      class pageHtmlAdminEmpList
11      {
12          public void VerifyEmployeeList()
13          {
14              String[][] rptTable = GetEmployeeListData( ↵
                    ↪ repHtmlAdminEmpList.Table_EmployeesList);
15
16              for (int ii = 1; ii < rptTable.Length; ii++)
17              {
18                  string stringSQL = "SELECT [EmployeeID], ↵
                        ↪ [Title], [Name], [Gender], ↵
                        ↪ Convert(varchar(10), ↵
                        ↪ CONVERT(date,[DateOfBirth],106),103) ↵
                        ↪ [DateOfBirth], [ContractJob]" + ↵
                        ↪ "\r\n";
19                  stringSQL = stringSQL + "FROM ↵
                        ↪ [dbo].[Employees] where EmployeeID = ↵
                        ↪ '" + rptTable[ii][0] + "'";
20
21                  Utility.Log.Info("SQL is: " + ↵
                        ↪ stringSQL);
22
23                  String actEmpId = "", actTitle = "", ↵
                        ↪ actName = "", actGender = "", actDob ↵
                        ↪ = "", actContract = "";
24
25                  using (SqlConnection con = new ↵
                        ↪ SqlConnection(Config.connectionString))
26                  {
27                      con.Open();
28
29                      using (SqlCommand command = new ↵
```

```
                        ↪ SqlCommand(stringSQL, con))
30              using (SqlDataReader reader = ↩
                        ↪ command.ExecuteReader())
31                  {
32                      while (reader.Read())
33                      {
34                          actEmpId = reader.GetString(0);
35                          actTitle = reader.GetString(1);
36                          actName = reader.GetString(2);
37                          actGender = reader.GetString(3);
38                          actDob = reader.GetString(4);
39                          actContract = ↩
                                ↪ reader.GetString(5);
40                      }
41                  }
42              }
43
44              Utility.ReportExpectedVsActual( ↩
                    ↪ rptTable[ii][0], actEmpId);
45              Utility.ReportExpectedVsActual( ↩
                    ↪ rptTable[ii][1], actTitle);
46              Utility.ReportExpectedVsActual( ↩
                    ↪ rptTable[ii][2], actName);
47              Utility.ReportExpectedVsActual( ↩
                    ↪ rptTable[ii][3], ↩
                    ↪ Utility.DecodeGender(actGender));
48              Utility.ReportExpectedVsActual( ↩
                    ↪ rptTable[ii][4], actDob);
49              Utility.ReportExpectedVsActual( ↩
                    ↪ rptTable[ii][5], ↩
                    ↪ Utility.DecodeContract(actContract));
50
51              Utility.ReportExpectedVsActual( ↩
                    ↪ Utility.GetValue(repHtmlAdminEmpList. ↩
                    ↪ Span_TotalEmployees), ↩
                    ↪ Utility.GetCountOfRecs("Select ↩
                    ↪ Count(*) from ↩
                    ↪ [dbo].[Employees]").ToString());
52          }
53      }
54
55      private static String[][] ↩
            ↪ GetEmployeeListData(Object obj)
56      {
57          String[][] tblData = { };
```

```
58
59              try
60              {
61                  switch (obj.GetType().ToString())
62                  {
63                      case Config.HTML_TABLE:
64                          ((HtmlTable)obj).WaitForControlExist( ↵
                            ↪ Config.TIMEOUT_MILLISEC);
65                          ((HtmlTable)obj).WaitForControlReady( ↵
                            ↪ Config.TIMEOUT_MILLISEC);
66                          Utility.Log.Info("GetValue ↵
                            ↪ HtmlTable: Id - " + ↵
                            ↪ ((HtmlTable)obj).Id + "  ↵
                            ↪ (Name - " + ↵
                            ↪ ((HtmlTable)obj).Name + ")");
67
68                          int rowCount = ↵
                            ↪ ((HtmlTable)obj).RowCount;
69
70                          Array.Resize(ref tblData, rowCount);
71
72                          for (int i = 0; i < rowCount; i++)
73                          {
74                              int colCount = ↵
                                ↪ ((HtmlTable)obj).ColumnCount;
75                              Array.Resize(ref tblData[i], ↵
                                ↪ colCount);
76
77                              for (int j = 0; j < colCount; ↵
                                ↪ j++)
78                              {
79                                  String stg = null;
80                                  if (j == 5)
81                                  {
82                                      var children = ↵
                                        ↪ ((HtmlTable)obj). ↵
                                        ↪ GetCell(i, j). ↵
                                        ↪ GetChildren();
83                                      foreach (var child in ↵
                                        ↪ children)
84                                      {
85                                          if (child. ↵
                                            ↪ ControlType ↵
                                            ↪ == ↵
                                            ↪ "CheckBox")
```

```
 86                                          {
 87                                             stg = (( ↵
                                                 ↪ HtmlCheckBox ↵
                                                 ↪ )child). ↵
                                                 ↪ Checked. ↵
                                                 ↪ ToString();
 88                                          }
 89                                      }
 90                                  }
 91                              else
 92                                  stg = ↵
                                     ↪ ((HtmlTable)obj). ↵
                                     ↪ GetCell(i, j). ↵
                                     ↪ InnerText;
 93
 94                              tblData[i][j] = stg;
 95                              Utility.Log.Info("Row: " ↵
                                 ↪ + i + " Col: " + j ↵
                                 ↪ + "   Value: " + ↵
                                 ↪ tblData[i][j]);
 96                          }
 97                      }
 98                      break;
 99
100                  default:
101                      Utility.Log.Error("Error, Unknown ↵
                         ↪ object type: " + ↵
                         ↪ obj.GetType().ToString());
102                      Utility.ReportExpectedVsActual( ↵
                         ↪ "Error", "Not Implemented");
103                      break;
104              }
105
106          return tblData;
107      }
108      catch (Exception exception)
109      {
110          Utility.Log.Error("GetEmployeeListData ↵
                 ↪ Exception: " + exception.ToString());
111          throw exception;
112      }
113  }
114
115  public void VerifyEmployeeById(String empId)
116  {
```

```
117        Utility.ClickCellWithValue(repHtmlAdminEmpList. ↵
               ↪ Table_EmployeesList, empId);
118
119        string stringSQL = "SELECT [EmployeeID], ↵
               ↪ [Title], [Name], [Gender], ↵
               ↪ [DateOfBirth], [Email], [ContractJob], ↵
               ↪ [Postcode]" + "\r\n";
120        stringSQL = stringSQL + "FROM ↵
               ↪ [dbo].[Employees] where EmployeeID = '" ↵
               ↪ + empId + "'";
121
122        Utility.Log.Info("SQL is: " + stringSQL);
123
124        String expEmpId = "", expTitle = "", expName ↵
               ↪ = "", expGender = "", expDob = "", ↵
               ↪ expEmail = "", expContract = "", ↵
               ↪ expPostcode = "";
125
126        using (SqlConnection con = new ↵
               ↪ SqlConnection(Config.connectionString))
127        {
128            con.Open();
129
130            using (SqlCommand command = new ↵
                   ↪ SqlCommand(stringSQL, con))
131            using (SqlDataReader reader = ↵
                   ↪ command.ExecuteReader())
132            {
133                while (reader.Read())
134                {
135                    expEmpId = reader.GetString(0);
136                    expTitle = reader.GetString(1);
137                    expName = reader.GetString(2);
138                    expGender = reader.GetString(3);
139                    expDob = ↵
                           ↪ reader.GetDateTime(4).ToString();
140                    expEmail = reader.GetString(5);
141                    expContract = reader.GetString(6);
142                    expPostcode = ↵
                           ↪ reader.GetString(7);
143                }
144            }
145        }
146
147        Utility.ReportExpectedVsActual(expEmpId, ↵
```

```
           ↪ Utility.GetValue(repHtmlEmployeeDetail. ↩
           ↪ EditBox_EmployeeId));
148    Utility.ReportExpectedVsActual(expTitle, ↩
           ↪ Utility.GetValue(repHtmlEmployeeDetail. ↩
           ↪ ComboBox_Title));
149    Utility.ReportExpectedVsActual(expName, ↩
           ↪ Utility.GetValue(repHtmlEmployeeDetail. ↩
           ↪ EditBox_Name));
150
151    if (Utility.DecodeGender(expGender) == ↩
           ↪ Config.MALE_TEXT)
152    {
153        Utility.Log.Info("Verifying... " + ↩
               ↪ Config.MALE_TEXT);
154        Utility.ReportExpectedVsActual(Config.TRUE, ↩
               ↪ Utility.GetValue(repHtmlEmployeeDetail. ↩
               ↪ RadioButton_GenderMale));
155    }
156    else if (Utility.DecodeGender(expGender) == ↩
           ↪ Config.FEMALE_TEXT)
157    {
158        Utility.Log.Info("Verifying... " + ↩
               ↪ Config.FEMALE_TEXT);
159        Utility.ReportExpectedVsActual(Config.TRUE, ↩
               ↪ Utility.GetValue(repHtmlEmployeeDetail. ↩
               ↪ RadioButton_GenderFemale));
160    }
161    else
162        Utility.ReportExpectedVsActual("Invalid ↩
               ↪ Value*** ", ↩
               ↪ Utility.DecodeGender(expGender));
163
164    Utility.ReportExpectedVsActual(expDob. ↩
           ↪ Substring(0, 10), ↩
           ↪ Utility.GetValue(repHtmlEmployeeDetail. ↩
           ↪ EditBox_DateOfBirth));
165    Utility.ReportExpectedVsActual(expEmail, ↩
           ↪ Utility.GetValue(repHtmlEmployeeDetail. ↩
           ↪ EditBox_Email));
166    Utility.ReportExpectedVsActual(Utility. ↩
           ↪ DecodeContract(expContract), ↩
           ↪ Utility.GetValue(repHtmlEmployeeDetail. ↩
           ↪ CheckBox_Contract));
167    Utility.ReportExpectedVsActual(expPostcode, ↩
           ↪ Utility.GetValue(repHtmlEmployeeDetail. ↩
```

```
                                    ↪ EditBox_Postcode));
168             }
169
170         public void VerifyEmployeeWithDBRandom()
171         {
172             string stringSQL = "SELECT TOP 1 ↩
                    ↪ [EmployeeID], [Title], [Name], [Gender], ↩
                    ↪ [DateOfBirth], [Email], [ContractJob], ↩
                    ↪ [Postcode]" + "\r\n";
173             stringSQL = stringSQL + "FROM ↩
                    ↪ [dbo].[Employees] Order by NEWID()";
174
175             Utility.Log.Info("SQL is: " + stringSQL);
176
177             String expEmpId = "", expTitle = "", expName ↩
                    ↪ = "", expGender = "", expDob = "", ↩
                    ↪ expEmail = "", expContract = "", ↩
                    ↪ expPostcode = "";
178
179             using (SqlConnection con = new ↩
                    ↪ SqlConnection(Config.connectionString))
180             {
181                 con.Open();
182
183                 using (SqlCommand command = new ↩
                        ↪ SqlCommand(stringSQL, con))
184                 using (SqlDataReader reader = ↩
                        ↪ command.ExecuteReader())
185                 {
186                     while (reader.Read())
187                     {
188                         expEmpId = reader.GetString(0);
189                         expTitle = reader.GetString(1);
190                         expName = reader.GetString(2);
191                         expGender = reader.GetString(3);
192                         expDob = ↩
                            ↪ reader.GetDateTime(4).ToString();
193                         expEmail = reader.GetString(5);
194                         expContract = reader.GetString(6);
195                         expPostcode = reader.GetString(7);
196                     }
197                 }
198             }
199
200             Utility.ClickCellWithValue(repHtmlAdminEmpList. ↩
```

```
              ↪ Table_EmployeesList , expEmpId);
201
202           Utility.ReportExpectedVsActual(expEmpId , ↩
                  ↪ Utility.GetValue(repHtmlEmployeeDetail . ↩
                  ↪ EditBox_EmployeeId));
203           Utility.ReportExpectedVsActual(expTitle , ↩
                  ↪ Utility.GetValue(repHtmlEmployeeDetail . ↩
                  ↪ ComboBox_Title));
204           Utility.ReportExpectedVsActual(expName , ↩
                  ↪ Utility.GetValue(repHtmlEmployeeDetail . ↩
                  ↪ EditBox_Name));
205
206           if (Utility.DecodeGender(expGender) == ↩
                  ↪ Config.MALE_TEXT)
207               Utility.ReportExpectedVsActual(Config.TRUE , ↩
                      ↪ Utility.GetValue(repHtmlEmployeeDetail . ↩
                      ↪ RadioButton_GenderMale));
208           else if (Utility.DecodeGender(expGender) == ↩
                  ↪ Config.FEMALE_TEXT)
209               Utility.ReportExpectedVsActual(Config.TRUE , ↩
                      ↪ Utility.GetValue(repHtmlEmployeeDetail . ↩
                      ↪ RadioButton_GenderFemale));
210           else
211               Utility.ReportExpectedVsActual("Invalid ↩
                      ↪ Value*** ", ↩
                      ↪ Utility.DecodeGender(expGender));
212
213           Utility.ReportExpectedVsActual(expDob. ↩
                  ↪ Substring(0, 10), ↩
                  ↪ Utility.GetValue(repHtmlEmployeeDetail . ↩
                  ↪ EditBox_DateOfBirth));
214           Utility.ReportExpectedVsActual(expEmail , ↩
                  ↪ Utility.GetValue(repHtmlEmployeeDetail . ↩
                  ↪ EditBox_Email));
215           Utility.ReportExpectedVsActual(Utility. ↩
                  ↪ DecodeContract(expContract), ↩
                  ↪ Utility.GetValue(repHtmlEmployeeDetail . ↩
                  ↪ CheckBox_Contract));
216           Utility.ReportExpectedVsActual(expPostcode , ↩
                  ↪ Utility.GetValue(repHtmlEmployeeDetail . ↩
                  ↪ EditBox_Postcode));
217       }
218   }
219 }
```

◈ Line 12: Page logic to verify the employee list data.

◈ Line 14: Gets the table data into an array-of-arrays.

◈ Line 16: Iterates through the array-of-arrays from row 1 onwards. We are skipping row 0 which is the header row of the table. Note that `C#` arrays are zero indexed i.e. the array indexes start at zero.

◈ Lines 18 - 19: Construct the SQL Query to fetch data from the database table for the given employee id. Note that `rptTable[ii][0]` denotes first column of the table which stores the employee id.

◈ Line 21: Logs the SQL Query.

◈ Line 23: Initialises variables to store data fetched from the SQL Query.

◈ Lines 34 - 39: Store data fetched from the SQL Query into variables.

◈ Lines 44 - 49: Compare the expected values in the array with the actual values fetched from the database table and report the outcome.

◈ Line 47: Uses the Utility function `DecodeGender` to decode the gender.

◈ Line 49: Uses the Utility function `DecodeContract` to decode the contract.

◈ Line 51: Compares the expected value of the total displayed on the web page with the actual count retrieved via the SQL Query and reports the outcome.

◈ Line 55: Defines the `private` function `GetEmployeeListData` to retrieve the employee list. Note that we have defined this function as `private` and will be accessible only within the body of the class. We think that the logic to retrieve *Employee List* data is specific to this page only and that is why we haven't implemented this function in the 'Utility.cs' class.

◈ Line 80: The sixth column which contains a `CheckBox`, needs a special treatment to retrieve its value.

◈ Line 82: Retrieves all the child elements in the specified cell.

◈ Line 83: Loops through all the child elements.

◈ Lines 85 - 87: If child element is of type `CheckBox` then note down its `Checked` status.

◈ Line 92: If it is not the sixth column, in that case, just gets its `InnerText`.

◈ Line 115: Verifies an employee with the values stored in the database for a given employee id - `empId`.

◈ Line 117: Clicks the table row containing the employee id.

◈ Lines 18 - 19: Construct the SQL Query to fetch data for the `empId`.

◈ Lines 35 - 42: Store data fetched from the SQL Query into variables. Note the use of `ToString()` function to convert datetime into a string value.

◈ Lines 151 - 162: Pass the expected value of gender (`expGender`) to the generic function `DecodeGender`, compare it with the actual value on the web page and report the outcome.

◈ Line 164: Note the use of `Substring` function to retrieve first 10 characters.

◈ Line 166: Passes the expected value of contract (`expContract`) to the generic function `DecodeContract`, compares it with the actual value on the web page and reports the outcome.

◈ Line 170: Verifies a randomly selected employee from the database with the corresponding values on the web page.

◈ Line 172: Uses `SELECT TOP` clause to specify the number of records to return, which is *one* in our case.

◈ Line 173: The `Order by NEWID()` statement selects different record(s) each time the SQL Query is executed.

◈ Line 200: Clicks the corresponding Employee Id in the web page table as fetched from the database table.

5.3.5 Creating Tests

Add new tests to the 'WebHtmlTests.cs' file as shown in Listing 5.15.

Listing 5.15: 'WebHtmlTests.cs' - Additional tests

```
1  [TestMethod]
2  public void WebHtmlAdminVerifyEmployeeList()
3  {
4      Utility.Log.Info("Starting Test ***** " + ↵
         ↪ Utility.TestName + " *****");
5
6      try
7      {
8          Utility.LaunchWebApp();
9
10         pageHtmlHome Home = new pageHtmlHome();
11         Home.ClickLogin();
12
13         pageHtmlLogin Login = new pageHtmlLogin();
14         Login.LoginUser("Admin", "Admin123");
15
16         pageHtmlAdminHome homeAdmin = new ↵
            ↪ pageHtmlAdminHome();
17         homeAdmin.ClickEmployeeList();
18
19         pageHtmlAdminEmpList emplist = new ↵
            ↪ pageHtmlAdminEmpList();
20         emplist.VerifyEmployeeList();
21
22         homeAdmin.ClickLogout();
23         Utility.CloseWebApp();
24         Utility.ReportResult();
25     }
26     catch (Exception exception)
27     {
28         Utility.ReportExpectedVsActual(Utility.TestName, ↵
            ↪ "Exception occurred");
29         Utility.Log.Error("Exception: " + ↵
            ↪ exception.ToString());
```

```
30          throw exception;
31      }
32 }
33
34 [TestMethod]
35 public void WebHtmlAdminVerifyEmployeeById()
36 {
37      Utility.Log.Info("Starting Test ***** " + ↵
            ↪ Utility.TestName + " *****");
38
39      try
40      {
41          Utility.LaunchWebApp();
42
43          pageHtmlHome Home = new pageHtmlHome();
44          Home.ClickLogin();
45
46          pageHtmlLogin Login = new pageHtmlLogin();
47          Login.LoginUser("Admin", "Admin123");
48
49          pageHtmlAdminHome homeAdmin = new ↵
                ↪ pageHtmlAdminHome();
50          homeAdmin.ClickEmployeeList();
51
52          pageHtmlAdminEmpList emplist = new ↵
                ↪ pageHtmlAdminEmpList();
53          emplist.VerifyEmployeeById("10003");
54
55          homeAdmin.ClickLogout();
56          Utility.CloseWebApp();
57          Utility.ReportResult();
58      }
59      catch (Exception exception)
60      {
61          Utility.ReportExpectedVsActual(Utility.TestName, ↵
                ↪ "Exception occurred");
62          Utility.Log.Error("Exception: " + ↵
                ↪ exception.ToString());
63          throw exception;
64      }
65 }
66
67 [TestMethod]
68 public void WebHtmlAdminVerifyEmployeeByIdRandom()
69 {
```

```
70      Utility.Log.Info("Starting Test ***** " + ↵
            ↳ Utility.TestName + " *****");
71
72      try
73      {
74          Utility.LaunchWebApp();
75
76          pageHtmlHome Home = new pageHtmlHome();
77          Home.ClickLogin();
78
79          pageHtmlLogin Login = new pageHtmlLogin();
80          Login.LoginUser("Admin", "Admin123");
81
82          pageHtmlAdminHome homeAdmin = new ↵
                ↳ pageHtmlAdminHome();
83          homeAdmin.ClickEmployeeList();
84
85          pageHtmlAdminEmpList emplist = new ↵
                ↳ pageHtmlAdminEmpList();
86          emplist.VerifyEmployeeWithDBRandom();
87
88          homeAdmin.ClickLogout();
89          Utility.CloseWebApp();
90          Utility.ReportResult();
91      }
92      catch (Exception exception)
93      {
94          Utility.ReportExpectedVsActual(Utility.TestName, ↵
                ↳ "Exception occurred");
95          Utility.Log.Error("Exception: " + ↵
                ↳ exception.ToString());
96          throw exception;
97      }
98 }
```

◈ Line 1: New test `WebHtmlAdminVerifyEmployeeList`.

◈ Line 17: Clicks the *View Employee List* link in Admin user's *Home* Page.

◈ Line 20: Calls the `VerifyEmployeeList` function in the page logic.

◈ Line 34: New test `WebHtmlAdminVerifyEmployeeById`.

◈ Line 50: Clicks the *View Employee List* link in Admin user's *Home* Page.

◈ Line 53: Calls the `VerifyEmployeeWithDB` function with employee id "10003".

◈ Line 67: New test `WebHtmlAdminVerifyEmployeeByIdRandom`.

◈ Line 83: Clicks the *View Employee List* link in Admin user's *Home* Page.

◈ Line 86: Calls the `VerifyEmployeeWithDBRandom` function to randomly select a record from the database and verifies corresponding values in the web page.

5.3.6 Executing Tests

Execute the new tests and you will see a Test Summary report as shown in Figure 5.2. The tests should execute successfully.

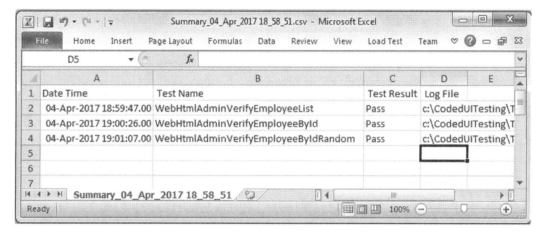

Figure 5.2: Employee List Output

Chapter 6

Data Driven Testing

Data Driven Testing

In this chapter, we will learn:

- *About Data Driven Testing*

- *How to use Excel® XLS and XLSX files as a data source for the automated testing*

- *About adding some important features to our Automation Framework*

So let's get on with it...

DATA Driven Testing (DDT) is the creation of automated test scripts where the test data is read from a data file instead of using the same hard-coded values, each time the test runs. By using the Data Driven Testing approach, we can effectively test how the Application Under Test handles various inputs. To get a larger test coverage, you should perform automated tests with different input data. Consider a scenario where we add an employee or view an employee via automated test. The automated test contains only those values that you entered during the coding and (most likely) these values do not cause any errors in the Application Under Test, however other data may cause them. Therefore, we should run our automated tests with different sets of input data to ensure that the Application Under Test works as expected for various input values. This approach is called *Data Driven Testing.*

A data driven test will read data from a storage (an Excel file in our case) rather than use hard-coded values. Such a separation of data makes a test simpler and easy to maintain. On the other hand, a test containing several sets of hard-coded values can be rather difficult to maintain. If you need more input data, you will have to modify the test itself e.g. in order to verify an employee whose id is "10004" instead of "10002", you have to either update the existing test or write a new test. However, if the test is written with the Data Driven Testing approach, you can have all the employee data in an Excel file and randomly pick an employee's id during the test execution, hence giving you more data coverage at runtime. There is no need to modify the existing test or write a new test with this approach. We will cover two Excel formats – XLSX and XLS (Excel 97 – 2003) for the data sources.

In order to use Excel as the data source, we will use NPOI which is the .NET version of POI Java project (`http://poi.apache.org/`). POI is an open source project which helps you read and write Excel files. Download NPOI and extract to the 'C:\NPOI' folder. You may extract to a different folder that suites you but the book assumes you have chosen 'C:\NPOI' folder.

6.1 Adding Necessary References

First of all, let's add the necessary references to support Excel files.

- In the *Solution Explorer* window, right click on *References* and select *Add Reference*.

- Click the *Browse...* button and navigate to 'C:\NPOI\dotnet4' folder. Your location may differ depending on where you extracted NPOI files.

- Select files 'NPOI.dll', 'NPOI.OOXML.dll' and 'NPOI.OpenXml4Net.dll' as shown in Figure 6.1. Use the Ctrl key to select multiple files.

- Click the *Add* button and then press *OK*.

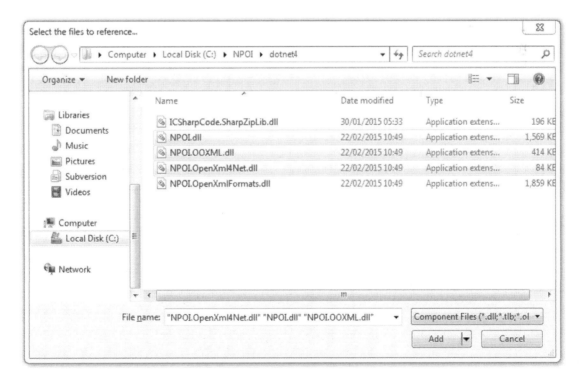

Figure 6.1: Adding References to Support Excel Files

6.2 Excel XLS Format

6.2.1 Utility Functions

Let us define some new Utility functions as:

GetSpreadSheetXLS - Gets the Spreadsheet data in XLS format into an array-of-arrays		
Input Parameters	*pathName*	Path and name of the XLS file to read
	sheetNumber	Sheet number of the XLS file to read
Return Value	*jaggedArray*	Returns the Spreadsheet data as an array-of-arrays

ExcelDateParse - Converts an Excel date to a defined date format		
Input Parameters	*ExcelDate*	Date in Excel format
Return Value	*date*	Returns the date in java.util.Date format

Add Listing 6.1 code to the 'Utility.cs' file.

Listing 6.1: 'Utility.cs' - Changes to support XLS file format

```
1  using NPOI.HSSF.UserModel;
2
3  public static String[][] GetSpreadSheetXLS(String ←
       ↪ pathName, int sheetNumber)
4  {
5      Utility.Log.Info("GetSpreadSheetXLS....... File: " + ←
           ↪ pathName + "       Sheet: " + sheetNumber);
6      String[][] ssData = { };
7
8      try
9      {
10         FileStream ExcelFileToRead = new ←
               ↪ FileStream(pathName, FileMode.Open, ←
               ↪ FileAccess.Read);
11         HSSFWorkbook workbk = new ←
               ↪ HSSFWorkbook(ExcelFileToRead);
12
13         HSSFSheet sheet = ←
               ↪ (HSSFSheet)workbk.GetSheetAt(sheetNumber);
14
15         Utility.Log.Info("SHEET Name: " + ←
               ↪ sheet.SheetName);
```

```
16
17          Utility.Log.Info("SHEET LastRowNum: " + ←
                ↪ sheet.LastRowNum);
18          Utility.Log.Info("SHEET ColumnCount: " + ←
                ↪ sheet.GetRow(0).Cells.Count);
19
20          int rowCount = sheet.LastRowNum + 1;
21          int colCount = sheet.GetRow(0).Cells.Count;
22
23          Array.Resize(ref ssData, rowCount);
24
25          int i = 0;
26
27          while (sheet.GetRow(i) != null)
28          {
29              Array.Resize(ref ssData[i], colCount);
30
31              for (int j = 0; j < ←
                    ↪ sheet.GetRow(i).Cells.Count; j++)
32              {
33                  var cell = sheet.GetRow(i).GetCell(j);
34
35                  if (cell != null)
36                  {
37                      Utility.Log.Info("CellType: " + ←
                            ↪ cell.CellType);
38
39                      switch (cell.CellType)
40                      {
41                          case NPOI.SS.UserModel.CellType. ←
                                ↪ Numeric:
42                              ssData[i][j] = ←
                                    ↪ sheet.GetRow(i).GetCell(j). ←
                                    ↪ NumericCellValue.ToString();
43                              break;
44                          case NPOI.SS.UserModel.CellType. ←
                                ↪ String:
45                              ssData[i][j] = ←
                                    ↪ sheet.GetRow(i).GetCell(j). ←
                                    ↪ StringCellValue.ToString();
46                              break;
47                      }
48
49                      Utility.Log.Info("Row: " + (i) + " ←
                            ↪ Col: " + (j) + " " + ←
```

```
                                  ↪ ssData[i][j] + " ");
50                    }
51                }
52
53                i++;
54            }
55
56            return ssData;
57        }
58        catch (Exception exception)
59        {
60            Utility.Log.Error("GetSpreadSheetXLS Exception: " ↩
                  ↪ + exception.ToString());
61            throw exception;
62        }
63 }
64
65 public static String ExcelDateParse(String ExcelDate)
66 {
67     double dt = Double.Parse(ExcelDate);
68
69     DateTime dt1 = ↩
              ↪ NPOI.SS.UserModel.DateUtil.GetJavaDate(dt);
70
71     return dt1.ToString();
72 }
```

◈ Line 1: Additional import required to support the functionality.

◈ Line 5: Logs the received parameters.

◈ Line 6: Initialises an array-of-arrays.

◈ Line 10: Initialises a new instance of the `FileStream` class with the specified pathname, creation mode and access permission:

- PathName - path and name of the XLS file.

- FileMode `Open` - the operating system should open an existing file.

- FileAccess `Read` - read access to the file. Data can be read from the file.

◈ Line 11: Initialises a new instance of the `HSSFWorkbook` class - high level representation of a workbook.

◈ Line 13: Gets the worksheet specified by the sheet number.

◈ Line 15: Logs the sheet name.

◈ Line 17: Logs the last row number in the sheet.

◈ Line 18: Logs the column count of the first row.

◈ Line 20: Initialises a variable for the row count.

◈ Line 21: Initialises a variable for the column count

◈ Line 23: Resizes the data array to the row count - to accommodate all the rows.

◈ Line 25: Initialises a row variable.

◈ Line 27: Loops while there are rows in the worksheet.

◈ Line 29: Resizes current row of the data array to the column count - to accommodate all the columns.

◈ Line 31: Loops while there are columns in the current row.

◈ Line 33: Gets the cell at the current row and column position.

◈ Line 35: Ensures that the cell is not `null`.

◈ Line 41: If the cell type is `Numeric`, gets its numeric value and stores it in the array-of-arrays at the current row and column position.

◈ Line 44: If the cell type is `String`, gets its string value and stores it in the array-of-arrays at the current row and column position.

◈ Line 49: Logs the array data at the current row and column position.

◈ Line 53: Increments the row variable.

◈ Line 56: Returns the spreadsheet data.

◈ Line 65: Converts an Excel date using 1900 date windowing to a `java.util.Date`.

◈ Line 67: Parses the Excel date in string format to a double value.

◈ Line 69: Gets the java date of the double value.

◈ Line 71: Returns the date as a string.

6.2.2 Data Driven - Login

Let's write a data driven login test that will read data from an Excel file in XLS format, rather than hard-coded values. We will perform the following Test Scenario to demonstrate data driven login:

- Launch the demo website.

- Click on the *Login* link.

- Read the user credentials from the test data file in XLS format.

- Login the general user with the credentials read above.

6.2.2.1 Test Data File

As you know, the demo website has two users - 'Tester' and 'Admin'. We will create the login credentials for both of these users in the data source. Here are the steps to create the test data file in XLS format:

- Open Excel and create the test data as shown in Figure 6.2.

- Row 1 is the header row.

- Column A contains the *User id* and Column B contains the *Password*.

- Rename the worksheet as 'Login'.

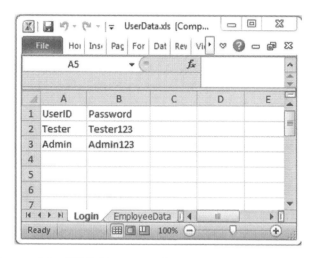

Figure 6.2: XLS Format- Creating Login Test Data

- Save the data file as 'UserData.xls' in the 'C:\CodedUITesting\CodedUITesting\TestData' folder. Ensure that the "Save as type" is 'Excel 97-2003 Workbook (*.xls)'.

- Close Excel.

6.2.2.2   Creating Test

Add Listing 6.2 code to the 'WebHtmlTests.cs' file.

Listing 6.2: 'WebHtmlTests.cs' - Code for test WebHtmlTesterLoginXLSData

```
1  [TestMethod]
2  public void WebHtmlTesterLoginXLSData()
3  {
4      Utility.Log.Info("Starting Test ***** " + ↵
           ↪ Utility.TestName + " *****");
5
6      try
7      {
8          Utility.LaunchWebApp();
9
10         pageHtmlHome Home = new pageHtmlHome();
11         Home.ClickLogin();
12
13         String[][] data = Utility.GetSpreadSheetXLS( ↵
               ↪ @"C:\CodedUITesting\CodedUITesting\TestData\ ↵
               ↪ UserData.xls", 0);
14
15         pageHtmlLogin Login = new pageHtmlLogin();
16         Login.LoginUser(data[1][0], data[1][1]);
17
```

```
18          Utility.CloseWebApp();
19          Utility.ReportResult();
20      }
21  catch (Exception exception)
22  {
23          Utility.ReportExpectedVsActual(Utility.TestName, ↵
            ↪ "Exception occurred");
24          Utility.Log.Error("Exception: " + ↵
            ↪ exception.ToString());
25      throw exception;
26  }
27 }
```

◈ Line 2: New login test that uses Excel XLS file as a data source.

◈ Line 13: Gets the spreadsheet data in an array-of-arrays. Note that the second parameter 0 corresponds to the first worksheet i.e. 'Login'.

◈ Line 16: Calls the `Login` function with the data read from the XLS file. Parameter `data[1][0]` is the user id *Tester* and `data[1][1]` is its password i.e. *Tester123*. Note that C# arrays are zero indexed.

6.2.2.3   Executing Test

Execute the test `WebHtmlTesterLoginXLSData` and you will see an output as shown in Figure 6.3. The login credentials are read from the XLS file and the user is logged in successfully.

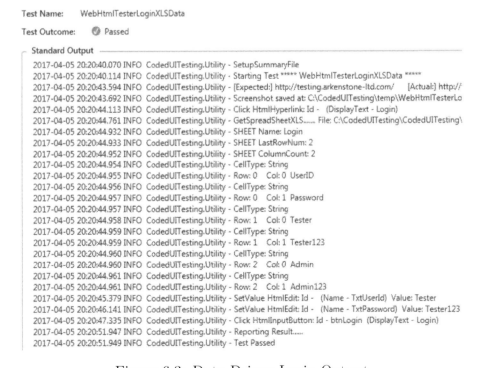

Figure 6.3: Data Driven Login Output

☞ If the Test Data file in Excel has not been closed, you may get the error "System.IO.IOException: The process cannot access the file 'C:\CodedUITesting\CodedUITesting\TestData\UserData.xls' because it is being used by another process." Please ensure that the Test Data file in Excel is closed before executing the test.

6.2.3 Data Driven - Add Employee

Let's write a data driven test to add an employee as per the following Test Scenario:

- Launch the demo website.

- Click on the *Login* link.

- Read user credentials from the test data file in XLS format.

- Login the general user with the credentials read above.

- Click on the *Add Employee* link.

- Read the employee data to be added from the test data file in XLS format.

- Add the employee using the data read above

6.2.3.1 Test Data File

- Open the 'UserData.xls' file, add a new worksheet and create the test data as shown in Figure 6.4.

- Row 1 is the header row.

- Rename the worksheet as 'EmployeeData'.

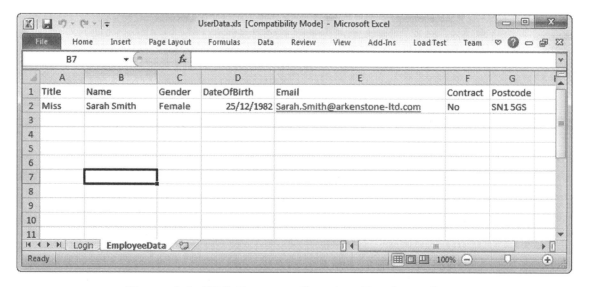

Figure 6.4: XLS Format - Creating Employee Data

- Save the data file. Ensure that the "Save as type" is 'Excel 97-2003 Workbook (*.xls)'.

- Close Excel.

6.2.3.2 Page Logic

We will add a new action to the *Add Employee* page's logic as follows:

Action	Description
AddEmployeeXLSData()	This action will add an employee using data read from an XLS file.

Let's now add the page logic to the 'pageHtmlTesterAddEmployee.cs' file as shown in Listing 6.3.

Listing 6.3: 'pageHtmlTesterAddEmployee.cs' - New function AddEmployeeXLSData

```
1  using System;
2
3  public void AddEmployeeXLSData()
4  {
5      String[][] data = Utility.GetSpreadSheetXLS( ↵
           ↳ @"C:\CodedUITesting\CodedUITesting\TestData\ ↵
           ↳ UserData.xls", 1);
6
7      Utility.SetValue(repHtmlEmployeeDetail. ↵
           ↳ ComboBox_Title, data[1][0]);
8      Utility.SetValue(repHtmlEmployeeDetail.EditBox_Name, ↵
           ↳ data[1][1]);
9
10     if (data[1][2].Equals(Config.FEMALE_TEXT))
11         Utility.Click(repHtmlEmployeeDetail. ↵
               ↳ RadioButton_GenderFemale);
12     else if (data[1][2].Equals(Config.MALE_TEXT))
13         Utility.Click(repHtmlEmployeeDetail. ↵
               ↳ RadioButton_GenderMale);
14     else
15         Utility.ReportExpectedVsActual("Unknown Gender ↵
               ↳ Code", data[1][2]);
16
17     Utility.SetValue(repHtmlEmployeeDetail. ↵
           ↳ EditBox_DateOfBirth, Utility.ExcelDateParse( ↵
           ↳ data[1][3]).Substring(0,10));
```

```
18      Utility.SetValue(repHtmlEmployeeDetail.EditBox_Email, ↵
            ↪ data[1][4]);
19
20      if (data[1][5].Equals(Config.YES))
21          Utility.SetValue(repHtmlEmployeeDetail. ↵
                ↪ CheckBox_Contract, Config.TRUE);
22
23      Utility.SetValue(repHtmlEmployeeDetail.EditBox_Postcode, ↵
            ↪ data[1][6]);
24
25      Utility.SaveScreenshot("AddEmployee");
26
27      Utility.Click(repHtmlEmployeeDetail.Button_Add);
28
29      Utility.HandleBrowserDialog();
30  }
```

◈ Line 3: Page logic to add an employee using Excel XLS file as the data source.

◈ Line 5: Gets the spreadsheet data in an array-of-arrays. Note that the second parameter 1 corresponds to the second worksheet i.e. 'EmployeeData'.

◈ Line 7: Parameter `data[1][0]` is the Title 'Miss'.

◈ Line 8: Parameter `data[1][1]` is the Name 'Sarah Smith'.

◈ Line 10: Parameter `data[1][2]` is the Gender 'Female'.

◈ Line 17: Parameter `data[1][3]` is the DateOfBirth '25/12/1982'.

◈ Line 18: Parameter `data[1][4]` is the Email 'Sarah.Smith@arkenstone-ltd.com'.

◈ Line 20: Parameter `data[1][5]` is the Contract 'No'.

◈ Line 23: Parameter `data[1][6]` is the Postcode 'SN1 5GS'.

◈ Line 25: Takes a screenshot of the page.

◈ Line 27: Clicks the *Add* button.

◈ Line 29: Handles the browser dialog message.

6.2.3.3   Creating Test

Add Listing 6.4 code to the 'WebHtmlTests.cs' file.

Listing 6.4: 'WebHtmlTests.cs' - New test WebHtmlTesterAddEmployeeXLSData

```
1  [TestMethod]
2  public void WebHtmlTesterAddEmployeeXLSData()
3  {
4      Utility.Log.Info("Starting Test ***** " + ↵
            ↪ Utility.TestName + " *****");
5
6      try
```

```
 7      {
 8              Utility.LaunchWebApp();
 9
10              pageHtmlHome Home = new pageHtmlHome();
11              Home.ClickLogin();
12
13              String[][] data = Utility.GetSpreadSheetXLS( ↵
                    ↪ @"C:\CodedUITesting\CodedUITesting\TestData\ ↵
                    ↪ UserData.xls", 0);
14
15              pageHtmlLogin Login = new pageHtmlLogin();
16              Login.LoginUser(data[1][0], data[1][1]);
17
18              pageHtmlTesterHome homeTester = new ↵
                    ↪ pageHtmlTesterHome();
19              homeTester.ClickAddEmployee();
20
21              pageHtmlTesterAddEmployee emp = new ↵
                    ↪ pageHtmlTesterAddEmployee();
22              emp.AddEmployeeXLSData();
23
24              homeTester.ClickLogout();
25
26              Utility.CloseWebApp();
27
28              Utility.ReportResult();
29      }
30      catch (Exception exception)
31      {
32              Utility.ReportExpectedVsActual(Utility.TestName, ↵
                    ↪ "Exception occurred");
33              Utility.Log.Error("Exception: " + ↵
                    ↪ exception.ToString());
34              throw exception;
35      }
36 }
```

◇ Line 1: New test to add an employee using Excel XLS file as the data source.

◇ Line 13: Gets the spreadsheet data in an array-of-arrays. Note that the second parameter 0 corresponds to the first worksheet.

◇ Line 16: Logins with the data read from the first worksheet.

◇ Line 22: Adds employee using data read from the second worksheet.

6.2.3.4 Executing Test

Execute the test `WebHtmlTesterAddEmployeeXLSData` and you will see an output as shown in Figure 6.5. The employee was added using data read from the XLS file.

Test Name: WebHtmlTesterAddEmployeeXLSData

Test Outcome: ⊘ Passed

```
Standard Output
2017-04-05 20:27:55.737 INFO  CodedUITesting.Utility - SetupSummaryFile
2017-04-05 20:27:55.826 INFO  CodedUITesting.Utility - Starting Test ***** WebHtmlTesterAddEmployeeXLSData *****
2017-04-05 20:28:00.093 INFO  CodedUITesting.Utility - [Expected:] http://testing.arkenstone-ltd.com/     [Actual:] http://testing.arkenstone-ltd.com/     [Ste
2017-04-05 20:28:00.262 INFO  CodedUITesting.Utility - Screenshot saved at: C:\CodedUITesting\temp\WebHtmlTesterAddEmployeeXLSData_Home_2017-0
2017-04-05 20:28:01.051 INFO  CodedUITesting.Utility - Click HtmlHyperlink: Id -  (DisplayText - Login)
2017-04-05 20:28:02.105 INFO  CodedUITesting.Utility - GetSpreadSheetXLS....... File: C:\CodedUITesting\CodedUITesting\TestData\UserData.xls     Sheet: 0
2017-04-05 20:28:02.464 INFO  CodedUITesting.Utility - SHEET Name: Login
2017-04-05 20:28:02.466 INFO  CodedUITesting.Utility - SHEET LastRowNum: 2
2017-04-05 20:28:02.471 INFO  CodedUITesting.Utility - SHEET ColumnCount: 2
2017-04-05 20:28:02.474 INFO  CodedUITesting.Utility - CellType: String
2017-04-05 20:28:02.476 INFO  CodedUITesting.Utility - Row: 0   Col: 0  UserID
2017-04-05 20:28:02.477 INFO  CodedUITesting.Utility - CellType: String
2017-04-05 20:28:02.478 INFO  CodedUITesting.Utility - Row: 0   Col: 1  Password
2017-04-05 20:28:02.478 INFO  CodedUITesting.Utility - CellType: String
2017-04-05 20:28:02.479 INFO  CodedUITesting.Utility - Row: 1   Col: 0  Tester
2017-04-05 20:28:02.480 INFO  CodedUITesting.Utility - CellType: String
2017-04-05 20:28:02.481 INFO  CodedUITesting.Utility - Row: 1   Col: 1  Tester123
2017-04-05 20:28:02.483 INFO  CodedUITesting.Utility - CellType: String
2017-04-05 20:28:02.484 INFO  CodedUITesting.Utility - Row: 2   Col: 0  Admin
2017-04-05 20:28:02.485 INFO  CodedUITesting.Utility - CellType: String
2017-04-05 20:28:02.487 INFO  CodedUITesting.Utility - Row: 2   Col: 1  Admin123
2017-04-05 20:28:03.084 INFO  CodedUITesting.Utility - SetValue HtmlEdit: Id -  (Name - TxtUserId) Value: Tester
2017-04-05 20:28:04.318 INFO  CodedUITesting.Utility - SetValue HtmlEdit: Id -  (Name - TxtPassword) Value: Tester123
2017-04-05 20:28:05.851 INFO  CodedUITesting.Utility - Click HtmlInputButton: Id - btnLogin (DisplayText - Login)
2017-04-05 20:28:10.182 INFO  CodedUITesting.Utility - Click HtmlHyperlink: Id -  (DisplayText - Add Employee)
2017-04-05 20:28:10.833 INFO  CodedUITesting.Utility - GetSpreadSheetXLS....... File: C:\CodedUITesting\CodedUITesting\TestData\UserData.xls     Sheet: 1
2017-04-05 20:28:10.836 INFO  CodedUITesting.Utility - SHEET Name: EmployeeData
2017-04-05 20:28:10.838 INFO  CodedUITesting.Utility - SHEET LastRowNum: 1
2017-04-05 20:28:10.839 INFO  CodedUITesting.Utility - SHEET ColumnCount: 7
```

Figure 6.5: Data Driven Add Employee Output

6.2.4 Data Driven - View Employee Verification

Let's write a data driven test to verify an employee with the data read from the Excel file as per the following Test Scenario:

- Launch the demo website.

- Click on the *Login* link.

- Read the user credentials from the test data file in XLS format.

- Login the general user with the credentials read above.

- Click on the *View Employee* link.

- Read the employee data to be verified from the test data file in XLS format.

- Verify the employee using data read above

6.2.4.1 Page Logic

We will now add a new action to the *View Employee* page's logic as follows:

Action	Description
VerifyEmployeeXLSData()	This action will verify the employee detail displayed on the web page with data read from the XLS file.

Let's now add the page logic to the 'pageHtmlTesterViewEmployee.cs' file as shown in Listing 6.5.

Listing 6.5: 'pageHtmlTesterViewEmployee.cs' - Code for VerifyEmployeeXLSData

```
1  using System;
2
3  public void VerifyEmployeeXLSData()
4  {
5      String[][] data = Utility.GetSpreadSheetXLS( ↵
         ↪ @"C:\CodedUITesting\CodedUITesting\TestData\ ↵
         ↪ UserData.xls", 1);
6
7      Utility.ReportExpectedVsActual("10004", ↵
         ↪ Utility.GetValue(repHtmlEmployeeDetail. ↵
         ↪ EditBox_EmployeeId));
8      Utility.ReportExpectedVsActual(data[1][0], ↵
         ↪ Utility.GetValue(repHtmlEmployeeDetail. ↵
         ↪ ComboBox_Title));
9      Utility.ReportExpectedVsActual(data[1][1], ↵
         ↪ Utility.GetValue(repHtmlEmployeeDetail. ↵
         ↪ EditBox_Name));
10
11     if (data[1][2].Equals(Config.FEMALE_TEXT))
12         Utility.ReportExpectedVsActual(Config.TRUE, ↵
            ↪ Utility.GetValue(repHtmlEmployeeDetail. ↵
            ↪ RadioButton_GenderFemale));
13     else if (data[1][2].Equals(Config.MALE_TEXT))
14         Utility.ReportExpectedVsActual(Config.TRUE, ↵
            ↪ Utility.GetValue(repHtmlEmployeeDetail. ↵
            ↪ RadioButton_GenderMale));
15     else
16         Utility.ReportExpectedVsActual("Unknown Gender ↵
            ↪ Code", data[1][2]);
```

```
17
18      Utility.ReportExpectedVsActual(Utility.ExcelDateParse( ↵
            ↪ data[1][3]).Substring(0, 10), Utility.GetValue( ↵
            ↪ repHtmlEmployeeDetail.EditBox_DateOfBirth));
19      Utility.ReportExpectedVsActual(data[1][4].ToLower(), ↵
            ↪ Utility.GetValue(repHtmlEmployeeDetail. ↵
            ↪ EditBox_Email));
20      Utility.ReportExpectedVsActual(Utility.DecodeContract( ↵
            ↪ data[1][5]), Utility.GetValue( ↵
            ↪ repHtmlEmployeeDetail.CheckBox_Contract));
21      Utility.ReportExpectedVsActual(data[1][6], Utility. ↵
            ↪ GetValue(repHtmlEmployeeDetail.EditBox_Postcode));
22
23      Utility.Click(repHtmlEmployeeDetail.Button_Close);
24  }
```

◈ Line 5: Gets the spreadsheet data in an array-of-arrays from the second worksheet.

◈ Lines 7 - 21: Verify values with the data read from the worksheet.

6.2.4.2 Creating Test

Add Listing 6.6 code to the 'WebHtmlTests.cs' file.

Listing 6.6: 'WebHtmlTests.cs' - Code for WebHtmlTesterVerifyEmployeeXLSData

```
1   [TestMethod]
2   public void WebHtmlTesterVerifyEmployeeXLSData()
3   {
4       Utility.Log.Info("Starting Test ***** " + ↵
            ↪ Utility.TestName + " *****");
5
6       try
7       {
8           Utility.LaunchWebApp();
9
10          pageHtmlHome Home = new pageHtmlHome();
11          Home.ClickLogin();
12
13          String[][] data = Utility.GetSpreadSheetXLS( ↵
                ↪ @"C:\CodedUITesting\CodedUITesting\TestData\ ↵
                ↪ UserData.xls", 0);
14
15          pageHtmlLogin Login = new pageHtmlLogin();
16          Login.LoginUser(data[1][0], data[1][1]);
```

```
17
18              pageHtmlTesterHome homeTester = new ↵
                  ↳ pageHtmlTesterHome();
19              homeTester.ClickViewEmployee();
20
21              pageHtmlTesterViewEmployee emp = new ↵
                  ↳ pageHtmlTesterViewEmployee();
22              emp.VerifyEmployeeXLSData();
23
24              Playback.Wait(2000);
25              homeTester.ClickLogout();
26
27              Utility.CloseWebApp();
28
29              Utility.ReportResult();
30          }
31      catch (Exception exception)
32      {
33              Utility.ReportExpectedVsActual(Utility.TestName, ↵
                  ↳ "Exception occurred");
34              Utility.Log.Error("Exception: " + ↵
                  ↳ exception.ToString());
35              throw exception;
36      }
37 }
```

◈ Line 1: New test to verify an employee using Excel XLS file as the data source.

◈ Line 13: Gets the spreadsheet data in an array-of-arrays. Note that the second parameter 0 corresponds to the first worksheet.

◈ Line 16: Logins with the data read from the first worksheet.

◈ Line 22: Verifies the employee using data read from the second worksheet.

6.2.4.3 Executing Test

Execute the test WebHtmlTesterVerifyEmployeeXLSData and you will see an output as shown in Figure 6.6. The employee is verified with the data read from the data file in XLS format.

Test Name: WebHtmlTesterVerifyEmployeeXLSData

Test Outcome: ⓥ Passed

```
Standard Output
2017-04-05 20:41:54.314 INFO  CodedUITesting.Utility - SetupSummaryFile
2017-04-05 20:41:54.404 INFO  CodedUITesting.Utility - Starting Test ***** WebHtmlTesterVerifyEmployeeXLSData *****
2017-04-05 20:41:58.513 INFO  CodedUITesting.Utility - [Expected:] http://testing.arkenstone-ltd.com/   [Actual:] http://testing.arkenstone-ltd.com/   [Ste
2017-04-05 20:41:58.647 INFO  CodedUITesting.Utility - Screenshot saved at: C:\CodedUITesting\temp\WebHtmlTesterVerifyEmployeeXLSData_Home_2017-
2017-04-05 20:41:59.423 INFO  CodedUITesting.Utility - Click HtmlHyperlink: Id -  (DisplayText - Login)
2017-04-05 20:42:00.303 INFO  CodedUITesting.Utility - GetSpreadSheetXLS........ File: C:\CodedUITesting\CodedUITesting\TestData\UserData.xls     Sheet: 0
2017-04-05 20:42:00.771 INFO  CodedUITesting.Utility - SHEET Name: Login
2017-04-05 20:42:00.773 INFO  CodedUITesting.Utility - SHEET LastRowNum: 2
2017-04-05 20:42:00.778 INFO  CodedUITesting.Utility - SHEET ColumnCount: 2
2017-04-05 20:42:00.781 INFO  CodedUITesting.Utility - CellType: String
2017-04-05 20:42:00.784 INFO  CodedUITesting.Utility - Row: 0  Col: 0  UserID
2017-04-05 20:42:00.784 INFO  CodedUITesting.Utility - CellType: String
2017-04-05 20:42:00.785 INFO  CodedUITesting.Utility - Row: 0  Col: 1  Password
2017-04-05 20:42:00.786 INFO  CodedUITesting.Utility - CellType: String
2017-04-05 20:42:00.787 INFO  CodedUITesting.Utility - Row: 1  Col: 0  Tester
2017-04-05 20:42:00.788 INFO  CodedUITesting.Utility - CellType: String
2017-04-05 20:42:00.789 INFO  CodedUITesting.Utility - Row: 1  Col: 1  Tester123
2017-04-05 20:42:00.790 INFO  CodedUITesting.Utility - CellType: String
2017-04-05 20:42:00.792 INFO  CodedUITesting.Utility - Row: 2  Col: 0  Admin
2017-04-05 20:42:00.793 INFO  CodedUITesting.Utility - CellType: String
2017-04-05 20:42:00.793 INFO  CodedUITesting.Utility - Row: 2  Col: 1  Admin123
2017-04-05 20:42:01.480 INFO  CodedUITesting.Utility - SetValue HtmlEdit: Id -  (Name - TxtUserId)  Value: Tester
2017-04-05 20:42:02.703 INFO  CodedUITesting.Utility - SetValue HtmlEdit: Id -  (Name - TxtPassword)  Value: Tester123
2017-04-05 20:42:04.668 INFO  CodedUITesting.Utility - Click HtmlInputButton: Id - btnLogin  (DisplayText - Login)
2017-04-05 20:42:09.277 INFO  CodedUITesting.Utility - Click HtmlHyperlink: Id -  (DisplayText - View Employee)
2017-04-05 20:42:09.925 INFO  CodedUITesting.Utility - GetSpreadSheetXLS........ File: C:\CodedUITesting\CodedUITesting\TestData\UserData.xls     Sheet: 1
2017-04-05 20:42:09.928 INFO  CodedUITesting.Utility - SHEET Name: EmployeeData
2017-04-05 20:42:09.931 INFO  CodedUITesting.Utility - SHEET LastRowNum: 1
2017-04-05 20:42:09.933 INFO  CodedUITesting.Utility - SHEET ColumnCount: 7
```

Figure 6.6: Data Driven Verify Employee Output

6.3 Excel XLSX Format

6.3.1 Utility Functions

Let us define a new Utility function as:

GetSpreadSheetXLSX - Gets the Spreadsheet data in XLSX format into an array-of-arrays		
Input Parameters	*pathName*	Path and name of the XLSX file to read
	sheetNumber	Sheet number of the XLSX file to read
Return Value	*jaggedArray*	Returns the Spreadsheet data in an array-of-arrays

Add Listing 6.7 code to the 'Utility.cs' file.

Listing 6.7: 'Utility.cs' - Code for GetSpreadSheetXLSX

```
1  using NPOI.XSSF.UserModel;
2
3  public static String[][] GetSpreadSheetXLSX(String ↵
       ↪ pathName, int sheetNumber)
```

```
 4   {
 5        Utility.Log.Info("GetSpreadSheetXLSX....... File: " + ←
             ↪ pathName + "       Sheet: " + sheetNumber);
 6        String[][] ssData = { };
 7
 8        try
 9        {
10            FileStream ExcelFileToRead = new ←
                 ↪ FileStream(pathName, FileMode.Open, ←
                 ↪ FileAccess.Read);
11            XSSFWorkbook workbk = new ←
                 ↪ XSSFWorkbook(ExcelFileToRead);
12
13            XSSFSheet sheet = ←
                 ↪ (XSSFSheet)workbk.GetSheetAt(sheetNumber);
14
15            Utility.Log.Info("SHEET Name: " + ←
                 ↪ sheet.SheetName);
16
17            Utility.Log.Info("SHEET LastRowNum: " + ←
                 ↪ sheet.LastRowNum);
18            Utility.Log.Info("SHEET ColumnCount: " + ←
                 ↪ sheet.GetRow(0).Cells.Count);
19
20            int rowCount = sheet.LastRowNum + 1;
21            int colCount = sheet.GetRow(0).Cells.Count;
22
23            Array.Resize(ref ssData, rowCount);
24
25            int i = 0;
26
27            while (sheet.GetRow(i) != null)
28            {
29                Array.Resize(ref ssData[i], colCount);
30
31                for (int j = 0; j < ←
                     ↪ sheet.GetRow(i).Cells.Count; j++)
32                {
33                    var cell = sheet.GetRow(i).GetCell(j);
34
35                    if (cell != null)
36                    {
37                        Utility.Log.Info("CellType: " + ←
                             ↪ cell.CellType);
38
```

```
39                            switch (cell.CellType)
40                            {
41                                case NPOI.SS.UserModel.CellType. ↵
                                    ↳ Numeric:
42                                    ssData[i][j] = sheet. ↵
                                        ↳ GetRow(i).GetCell(j). ↵
                                        ↳ NumericCellValue.ToString();
43                                    break;
44                                case NPOI.SS.UserModel.CellType. ↵
                                    ↳ String:
45                                    ssData[i][j] = sheet. ↵
                                        ↳ GetRow(i).GetCell(j). ↵
                                        ↳ StringCellValue.ToString();
46                                    break;
47                            }
48
49                            Utility.Log.Info("Row: " + (i) + "      ↵
                                ↳ Col: " + (j) + "    " + ↵
                                ↳ ssData[i][j] + " ");
50                        }
51                    }
52
53                    i++;
54                }
55
56            return ssData;
57        }
58    catch (Exception exception)
59    {
60        Utility.Log.Error("GetSpreadSheetXLS Exception: " ↵
            ↳ + exception.ToString());
61        throw exception;
62    }
63 }
```

◈ Line 1: Additional import required to support the functionality.
◈ Line 5: Logs the received parameters.
◈ Line 6: Initialises an array-of-arrays.
◈ Line 10: Initialises a new instance of the FileStream class with the specified pathname, creation mode and access permission:

- PathName - path and name of the XLSX file.

- FileMode Open - the operating system should open an existing file.

- FileAccess Read - read access to the file. Data can be read from the file.

◈ Line 11: Initialises a new instance of the `XSSFWorkbook` class - high level representation of a workbook.

◈ Line 13: Gets the worksheet specified by the sheet number.

◈ Line 15: Logs the sheet name.

◈ Line 17: Logs the last row number in the sheet.

◈ Line 18: Logs the column count of the first row.

◈ Line 20: Initialises a variable for the row count.

◈ Line 21: Initialises a variable for the column count

◈ Line 23: Resizes the data array to the row count - to accommodate all the rows.

◈ Line 25: Initialises a row variable.

◈ Line 27: Loops while there are further rows in the worksheet.

◈ Line 29: Resizes current row of the data array to the column count - to accommodate all the columns.

◈ Line 31: Loops while there are further columns in the current row.

◈ Line 33: Gets the cell at the current row and column position.

◈ Line 35: Ensures that the cell is not null.

◈ Line 41: If the cell type is `Numeric`, gets its numeric value and stores it in an array-of-arrays at the current row and column position.

◈ Line 44: If the cell type is `String`, gets its string value and stores it in an array-of-arrays at the current row and column position.

◈ Line 49: Logs the array data at the current row and column position.

◈ Line 53: Increments the row variable.

◈ Line 56: Returns the spreadsheet data.

6.3.2   Data Driven - Employee List Verification

Let's write a test to verify the *Employee List* for the Admin user that will read data from the Excel file in XLSX format as per the following Test Scenario:

- Launch the demo website.

- Click on the *Login* link.

- Read the user credentials from the test data file in XLSX format.

- Login the admin user with the credentials read above.

- Click on the *Employee List* link.

- Read the 'employee list' data to be verified from the test data file in XLSX format.

- Verify the employee list using the data read above

6.3.2.1   Test Data File

Here are the steps to create the test data in XLSX format.

- Open Excel and create the test data as shown in Figure 6.7.

- Row 1 is the header row.

- Column A contains the *User id* and Column B contains the *Password.*

- Rename the worksheet as 'Login'.

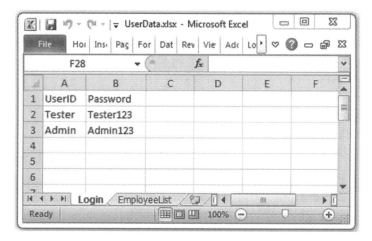

Figure 6.7: XLSX Format - Creating Login Test Data

- Add a new worksheet and create the test data as shown in Figure 6.8.

- Row 1 is the header row.

- Rename the worksheet as 'EmployeeList'.

- Save the data file as 'UserData.xlsx' in 'C:\CodedUITesting\CodedUITesting\TestData' folder. Ensure that the "Save as type" is 'Excel Workbook (*.xlsx)'.

- Close Excel.

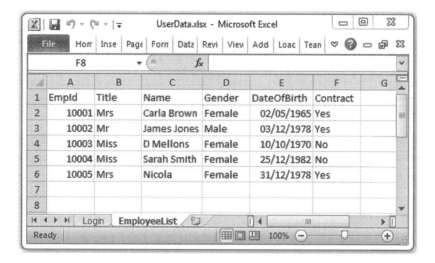

Figure 6.8: XLSX Format - Creating Employee List Test Data

6.3.2.2 Page Logic

We will add a new action to the *Employee List* page's logic as follows:

Action	Description
VerifyEmployeeListXLSXData()	This action will verify the employees' details displayed in the web page with the data fetched from the XLSX file.

Let's now add the page logic to the 'pageHtmlAdminEmpList.cs' file as shown in Listing 6.8.

Listing 6.8: 'pageHtmlAdminEmpList.cs' - Code for VerifyEmployeeListXLSXData

```
1  public void VerifyEmployeeListXLSXData()
2  {
3      String[][] rptTable = GetEmployeeListData( ↵
            ↳ repHtmlAdminEmpList.Table_EmployeesList);
4
5      String[][] xlsxData = Utility.GetSpreadSheetXLSX( ↵
            ↳ @"C:\CodedUITesting\CodedUITesting\TestData\ ↵
            ↳ UserData.xlsx", 1);
6
7      for (int ii = 1; ii < rptTable.Length; ii++)
8      {
9          Utility.ReportExpectedVsActual(rptTable[ii][0], ↵
                ↳ xlsxData[ii][0]);
10         Utility.ReportExpectedVsActual(rptTable[ii][1], ↵
                ↳ xlsxData[ii][1]);
11         Utility.ReportExpectedVsActual(rptTable[ii][2], ↵
                ↳ xlsxData[ii][2]);
12         Utility.ReportExpectedVsActual(rptTable[ii][3], ↵
                ↳ xlsxData[ii][3]);
13         Utility.ReportExpectedVsActual(rptTable[ii][4], ↵
                ↳ Utility.ExcelDateParse(xlsxData[ii][4]). ↵
                ↳ Substring(0, 10));
14         Utility.ReportExpectedVsActual(rptTable[ii][5], ↵
                ↳ Utility.DecodeContract(xlsxData[ii][5]));
15     }
16
17     Utility.ReportExpectedVsActual(Utility.GetValue( ↵
            ↳ repHtmlAdminEmpList.Span_TotalEmployees), ↵
            ↳ Utility.GetCountOfRecs("Select Count(*) from ↵
            ↳ [dbo].[Employees]").ToString());
```

18 }

◈ Line 3: Gets the web page table data in an array-of-arrays.
◈ Line 5: Gets the spreadsheet data in an array-of-arrays from the second worksheet.
◈ Lines 9 - 14: Verify the values read from the web page table with the data read from the worksheet.

6.3.2.3 Creating Test

Add Listing 6.9 code to the 'WebHtmlTests.cs' file.

Listing 6.9: 'WebHtmlTests.cs' - WebHtmlAdminVerifyEmployeeListXLSXData

```
1  [TestMethod]
2  public void WebHtmlAdminVerifyEmployeeListXLSXData()
3  {
4      Utility.Log.Info("Starting Test ***** " +
           Utility.TestName + " *****");
5
6      try
7      {
8          Utility.LaunchWebApp();
9
10         pageHtmlHome Home = new pageHtmlHome();
11         Home.ClickLogin();
12
13         String[][] data = Utility.GetSpreadSheetXLSX(
               @"C:\CodedUITesting\CodedUITesting\TestData\
               UserData.xlsx", 0);
14
15         pageHtmlLogin Login = new pageHtmlLogin();
16         Login.LoginUser(data[2][0], data[2][1]);
17
18         pageHtmlAdminHome homeAdmin = new
               pageHtmlAdminHome();
19         homeAdmin.ClickEmployeeList();
20
21         pageHtmlAdminEmpList emplist = new
               pageHtmlAdminEmpList();
22         emplist.VerifyEmployeeListXLSXData();
23
24         homeAdmin.ClickLogout();
25         Utility.CloseWebApp();
26         Utility.ReportResult();
27     }
```

```
28    catch (Exception exception)
29    {
30        Utility.ReportExpectedVsActual(Utility.TestName, ↵
             ↪ "Exception occurred");
31        Utility.Log.Error("Exception: " + ↵
             ↪ exception.ToString());
32        throw exception;
33    }
34 }
```

◈ Line 1: New test to verify employee list using Excel XLSX file as the data source.

◈ Line 13: Gets the spreadsheet data in an array-of-arrays. Note that the second parameter 0 corresponds to the first worksheet.

◈ Line 16: Logins with the data read from the first worksheet. Note that `data[2][0]` is the user id 'Admin' and `data[2][1]` is its password.

◈ Line 22: Verifies the employee list using data read from the second worksheet.

6.3.2.4 Executing Test

Execute the test `WebHtmlAdminVerifyEmployeeListXLSXData` and you will see an output as shown in Figure 6.9. The *Employee List* table data is verified with the data read from the Excel file in XLSX format.

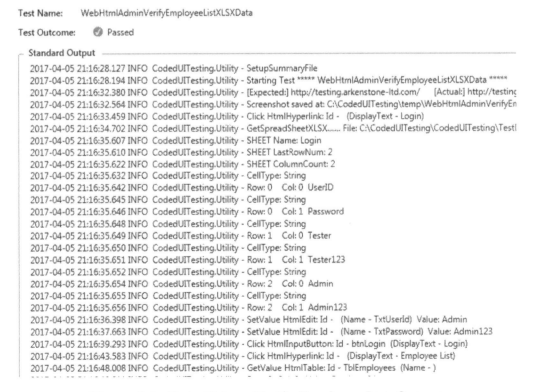

Figure 6.9: Data Driven Verify Employee List Output

6.4 Automation Framework - Adding More Features

6.4.1 Test Step Failure Threshold

Let us consider a scenario where you are executing a long test with many test steps. The current Automation Framework will execute all of the steps and only report any failures at the end. Sometimes, you may want to fail the test as soon as the first failure occurs. On the other hand, you may want to continue the test execution until you reach a predefined threshold of test step failures. So let's see how we can achieve this.

We will perform the following Test Scenario to demonstrate the test step failure threshold:

- Launch the demo website.

- Login with the user 'Tester'.

- Click on the *View Employee* link.

- Verify the employee with a test step failure threshold of 3 i.e. make the test fail once three test steps have failed.

6.4.1.1 Configuration Parameters

Double click on the 'Config.cs' file in the *Solution Explorer* and add Listing 6.10 code to it.

Listing 6.10: 'Config.cs' - Parameters for Test Step Failure Threshold

```
1 public static int STEP_PASS = 0;
2 public static int STEP_FAIL = 1;
3 public static int STEP_FAIL_THRESHOLD = 3;
```

◈ Line 1: Defines an integer value of a *Passed* step.
◈ Line 2: Defines an integer value of a *Failed* step.
◈ Line 3: Defines the test step failure threshold. A value of 3 means when the Automation Framework encounters 3 failures then it will stop executing further steps in the test.

6.4.1.2 Utility Functions

Let's define a new Utility function.

CheckFailureThreshold - Checks for the failure threshold; if reached then fails the test		
Input Parameters	*count*	Current count of failures
Return Value	*void*	Returns nothing

Add Listing 6.11 code to the 'Utility.cs' file.

Listing 6.11: 'Utility.cs' - Code for CheckFailureThreshold

```
1  public static void CheckFailureThreshold(int count)
2  {
3      if (count >= Config.STEP_FAIL_THRESHOLD)
4      {
5          Log.Error("Test Step Failure Threshold reached... ↵
                ↳ Failing Test.");
6          ReportResult();
7      }
8  }
```

◈ Line 3: If current failure count reaches the configured threshold, reports the result and fails the test.

We need to update the existing ReportExpectedVsActual function as defined below:

ReportExpectedVsActual - Reports the outcome of expected versus actual result comparison		
Input Parameters	*expected*	Expected result
	actual	Actual result
Return Value	*int*	Returns integer value of Pass or Fail configured parameters

Update 'Utility.cs' file as shown in Listing 6.12.

Listing 6.12: 'Utility.cs' - Updated code for ReportExpectedVsActual

```
1  public static int ReportExpectedVsActual(string expected, ↵
       ↳ string actual)
2  {
3      if (expected.Trim() == actual.Trim())
4      {
5          Log.Info("[Expected:] " + expected + "          ↵
                ↳ [Actual:] " + actual + "        [Step Passed]");
6          return Config.STEP_PASS;
7      }
8      else
9      {
10         Log.Error("[Expected:] " + expected + "          ↵
                ↳ [Actual:] " + actual + "        [Step Failed]");
```

```
11          TestResult = Config.FAIL;
12          SaveScreenshot(Config.FAIL);
13          return Config.STEP_FAIL;
14      }
15 }
```

◈ Line 1: Returns an `int` instead of `void`.

◈ Line 6: Returns `Config.STEP_PASS` if the test step passes.

◈ Line 13: Returns `Config.STEP_FAIL` if the test step fails.

6.4.1.3   Page Logic

We will add a new action to the *View Employee* page's logic as follows:

Action	Description
VerifyEmployeeWithFailureThreshold()	This action will verify the employee's detail with checks for the failure threshold.

Add the additional function in the page logic file 'pageHtmlTesterViewEmployee.cs' as shown in Listing 6.13.

Listing 6.13: 'pageHtmlTesterViewEmployee.cs' - Code to Verify Employee With Failure Threshold

```
1 public void VerifyEmployeeWithFailureThreshold()
2 {
3     int failedTimes = 0;
4
5     failedTimes += ↵
          ↪ Utility.ReportExpectedVsActual("10009", ↵
          ↪ Utility.GetValue(repHtmlEmployeeDetail. ↵
          ↪ EditBox_EmployeeId));
6     Utility.CheckFailureThreshold(failedTimes);
7
8     failedTimes += Utility.ReportExpectedVsActual("Mr", ↵
          ↪ Utility.GetValue(repHtmlEmployeeDetail. ↵
          ↪ ComboBox_Title));
9     Utility.CheckFailureThreshold(failedTimes);
10
11    failedTimes += Utility.ReportExpectedVsActual("Joe ↵
          ↪ Blog", Utility.GetValue(repHtmlEmployeeDetail. ↵
          ↪ EditBox_Name));
```

```
12      Utility.CheckFailureThreshold(failedTimes);
13
14      failedTimes += ↵
          ↪ Utility.ReportExpectedVsActual(Config.TRUE, ↵
          ↪ Utility.GetValue(repHtmlEmployeeDetail. ↵
          ↪ RadioButton_GenderFemale));
15      Utility.CheckFailureThreshold(failedTimes);
16
17      failedTimes += ↵
          ↪ Utility.ReportExpectedVsActual("29/12/1982", ↵
          ↪ Utility.GetValue(repHtmlEmployeeDetail. ↵
          ↪ EditBox_DateOfBirth));
18      Utility.CheckFailureThreshold(failedTimes);
19
20      failedTimes += Utility.ReportExpectedVsActual( ↵
          ↪ "joe.blog@arkenstone-ltd.com", ↵
          ↪ Utility.GetValue(repHtmlEmployeeDetail. ↵
          ↪ EditBox_Email));
21      Utility.CheckFailureThreshold(failedTimes);
22
23      failedTimes += ↵
          ↪ Utility.ReportExpectedVsActual(Config.FALSE, ↵
          ↪ Utility.GetValue(repHtmlEmployeeDetail. ↵
          ↪ CheckBox_Contract));
24      Utility.CheckFailureThreshold(failedTimes);
25
26      failedTimes += Utility.ReportExpectedVsActual("SN6 ↵
          ↪ 5GS", Utility.GetValue(repHtmlEmployeeDetail. ↵
          ↪ EditBox_Postcode));
27      Utility.CheckFailureThreshold(failedTimes);
28
29      Utility.Click(repHtmlEmployeeDetail.Button_Close);
30  }
```

◈ Line 3: Initialises a variable `failedTimes` to hold the value of *the number of times* the test step has failed.

◈ Line 5: Increments the value of variable `failedTimes` for each failed test step. Remember that the function `ReportExpectedVsActual` returns a zero value for a passed test step.

◈ Line 6: Checks if the failure count has reached the threshold value by passing its current value to the `CheckFailureThreshold` function.

6.4.1.4   Creating Test

Add Listing 6.14 code to the 'WebHtmlTests.cs' file.

```
1  [TestMethod]
2  public void ↵
      ↪ WebHtmlTesterVerifyEmployeeWithFailureThreshold()
3  {
4      Utility.Log.Info("Starting Test ***** " + ↵
          ↪ Utility.TestName + " *****");
5
6      try
7      {
8          Utility.LaunchWebApp();
9
10         pageHtmlHome Home = new pageHtmlHome();
11         Home.ClickLogin();
12
13         pageHtmlLogin Login = new pageHtmlLogin();
14         Login.LoginUser("Tester", "Tester123");
15
16         pageHtmlTesterHome homeTester = new ↵
              ↪ pageHtmlTesterHome();
17         homeTester.ClickViewEmployee();
18
19         pageHtmlTesterViewEmployee emp = new ↵
              ↪ pageHtmlTesterViewEmployee();
20         emp.VerifyEmployeeWithFailureThreshold();
21
22         Playback.Wait(2000);
23         homeTester.ClickLogout();
24
25         Utility.CloseWebApp();
26
27         Utility.ReportResult();
28     }
29     catch (Exception exception)
30     {
31         Utility.ReportExpectedVsActual(Utility.TestName, ↵
              ↪ "Exception occurred");
32         Utility.Log.Error("Exception: " + ↵
              ↪ exception.ToString());
33         throw exception;
34     }
35 }
```

◈ Line 1: New test to verify an employee with failure threshold.

◈ Line 20: Calls the page logic function `VerifyEmployeeWithFailureThreshold`.

6.4.1.5   Executing Test

Execute the test `WebHtmlTesterVerifyEmployeeWithFailureThreshold` and you will see the test failing after 3 test step failures as shown in Figure 6.10.

Figure 6.10: Step Failure Threshold Output

6.4.2   Log Failed Test Steps Only

The Automation Framework uses the generic function `ReportExpectedVsActual` to compare the expected and the actual values and report the outcome. If your test script is performing a lot of comparisons, your log file may become very large. In that case you may want to log expected vs. actual comparisons only if there is a failure. In other words, we don't log the passed steps, only the failed test steps. We need to add a feature to our Automation Framework which determines whether the framework should log all comparisons or only failures.

We will perform the following Test Scenario to demonstrate the logging of failed test steps only:

- Launch the demo website.

- Login with the user 'Tester'.

- Click on the *View Employee* link.

- Verify the employee - log failed test steps only.

6.4.2.1 Configuration Parameters

Double click on the 'Config.cs' file in the *Solution Explorer* and add Listing 6.15 code to it.

Listing 6.15: 'Config.cs' - Parameters to log all compares

```
1  public static bool LOG_ALL_COMPARE = false;
```

◈ Line 1: Defines a boolean configuration parameter to instruct whether to log all compares or not. A `false` value will log failures only.

6.4.2.2 Utility Functions

Update the `ReportExpectedVsActual` function in the 'Utility.cs' file as shown in Listing 6.16.

Listing 6.16: 'Utility.cs' - Updates to ReportExpectedVsActual

```
1  public static int ReportExpectedVsActual(string expected, ↵
       ↪ string actual)
2  {
3      if (expected.Trim() == actual.Trim())
4      {
5          if (Config.LOG_ALL_COMPARE)
6          {
7              Log.Info("[Expected:] " + expected + "        ↵
                   ↪ [Actual:] " + actual + "        [Step ↵
                   ↪ Passed]");
8          }
9          return Config.STEP_PASS;
10     }
11     else
12     {
13         Log.Error("[Expected:] " + expected + "        ↵
                   ↪ [Actual:] " + actual + "        [Step Failed]");
14         TestResult = Config.FAIL;
15         SaveScreenshot(Config.FAIL);
16         return Config.STEP_FAIL;
17     }
18  }
```

◈ Line 5: Additional condition that logs a passed test step if `Config.LOG_ALL_COMPARE` is true.

6.4.2.3 Executing Test

Let's now execute the test `WebHtmlTesterVerifyEmployeeWithFailureThreshold` and this time it will log the failed comparisons only, as shown in Figure 6.11.

Figure 6.11: Log Failed Test Steps Only Output

 At this point you may want to set the configuration parameter `Config.LOG_ALL_COMPARE` to `true` so that it logs all the comparisons.

6.4.3 Comparing Decimals With Tolerance

As a general rule, we can confidently use the `ReportExpectedVsActual` function to report the outcome of test steps where the parameters are passed on as strings. However, when we are comparing two decimal numbers (passed as strings), the function may report unnecessary failures. For example, if the values being compared are held in a different number of decimal places or if the difference between them is *insignificant*, the function will still report them as failures because it does an exact comparison. Also, the decimal values of the expected result may differ from the actual result because of the way the calculations are performed in the programming language being used. In this situation you may want to ignore any minor difference between the expected and the actual result e.g. if the expected result is 123.055556 and the actual result calculated by the application is 123.0555. You may want to ignore the difference of 0.000056 when reporting the result and pass the test step. So here is how we do it.

We will perform the following Test Scenario to demonstrate the comparison of decimal numbers with tolerance:

- Configure the difference threshold to '0.0001'

- Compare '123.055556' and '123.0555' and show that the difference of '0.000056' is ignored because it is below the threshold.

- Compare '123.0555' and '123.055556' and show that the difference of '-0.000056' is ignored because its absolute value is below the threshold.

6.4.3.1 Configuration Parameters

Let's add a new configuration variable. Double click on the 'Config.cs' file in the *Solution Explorer* and add Listing 6.17 code to it.

Listing 6.17: 'Config.cs' - Parameter for difference tolerance

```
1 public static double DIFFERENCE_TOLERANCE = 0.0001;
```

◈ Line 1: Ignores difference of 0.0001 between the expected and the actual result.

6.4.3.2 Utility Functions

Let's define a new Utility function as follows:

ReportExpectedVsActualWithTolerance - Reports the outcome of expected versus actual result comparison with a defined tolerance		
Input Parameters	*expected*	Expected result
	actual	Actual result
Return Value	*int*	Returns integer value of Pass or Fail configured parameters

Add Listing 6.18 to the 'Utility.cs' file.

Listing 6.18: 'Utility.cs' - Code for ReportExpectedVsActualWithTolerance

```
1 public static int ↵
     ↪ ReportExpectedVsActualWithTolerance(String exp, ↵
     ↪ String act)
2 {
3     exp = exp.Trim();
```

```
4        act = act.Trim();
5        double expDbl, actDbl, diff;
6
7        String expFormatted = String.Format("{0:#,0.0000}", ↵
             ↪ double.Parse(exp));
8        String actFormatted = String.Format("{0:#,0.0000}", ↵
             ↪ double.Parse(act));
9
10       expDbl = double.Parse(expFormatted);
11       actDbl = double.Parse(actFormatted);
12       diff = Math.Abs(expDbl * Config.DIFFERENCE_TOLERANCE);
13
14       if (expFormatted.Equals(actFormatted))
15       {
16           Log.Info("[Expected:] " + exp + "     [Actual:] " ↵
                 ↪ + act + "     [Step Passed]");
17
18           return Config.STEP_PASS;
19       }
20       else if (Math.Abs(actDbl - expDbl) <= diff)
21       {
22           Log.Info("Ignored minor difference of " + ↵
                 ↪ String.Format("{0:#,0.0000}", (actDbl - ↵
                 ↪ expDbl)) + " between expDbl = " + expDbl + " ↵
                 ↪ and actDbl = " + actDbl);
23           Log.Info("Original [Expected:] " + exp + "     ↵
                 ↪ Original [Actual:] " + act + "     [Step ↵
                 ↪ Passed]");
24
25           return Config.STEP_PASS;
26       }
27       else
28       {
29           Log.Error("[Expected:] " + exp + "     [Actual:] " ↵
                 ↪ + act + "     [Step FAILED]");
30           Log.Info("Difference of " + ↵
                 ↪ String.Format("{0:#,0.0000}", (actDbl - ↵
                 ↪ expDbl)) + " between expDbl = " + expDbl + " ↵
                 ↪ and actDbl = " + actDbl);
31           TestResult = Config.FAIL;
32
33           return Config.STEP_FAIL;
34       }
35   }
```

◇ Lines 7 and 8: Format the expected and the actual values to the same precision.

◇ Lines 10 and 11: Convert the expected and the actual values to the double format.

◇ Line 14: First of all, checks if the formatted values are equal.

◇ Line 20: Now checks if the double values are equal after ignoring the tolerance difference. Also logs additional information.

◇ Line 27: Otherwise reports a failure and logs additional information.

6.4.3.3   Creating Test

Add Listing 6.19 code to the 'WebHtmlTests.cs' file.

Listing 6.19: 'WebHtmlTests.cs' - Code for CompareDecimalNumbers

```
1  [TestMethod]
2  public void CompareDecimalNumbers()
3  {
4      try
5      {
6          Utility.Log.Info("Starting Test ***** " + ↵
               ↪ Utility.TestName + " *****");
7
8          Utility.ReportExpectedVsActualWithTolerance( ↵
               ↪ "123.055556", "123.0555");
9
10         Utility.ReportExpectedVsActualWithTolerance( ↵
               ↪ "123.0555", "123.055556");
11
12         Utility.ReportResult();
13     }
14     catch (Exception exception)
15     {
16         Utility.ReportExpectedVsActual(Utility.TestName, ↵
               ↪ "Exception occurred");
17         Utility.Log.Error("Exception: " + ↵
               ↪ exception.ToString());
18         throw exception;
19     }
20  }
```

◇ Lines 8 - 10: Call the `ReportExpectedVsActualWithTolerance` function. The test should pass after ignoring the difference.

6.4.3.4 Executing Test

Execute the test `CompareDecimalNumbers` and you will see an output as shown in Figure 6.12. The test passes after ignoring the difference.

Test Name: CompareDecimalNumbers

Test Outcome: Passed

```
Standard Output
2017-04-08 10:19:45.846 INFO  CodedUITesting.Utility - SetupSummaryFile
2017-04-08 10:19:45.932 INFO  CodedUITesting.Utility - Starting Test ***** CompareDecimalNumbers *****
2017-04-08 10:19:45.935 INFO  CodedUITesting.Utility - Ignored minor difference of -0.0001 between expDbl = 123.0556 and actDbl = 123.0555
2017-04-08 10:19:45.938 INFO  CodedUITesting.Utility - Original [Expected:] 123.055556   Original [Actual:] 123.0555    [Step Passed]
2017-04-08 10:19:45.939 INFO  CodedUITesting.Utility - Ignored minor difference of 0.0001 between expDbl = 123.0555 and actDbl = 123.0556
2017-04-08 10:19:45.941 INFO  CodedUITesting.Utility - Original [Expected:] 123.0555   Original [Actual:] 123.055556    [Step Passed]
2017-04-08 10:19:45.943 INFO  CodedUITesting.Utility - Reporting Result......
2017-04-08 10:19:45.945 INFO  CodedUITesting.Utility - Test Passed
2017-04-08 10:19:46.116 INFO  CodedUITesting.Utility - Source: C:\CodedUITesting\temp
2017-04-08 10:19:46.119 INFO  CodedUITesting.Utility - Destination: c:\CodedUITesting\TestResults\                    2017-04-(
2017-04-08 10:19:46.129 INFO  CodedUITesting.Utility - CreateSummaryFileEntry
```

Figure 6.12: Compare Decimals With Tolerance

Chapter 7

Cross Browser Testing

Cross Browser Testing

In this chapter, we will learn about:

- *Components needed for Cross Browser Testing in Coded UI*

- *Automating tests using commonly used browsers*

- *How to make test scripts browser compatible*

So let's get on with it...

CROSS Browser Testing is simply what its name suggests: to test the website in multiple browsers, ensuring that it works in a consistent and intended way. There are lots of web browsers these days and they have been developed in different ways. Some are exclusively compatible with certain operating systems, while some provide features that other browsers lack. Some browsers provide the means to restrict certain features to a specific operating system. As a tester, you may view the Web Application Under Test using Internet Explorer and it looks pretty cool. But when you view it in Firefox, it may not only look awful, but some of the vital features may not work at all. To make things even more challenging, these variations don't just exist between different browsers (e.g. Internet Explorer, Firefox, Chrome etc.) but even between different versions of the same browser! These variations make it essential to perform Cross Browser Testing to ensure that each browser renders pages as intended and allows the user to complete business transactions.

In this book, we will cover the following mostly used browsers for our Cross Browser Testing:

- Internet Explorer

- Mozilla Firefox

- Google Chrome

- Microsoft Edge

Before starting the tests, please ensure that you have installed the relevant browsers.

7.1   Components Needed for Cross Browser Testing

Download the required installer 'CodedUITestCrossBrowserSetup.msi' from the following location:

```
https://marketplace.visualstudio.com/items?itemName=AtinBansal.Seleniumc
omponentsforCodedUICrossBrowserTesting
```

The above web page also has a lot of information about installation and compatibility so please read it through.

Execute the 'msi' file and follow the on-screen instructions for installation. After the installation is complete, please verify that the 'Microsoft.VisualStudio.TestTools.UITe st.Extension.CrossBrowserProxy.dll' file exists at the following location:

For 32 bit workstations
C:\Program Files\Common Files\microsoft shared\VSTT\Cross Browser Selenium Components

For 64 bit workstations
C:\Program Files (x86)\Common Files\microsoft shared\VSTT\Cross Browser Selenium Components

☞   Here are a couple of points to note down before we set off on our Cross Browser Testing journey. The successful execution of tests with different browsers depend upon a number of factors. Some of the main ones are:

- Version number of the browser.

- Version number of the WebDriver (if there is one).

- Version number of the Selenium files (strongly typed).

- Last but not least, the version number of the Visual Studio® (and any patches).

So you may have to do a little bit of experimentation to find out which versions of the software are compatible with each other before you can execute Cross Browser Testing successfully in Coded UI.

7.2 Internet Explorer

7.2.1 Internet Explorer WebDriver

WebDriver is the core tool for automating web application testing. The WebDriver makes direct calls to the browser using each browser's native support for automation. How these direct calls are made and the features they support depend on the browser that we are using. In order to use the Internet Explorer browser, we don't need any WebDriver as it is supported by default in Coded UI.

7.2.2 Configuration Parameters

Let's add some configuration parameters which we will need later on. Double click on the 'Config.cs' file in *Solution Explorer* and add Listing 7.1 code to it.

Listing 7.1: 'Config.cs' - Parameters for Internet Explorer

```
1 public const string INTERNETEXPLORER = "IE";
2 public static string BROWSER = INTERNETEXPLORER;
```

◈ Line 1: Defines a constant string to hold the value "IE".
◈ Line 2: Defines a static string to hold the value of current browser which is set to the configuration parameter INTERNETEXPLORER. We will change the value of this parameter when we need to execute tests using a different browser as we will see later on.

7.2.3 Utility Functions

Update the LaunchWebApp function in the 'Utility.cs' file as shown in Listing 7.2.

Listing 7.2: 'Utility.cs' - Updated code for LaunchWebApp

```
1 public static void LaunchWebApp()
2 {
3     BrowserWindow.CurrentBrowser = Config.BROWSER;
4     Browser = BrowserWindow.Launch(Config.WEB_URL);
5     Browser.Maximized = true;
6
7     ReportExpectedVsActual( ↩
            ↪ "http://testing.arkenstone-ltd.com/", ↩
            ↪ Browser.Uri.ToString());
8 }
```

◈ Line 3: Sets the `CurrentBrowser` to the configured parameter `Config.BROWSER` which is `"IE"` in this case.

7.2.4 Executing Tests

As we have done before, execute the test `WebHtmlTesterAddEmployee` and you will see that it executes in Internet Explorer although this time we purposely specified `"IE"` for the test execution via `BrowserWindow.CurrentBrowser` option.

7.3 Mozilla Firefox

Let's see how we can use Mozilla Firefox for our Cross Browser Testing.

☞ Please ensure that Firefox is installed in the 'C:\Program Files (x86)\Mozilla Firefox' folder for 64 bit systems as I was having some difficulties in using Firefox initially because it was installed in 'C:\Program Files\Mozilla Firefox' folder.

7.3.1 Firefox WebDriver

In order to use the Firefox browser, we don't need any WebDriver as it is already built-into the Selenium dotnet binaries we installed in Section 7.1.

7.3.2 Configuration Parameters

Double click on the 'Config.cs' file in *Solution Explorer* and add Listing 7.3 code to it.

Listing 7.3: 'Config.cs' - Parameters for Firefox

```
1 public const string FIREFOX = "Firefox";
2 public static string BROWSER = FIREFOX;
```

◈ Line 1: Defines a constant string to hold the value `"Firefox"`.
◈ Line 2: Sets the current browser to `FIREFOX`. Please note that this line is not a new statement, it is just a code update where its previous value was `INTERNETEXPLORER`.

7.3.3 Executing Tests

Execute the test `WebHtmlTesterAddEmployee` and you will see it executing in the Firefox browser this time, as shown in Figure 7.1. The test should execute successfully.

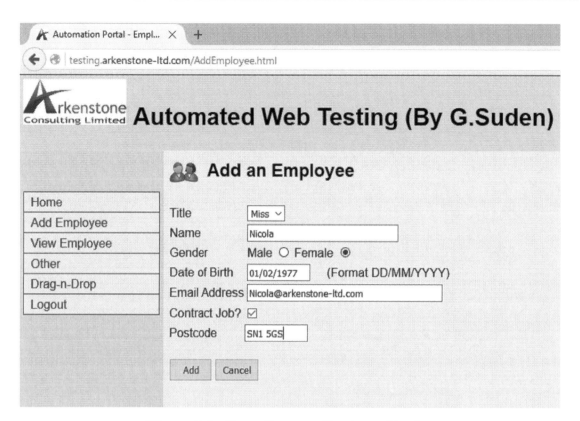

Figure 7.1: Cross Browser Testing - Firefox

7.4 Google Chrome

7.4.1 Chrome WebDriver

Although the ChromeDriver is automatically installed when you install the Cross Browser Components as per Section 7.1, you may have to download a compatible version to execute tests successfully with the Chrome browser. You may look at the following location to download a suitable ChromeDriver.

```
http://chromedriver.storage.googleapis.com/index.html
```

7.4.2 Configuration Parameters

Double click on the 'Config.cs' file in *Solution Explorer* and add Listing 7.4 code to it.

Listing 7.4: 'Config.cs' - Parameters for Chrome

```
1  public const string CHROME = "Chrome";
2  public static string BROWSER = CHROME;
```

◈ Line 1: Defines a constant string to hold the value `"Chrome"`.

◈ Line 2: Sets the current browser to `CHROME`.

7.4.3   Executing Tests

Execute the test `WebHtmlTesterLogin` and you will see a ChromeDriver window as shown in Figure 7.2 and the test execution starts.

Figure 7.2: ChromeDriver Window

Figure 7.3 shows the *Login* page during test execution.

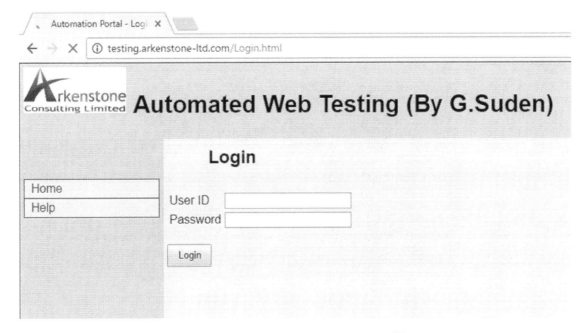

Figure 7.3: Cross Browser Testing - Chrome

7.5 Microsoft Edge

7.5.1 Microsoft Edge WebDriver

Download and install Microsoft WebDriver from the following location:

https://developer.microsoft.com/en-us/microsoft-edge/tools/webdriver/#do
wnloads

Please ensure to install the WebDriver in 'C:\Program Files (x86)\Microsoft Web Driver' folder.

7.5.2 Configuration Parameters

Double click on the 'Config.cs' file in *Solution Explorer* and add Listing 7.5 code to it.

Listing 7.5: 'Config.cs' - Parameters for Microsoft Edge

```
1  public const string EDGE = "MicrosoftEdge";
2  public static string BROWSER = EDGE;
```

◈ Line 1: Defines a constant string to hold the value "MicrosoftEdge".
◈ Line 2: Sets the current browser to EDGE.

7.5.3 Executing Tests

Execute the test WebHtmlAdminLogin and you will see a Microsoft WebDriver window, as shown in Figure 7.4, and the test execution starts.

Figure 7.4: Microsoft WebDriver Window

Figure 7.5 shows the Admin's *Home* page during test execution.

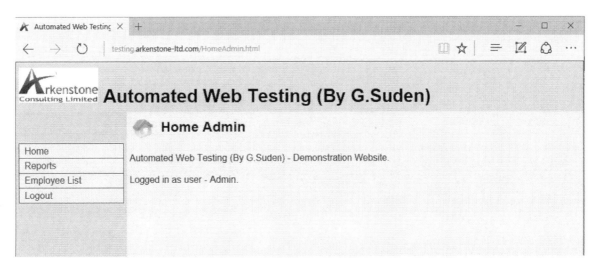

Figure 7.5: Cross Browser Testing - Microsoft Edge

7.6 Making Scripts Browser Compatible

Let me show you an issue which you might face when executing tests in different browsers. Execute the test `WebHtmlAdminVerifyEmployeeList` in Firefox (set `BROWSER = FIREFOX` in the 'Config.cs' file) and you will see that it fails. Figure 7.6 shows an excerpt from its CSV log file. By looking into the log file you will find that the `GetCell` function call on Firefox is returning an `HtmlRow` instead of an `HtmlCell` which results in the test failure.

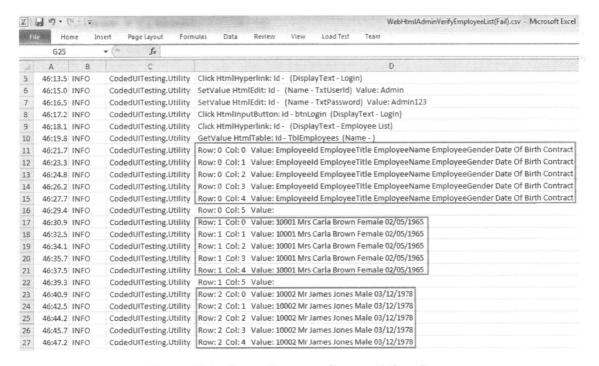

Figure 7.6: Cross Browser Compatibility Issue

Let's see how to fix this issue and make the test script compatible to work with Firefox.

7.6.1 Page Logic

Update the `GetEmployeeListData` function in the 'pageHtmlAdminEmpList.cs' file as shown in Listing 7.6.

Listing 7.6: 'pageHtmlAdminEmpList.cs' - Updated GetEmployeeListData

```
1  private static String[][] GetEmployeeListData(Object obj)
2  {
3      String[][] tblData = { };
4
5      try
6      {
7          switch (obj.GetType().ToString())
8          {
9              case Config.HTML_TABLE:
10                 ((HtmlTable)obj).WaitForControlExist( ↵
                       ↪ Config.TIMEOUT_MILLISEC);
11                 ((HtmlTable)obj).WaitForControlReady( ↵
                       ↪ Config.TIMEOUT_MILLISEC);
12
13                 Utility.Log.Info("GetValue HtmlTable: Id ↵
                       ↪ - " + ((HtmlTable)obj).Id + " (Name ↵
                       ↪ - " + ((HtmlTable)obj).Name + ")");
14
15                 int rowCount = ((HtmlTable)obj).RowCount;
16
17                 Array.Resize(ref tblData, rowCount);
18
19                 for (int i = 0; i < rowCount; i++)
20                 {
21                     int colCount = ↵
                           ↪ ((HtmlTable)obj).ColumnCount;
22                     Array.Resize(ref tblData[i], colCount);
23
24                     for (int j = 0; j < colCount; j++)
25                     {
26                         String stg = null;
27                         if (j == 5)
28                         {
29                             if ↵
                               ↪ (((HtmlTable)obj).GetCell(i, ↵
```

```
                                      ↪ j) is HtmlRow)
30                                    {
31                                        HtmlRow myRow = (HtmlRow) ←
                                            ↪ ((HtmlTable)obj). ←
                                            ↪ GetCell(i, j);
32
33                                        var children = ←
                                            ↪ myRow.Cells[j]. ←
                                            ↪ GetChildren();
34                                        foreach (var child in ←
                                            ↪ children)
35                                        {
36                                            if (child.ControlType ←
                                                ↪ == "CheckBox")
37                                            {
38                                                stg = ←
                                                    ↪ ((HtmlCheckBox) ←
                                                    ↪ child).Checked. ←
                                                    ↪ ToString();
39                                            }
40                                        }
41
42                                    }
43                                    else
44                                    {
45                                        var children = ←
                                            ↪ ((HtmlTable)obj). ←
                                            ↪ GetCell(i, ←
                                            ↪ j).GetChildren();
46                                        foreach (var child in ←
                                            ↪ children)
47                                        {
48                                            if (child.ControlType ←
                                                ↪ == "CheckBox")
49                                            {
50                                                stg = ←
                                                    ↪ ((HtmlCheckBox) ←
                                                    ↪ child).Checked. ←
                                                    ↪ ToString();
51                                            }
52                                        }
53                                    }
54                                }
55                                else
56                                {
```

```
57                                      if (((HtmlTable)obj). ↵
                                        ↳ GetCell(i, j) is ↵
                                        ↳ HtmlRow)
58                                      {
59                                          HtmlRow myRow = (HtmlRow) ↵
                                            ↳ ((HtmlTable)obj). ↵
                                            ↳ GetCell(i, j);
60                                          stg = myRow.Cells[j]. ↵
                                            ↳ GetProperty("InnerText"). ↵
                                            ↳ ToString();
61                                      }
62                                      else
63                                      {
64                                          stg = ((HtmlTable)obj). ↵
                                            ↳ GetCell(i, ↵
                                            ↳ j).InnerText;
65                                      }
66                                  }
67
68                                  tblData[i][j] = stg;
69                                  Utility.Log.Info("Row: " + i + " ↵
                                      ↳ Col: " + j + "   Value: " + ↵
                                      ↳ tblData[i][j]);
70                              }
71                          }
72                      break;
73
74              default:
75                      Utility.Log.Error("Error, Unknown object ↵
                          ↳ type: " + obj.GetType().ToString());
76                      Utility.ReportExpectedVsActual("Error", ↵
                          ↳ "Not Implemented");
77                      break;
78          }
79
80      return tblData;
81      }
82  catch (Exception exception)
83  {
84      Utility.Log.Error("GetEmployeeListData Exception: ↵
          ↳ " + exception.ToString());
85      throw exception;
86  }
87 }
```

◈ Line 29: Checks if the `GetCell` function call returns an `HtmlRow`.

◈ Line 31: Casts the cell to an `HtmlRow`.

◈ Line 33: Gets the cell at the `jth` position and proceeds with the normal logic.

◈ Line 57: Checks if the `GetCell` function call returns an `HtmlRow`.

◈ Line 59: Casts the cell to an `HtmlRow`.

◈ Line 60: Gets the `InnerText` of the cell at `jth` position.

7.6.2   Executing Tests

Re-execute the test `WebHtmlAdminVerifyEmployeeList` with Firefox and this time it should run successfully!

Chapter 8

Web Services Testing

Web Services Testing

In this chapter, we will learn:

- *About Web Services*

- *How to write a demo web service for our automated testing perspective*

- *How to automate Web Services testing via WebRequest method*

- *How to automate Web Services testing via HttpWebRequest SOAP method*

- *How to automate Web Services testing via Service Reference method*

So let's get on with it. . .

Wʜᴀᴛ is a Web Service? A web service is a piece of software that makes itself available over the internet and uses a standardised XML messaging system to code and decode data. By using web services, an application can publish its functions to the rest of the world. For example, we invoke a web service by sending the Employee ID in an XML *Request Message* and then wait for the Employee Details in an XML *Response Message*, as shown in Figure 8.1.

Interoperability is one of the most important features of web services. Interoperability is the ability for two different implementations of web services to communicate with one another. Interoperability is perhaps the most critical feature of web services, for without it, communication is not possible. Web services can exchange data between different applications and different platforms and hence solve the interoperability problem by giving different applications a way to link their data. We can build a web service in C# on a Windows platform that can be invoked from JavaServer pages running on a Linux platform.

A typical web service has the following features:

- Uses a standardised XML messaging system

- Is available over the internet

- Interoperable

- Platform independent

- Operating system independent

- Language independent

- Easily discoverable

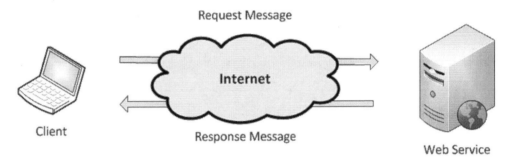

Figure 8.1: Web Services Overview

In this chapter, we will learn how to perform automated web services testing using Coded UI. Since we would need a web service to test against, we will write our own simple demo web service. Our demo web service will accept an Employee ID and will return the corresponding Employee Details. Don't worry if you are not familiar with web services, this chapter will provide step-by-step instructions on how to write a web service and subsequently test it using Coded UI. So let's get on with it.

8.1   Demo Web Service

Please follow these steps to create the demo web service:

- Launch Visual Studio® from its installed location or from the desktop shortcut.

- Open the *CodedUITesting* solution.

- Right click on *Solution* in the *Solution Explorer*.

- Click *Add ⇒ New Project...* as shown in Figure8.2

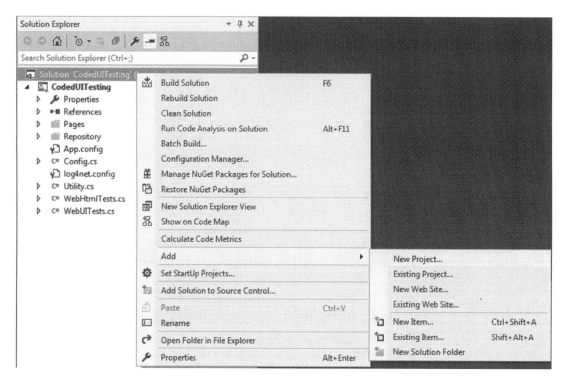

Figure 8.2: Add Web Service Project

- Select *ASP .NET Web Application* under *Web*.

- Type the *Name* as 'MyWebService' as shown in Figure8.3 and click the *OK* button.

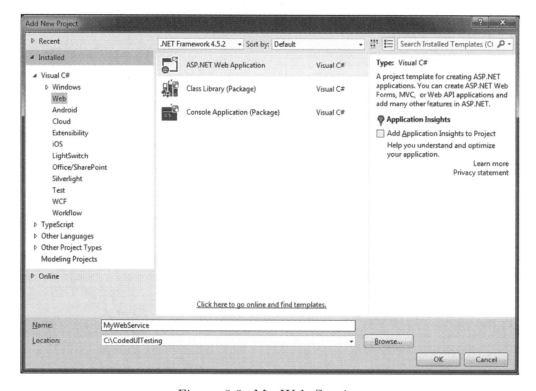

Figure 8.3: My Web Service

- In the next window, select the *Empty* Template.

- Ensure that *Host in the cloud* is not checked and leave everything else as default as shown in Figure8.4.

- Click the *OK* button.

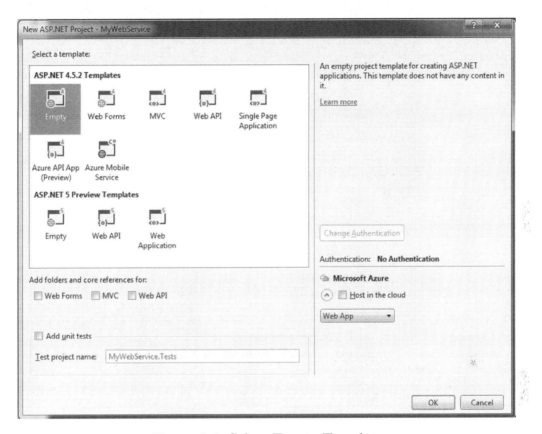

Figure 8.4: Select Empty Template

☞ If you are using a version of Visual Studio® that doesn't have *ASP .NET Web Application* listed under *Web*, you might have to perform the following steps:

- Close all instances of Visual Studio®.

- Go to the *Control Panel* on your workstation and select *Programs and Features*.

- Find Microsoft Visual Studio®, right click on it and select *Change*.

- Follow the on-screen instructions and then select *Modify*.

- Ensure that *Microsoft Web Developer Tools* is selected as shown in Figure 8.5 and follow the on-screen instructions to update Visual Studio®.

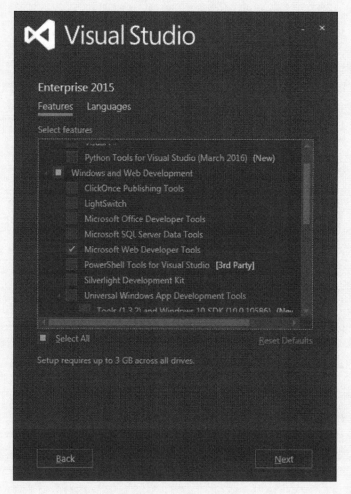

Figure 8.5: Web Developer Tools

8.1.1   Creating The Web Service

Let's now write the necessary code to create our demo web service.

- In the *Solution Explorer*, right click on *MyWebService* and select *Add → New Item...*

- Select *Web Service (ASMX)*.

- Type the *Name* as 'EmployeeWebService.asmx' as shown in Figure 8.6.

- Click the *Add* button.

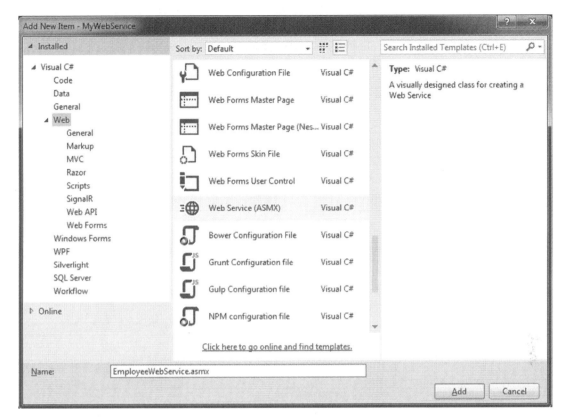

Figure 8.6: Employee Web Service

Add Listing 8.1 code to the 'EmployeeWebService.asmx' file.

 This is probably not the best way a developer would code a web service but it will give us something to test against!

Listing 8.1: 'EmployeeWebService.asmx' - Code for the Employee Web Service

```
1  /******************************************************
2   * All rights reserved. Copyright 2017 Arkenstone-ltd.com *
3   *****************************************************/
4  using System;
5  using System.Web.Services;
6
7  namespace MyWebService
8  {
9      [WebService(Namespace = "http://tempuri.org/")]
10     [WebServiceBinding(ConformsTo = ↵
            ↪ WsiProfiles.BasicProfile1_1)]
11     [System.ComponentModel.ToolboxItem(false)]
12
```

```
13      public class EmployeeWebService : ↵
          ↳ System.Web.Services.WebService
14      {
15
16          public class Employee
17          {
18              public string EmpID { get; set; }
19              public string Title { get; set; }
20              public string Name { get; set; }
21              public string Gender { get; set; }
22              public string BirthDate { get; set; }
23              public string Contract { get; set; }
24          }
25
26          [WebMethod]
27          public Employee GetEmployee(String employeeID)
28          {
29              Employee emp = new Employee();
30
31              switch (employeeID)
32              {
33                  case "10001":
34                      emp.EmpID = "10001";
35                      emp.Title = "Mrs";
36                      emp.Name = "Carla Brown";
37                      emp.Gender = "Female";
38                      emp.BirthDate = "02/05/1965";
39                      emp.Contract = "Yes";
40                      break;
41
42                  case "10002":
43                      emp.EmpID = "10002";
44                      emp.Title = "Mr";
45                      emp.Name = "James Jones";
46                      emp.Gender = "Male";
47                      emp.BirthDate = "03/12/1978";
48                      emp.Contract = "Yes";
49                      break;
50
51                  case "10003":
52                      emp.EmpID = "10003";
53                      emp.Title = "Miss";
54                      emp.Name = "D Mellons";
55                      emp.Gender = "Female";
56                      emp.BirthDate = "10/10/1970";
```

```
57              emp.Contract = "No";
58              break;
59
60          case "10004":
61              emp.EmpID = "10004";
62              emp.Title = "Miss";
63              emp.Name = "Sarah Smith";
64              emp.Gender = "Female";
65              emp.BirthDate = "25/12/1982";
66              emp.Contract = "No";
67              break;
68
69          case "10005":
70              emp.EmpID = "10005";
71              emp.Title = "Mrs";
72              emp.Name = "Nicola";
73              emp.Gender = "Female";
74              emp.BirthDate = "31/12/1978";
75              emp.Contract = "Yes";
76              break;
77
78          default:
79              emp.EmpID = "Invalid EmployeeID";
80              emp.Title = "Invalid EmployeeID";
81              emp.Name = "Invalid EmployeeID";
82              emp.Gender = "Invalid EmployeeID";
83              emp.BirthDate = "Invalid EmployeeID";
84              emp.Contract = "Invalid EmployeeID";
85              break;
86          }
87
88          return emp;
89      }
90   }
91 }
```

◈ Line 16: Defines the `Employee` record.

◈ Line 26: Attaching the `WebMethod` *Attribute* to a public method exposes the method as part of the XML web service and hence callable from the remote web clients.

◈ Line 31: Assigns values to the employee record based on the value of `employeeID`.

◈ Line 78: For any other value of the `employeeID`, just returns the value "Invalid EmployeeID".

◈ Line 88: Returns the `Employee` record.

8.1.2   Running The Web Service

Let's now run our demo web service so that it is ready to take any requests.

- In the *Solution Explorer*, right click on *MyWebService* and select *Set as StartUp Project* as shown in Figure 8.7.

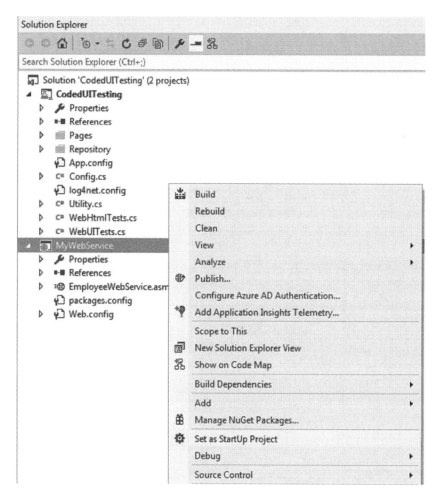

Figure 8.7: Set StartUp Project

- Select the *EmployeeWebService.asmx* file in the *Solution Explorer*.

- Press Ctrl + F5 and you should see a browser window launching as shown in Figure 8.8.

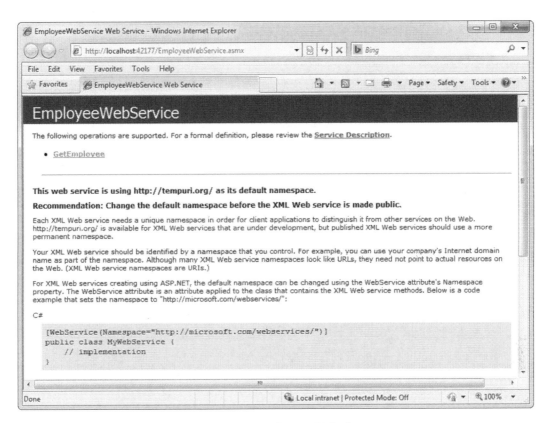

Figure 8.8: Localhost Web Service

If *Internet Information Services* (IIS) is turned off on your workstation, you may see an error window as shown in Figure 8.9.

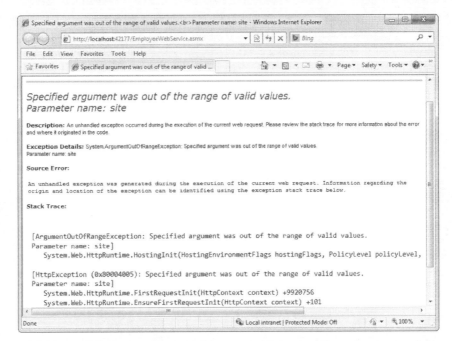

Figure 8.9: Internet Information Services Error

In order to resolve this issue, follow these steps:

- Go to the *Control Panel*.

- Select *Turn Windows features on or off*.

- Select *Internet Information Services* as shown in Figure 8.10 and click the *OK* button.

Figure 8.10: Internet Information Service Turned On

Now when you select the *EmployeeWebService.asmx* file in the *Solution Explorer* and press Ctrl + F5 , you should see a browser window as shown in Figure 8.8. You can ensure that IIS Express is running from the *Windows System Tray* as shown in Figure 8.11.

Figure 8.11: IIS Express Running

☞ The *Windows System Tray* is located in the *Windows Taskbar* (usually at the bottom right corner next to the clock). You may have to click the arrow (facing upward) to see all the icons.

8.1.3   Invoking The Web Service

Let's now invoke our web service. Click on the *GetEmployee* link (see Figure 8.8), and you will see a window as shown in Figure 8.12.

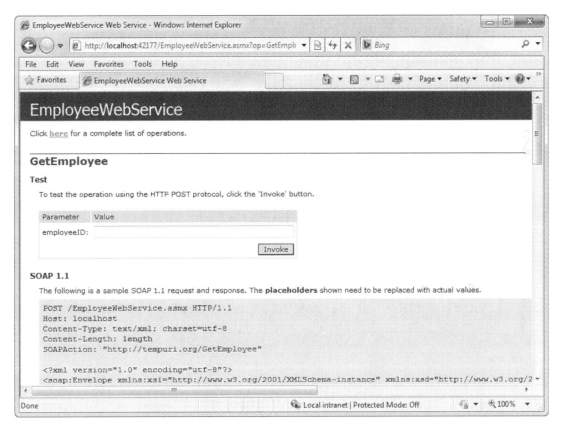

Figure 8.12: Get Employee Web Service

Enter 10004 in the *employeeID* field and press the *Invoke* button. You will see a result window as shown in Figure 8.13.

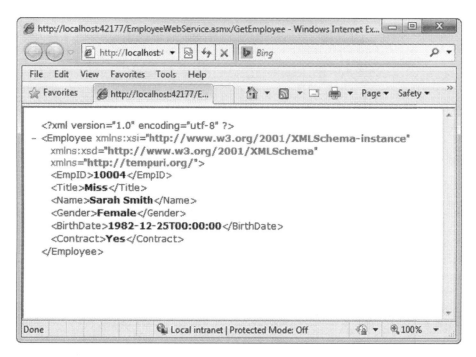

Figure 8.13: Get Employee Web Service Result

We have now successfully invoked the web service by calling it with an Employee ID 10004 and the result is displayed in the web browser. Try different Employee Id values and see if you get the right results. Let's now learn how to automate the testing of this web service using Coded UI.

8.2 Testing The Web Service via WebRequest

Let's perform the following Test Scenario to demonstrate accessing our web service via the WebRequest method:

- Setup an Employee record with the *expected result* values for the Employee ID = 10004.

- Call the demo web service via the WebRequest method with the Employee ID = 10004 to get the *actual result* values.

- Compare both the *expected* and the *actual result* values and report the outcome.

8.2.1 Adding Reference

First of all, let's add a necessary reference to our Coded UI project which is needed to support the functionality.

- In the *Solution Explorer*, right click on the *References* folder in the *CodedUITesting* project.

- Select *Add Reference...*

- In the left hand pane, click on *Assemblies.*

- In the right hand pane, type *system.xml* in the search area.

- Select *System.Xml* as shown in Figure 8.14.

- Click the *OK* button.

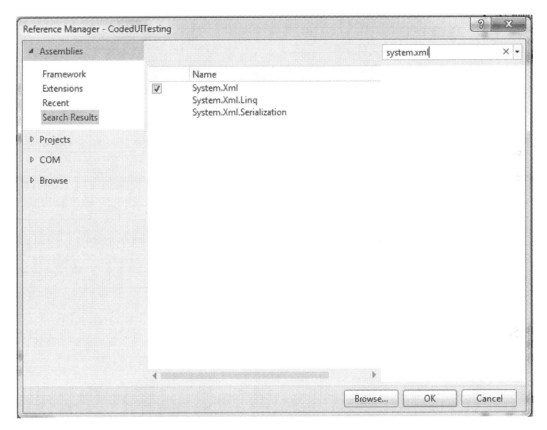

Figure 8.14: Add System.XML Reference

8.2.2 Utility Functions

Let's define two new Utility functions as follows:

GetEmployeeByWebRequest - Gets an employee's detail by the WebRequest method		
Input Parameters	*empId*	Employee Id
Return Value	*XmlDocument*	Returns the XmlDocument containing the employee record

VerifyEmployee - Compares an employee's record with the XML message and reports the outcome		
Input Parameters	*employeeRecord*	Expected values in the EmployeeRecord format
	XmlDocument	Actual values in the XML format
Return Value	*void*	Returns nothing

Add Listing 8.2 code to the 'Utility.cs' file.

Listing 8.2: 'Utility.cs' - Code for GetEmployeeByWebRequest and VerifyEmployee

```
1  using System.Net;
2  using System.Xml;
3  using System.Text;
4
5  public struct EmployeeRecord
6  {
7      public string EmpID;
8      public string Title;
9      public string Name;
10     public string Gender;
11     public string BirthDate;
12     public string Contract;
13 }
14
15 public static XmlDocument GetEmployeeByWebRequest(String ↵
    ↪ empId)
16 {
17     try
18     {
19         WebRequest request = WebRequest.Create( ↵
            ↪ "http://localhost:50380/EmployeeWebService.asmx ↵
            ↪ /GetEmployee");
20
21         request.Method = "POST";
22
23         string postData = "employeeID=" + empId;
24         byte[] byteArray = ↵
            ↪ Encoding.UTF8.GetBytes(postData);
25
26         request.ContentType = ↵
            ↪ "application/x-www-form-urlencoded";
27
```

```
28          request.ContentLength = byteArray.Length;
29
30          Stream dataStream = request.GetRequestStream();
31
32          dataStream.Write(byteArray, 0, byteArray.Length);
33
34          dataStream.Close();
35
36          WebResponse response = request.GetResponse();
37
38          Log.Info(((HttpWebResponse)response). ↵
                ↪ StatusDescription);
39
40          dataStream = response.GetResponseStream();
41
42          StreamReader reader = new ↵
                ↪ StreamReader(dataStream);
43
44          string responseFromServer = reader.ReadToEnd();
45
46          Log.Info(responseFromServer);
47
48          reader.Close();
49          dataStream.Close();
50          response.Close();
51
52          XmlDocument xml = new XmlDocument();
53          xml.LoadXml(responseFromServer);
54
55          return xml;
56      }
57      catch (Exception exception)
58      {
59          Utility.Log.Error("exception" + ↵
                ↪ exception.ToString());
60          throw exception;
61      }
62 }
63
64 public static void VerifyEmployee(EmployeeRecord emp, ↵
        ↪ XmlDocument xml)
65 {
66      ReportExpectedVsActual(emp.EmpID, ↵
            ↪ (xml.GetElementsByTagName("EmpID"))[0].InnerXml);
67      ReportExpectedVsActual(emp.Title, ↵
```

```
         ↪ xml.GetElementsByTagName("Title").Item(0).InnerXml);
68       ReportExpectedVsActual(emp.Name, ↵
         ↪ xml.GetElementsByTagName("Name").Item(0).InnerXml);
69       ReportExpectedVsActual(emp.Gender, ↵
         ↪ xml.GetElementsByTagName("Gender").Item(0).InnerXml);
70       ReportExpectedVsActual(emp.BirthDate, ↵
         ↪ (xml.GetElementsByTagName("BirthDate").Item(0). ↵
         ↪ InnerXml).Substring(0, 10));
71       ReportExpectedVsActual(emp.Contract, ↵
         ↪ xml.GetElementsByTagName("Contract").Item(0).InnerXml);
72 }
```

◈ Lines 1 - 3: Additional imports required to support the new functionality.

◈ Line 5: Creates a structure for the employee record.

◈ Line 19: Creates the `WebRequest`. Please change the port number (50380) to the value you see in your workstation's browser window

◈ Line 21: Sets the `Method` property of the request to "POST".

◈ Line 23: Creates the `POST` data.

◈ Line 24: Converts it to a byte array.

◈ Line 26: Sets the `ContentType` property of the `WebRequest`.

◈ Line 28: Sets the `ContentLength` property of the `WebRequest`.

◈ Line 30: Gets the request stream.

◈ Line 32: Writes the data to the request stream.

◈ Line 34: Closes the stream object.

◈ Line 36: Gets the response.

◈ Line 38: Logs the status.

◈ Line 40: Gets the stream containing content returned by the server.

◈ Line 42: Opens the stream using `StreamReader` for easy access.

◈ Line 44: Reads the content.

◈ Line 46: Logs the content.

◈ Lines 48 - 50: Clean up the streams.

◈ Line 52: Initialises a new instance of the `XmlDocument` class.

◈ Line 53: Loads the XML document with response from the server.

◈ Line 55: Returns the XML document.

◈ Line 64: A new function that compares employee record with the XML message and reports the outcome.

◈ Line 66: Uses notation `("EmpID"))[0].InnerXml` to read a tag value.

◈ Line 67: Uses notation `("Title").Item(0).InnerXml` to read a tag value.

◈ Line 70: Uses the `Substring` function to compare first 10 characters.

8.2.3   Creating Test

In the *Solution Explorer*, right click on the *CodedUITesting* project and click *Add* ⇒ *Class...* Name the class as 'WebServicesTests.cs' and click the *Add* button. Add Listing 8.3 code to it.

```
1   /*****************************************************************
2    * All rights reserved. Copyright 2017 Arkenstone-ltd.com *
3    *****************************************************************/
4   using Microsoft.VisualStudio.TestTools.UITesting;
5   using Microsoft.VisualStudio.TestTools.UnitTesting;
6   using System;
7   using System.IO;
8   using System.Xml;
9
10  namespace CodedUITesting
11  {
12      [CodedUITest]
13      public class WebServicesTests
14      {
15          public WebServicesTests()
16          {
17          }
18
19          [TestInitialize()]
20          public void Initialize()
21          {
22              Utility.TestResult = Config.PASS;
23              Utility.TestName = TestContext.TestName;
24              Utility.TestResultFolder = ←
                  ↪ TestContext.TestResultsDirectory;
25              Utility.TestRunFolder = ←
                  ↪ TestContext.TestRunDirectory;
26
27              log4net.Config.XmlConfigurator.ConfigureAndWatch( ←
                  ↪ new FileInfo(Config.PROJECT_FOLDER + ←
                  ↪ "log4net.config"));
28              Utility.SetupSummaryFile();
29          }
30
31          [TestCleanup()]
32          public void Cleanup()
33          {
34              Utility.MoveScreenshots();
35              string logFile = Utility.SaveLogFile();
36              Utility.CreateSummaryFileEntry(DateTime. ←
                  ↪ Now.ToString() + "," + ←
```

```
            ↳ TestContext.TestName + "," + ↵
            ↳ Utility.TestResult + "," + logFile);
37          Utility.CreateShortcut("TestSummary", ↵
            ↳ Utility.TestResultFolder, ↵
            ↳ Config.SUMMARY_PATHFILENAME);
38          Utility.CloseWebApp();
39          Playback.Cleanup();
40      }
41
42      [TestMethod]
43      public void WebServicesWebRequest()
44      {
45          Utility.Log.Info("Starting Test ***** " + ↵
            ↳ Utility.TestName + " *****");
46
47          try
48          {
49              Utility.EmployeeRecord empRec;
50
51              empRec.EmpID = "10004";
52              empRec.Title = "Miss";
53              empRec.Name = "Sarah Smith";
54              empRec.Gender = "Female";
55              empRec.BirthDate = "25/12/1982";
56              empRec.Contract = "No";
57
58              XmlDocument xmlRec = ↵
                 ↳ Utility.GetEmployeeByWebRequest("10004");
59
60              Utility.VerifyEmployee(empRec, xmlRec);
61
62              Utility.ReportResult();
63          }
64          catch (Exception exception)
65          {
66              Utility.ReportExpectedVsActual(Utility. ↵
                 ↳ TestName, "Exception occurred");
67              Utility.Log.Error("Exception: " + ↵
                 ↳ exception.ToString());
68              throw exception;
69          }
70      }
71
72      public TestContext TestContext
73      {
```

```
74              get
75              {
76                  return testContextInstance;
77              }
78              set
79              {
80                  testContextInstance = value;
81              }
82          }
83          private TestContext testContextInstance;
84      }
85  }
```

◈ Line 49: Declares a record of type `EmployeeRecord`.

◈ Lines 51 - 56: Assign expected result values.

◈ Line 58: Gets the actual result values of employee data via the web service.

◈ Line 60: Verifies both records by calling the Utility function `VerifyEmployee` that we created earlier.

 Note that there is no need to launch the browser window as we don't require it for web services testing.

8.2.4 Executing Tests

Ensure that 'IIS Express' is running as shown in Figure 8.11. The output is shown in Figure 8.15 for a successful execution.

Test Name: WebServicesWebRequest

Test Outcome: ⊘ Passed

Standard Output

```
2017-04-08 10:11:01.376 INFO  CodedUITesting.Utility - SetupSummaryFile
2017-04-08 10:11:01.450 INFO  CodedUITesting.Utility - Starting Test ***** WebServicesWebRequest *****
2017-04-08 10:11:01.532 INFO  CodedUITesting.Utility - OK
2017-04-08 10:11:01.534 INFO  CodedUITesting.Utility - <?xml version="1.0" encoding="utf-8"?>
<Employee xmlns:xsi="http://www.w3.org/2001/XMLSchema-instance" xmlns:xsd="http://www.w3.org/2001/XMLSchema"
  <EmpID>10004</EmpID>
  <Title>Miss</Title>
  <Name>Sarah Smith</Name>
  <Gender>Female</Gender>
  <BirthDate>25/12/1982</BirthDate>
  <Contract>No</Contract>
</Employee>
2017-04-08 10:11:01.537 INFO  CodedUITesting.Utility - [Expected:] 10004     [Actual:] 10004     [Step Passed]
2017-04-08 10:11:01.538 INFO  CodedUITesting.Utility - [Expected:] Miss      [Actual:] Miss      [Step Passed]
2017-04-08 10:11:01.539 INFO  CodedUITesting.Utility - [Expected:] Sarah Smith     [Actual:] Sarah Smith     [Step Passed]
2017-04-08 10:11:01.542 INFO  CodedUITesting.Utility - [Expected:] Female    [Actual:] Female    [Step Passed]
2017-04-08 10:11:01.544 INFO  CodedUITesting.Utility - [Expected:] 25/12/1982     [Actual:] 25/12/1982     [Step Passed]
2017-04-08 10:11:01.546 INFO  CodedUITesting.Utility - [Expected:] No     [Actual:] No     [Step Passed]
2017-04-08 10:11:01.548 INFO  CodedUITesting.Utility - Reporting Result......
2017-04-08 10:11:01.549 INFO  CodedUITesting.Utility - Test Passed
```

Figure 8.15: Web Services WebRequest Output

8.3 Testing The Web Service via HttpWebRequest SOAP

Let's perform the following Test Scenario to demonstrate accessing our web service via the `HttpWebRequest SOAP` method:

- Call the demo web service via `HttpWebRequest SOAP` method with the Employee ID = 10004 to get the *actual result* values.

- Read the *expected result* values from the database for Employee ID = 10004.

- Compare both the *expected* and the *actual result* values and report the outcome.

8.3.1 Utility Functions

First of all, let's define two new Utility functions as follows:

GetEmployeeByHttpWebRequest - Gets an employee's detail by the HttpWebRequest method		
Input Parameters	*empId*	Employee Id
Return Value	*XmlDocument*	Returns the XmlDocument containing the employee record

VerifyEmployeeWithDB - Compares the XML message with the database values and reports the outcome		
Input Parameters	*empId*	Expected result Employee Id (for data retrieval from the database)
	XmlDocument	Actual values in the XML format
Return Value	*void*	Returns nothing

Add Listing 8.4 code to the 'Utility.cs' file.

Listing 8.4: 'Utility.cs' - Additional code

```
1  public static XmlDocument ↵
      ↳ GetEmployeeByHttpWebRequest(String empId)
2  {
3      try
4      {
5          HttpWebRequest webRequest = ↵
              ↳ (HttpWebRequest)WebRequest.Create( ↵
              ↳ @"http://localhost:50380/EmployeeWebService. ↵
              ↳ asmx?op=GetEmployee");
```

```
 6        webRequest.Headers.Add(@"SOAP:Action");
 7        webRequest.ContentType = ←
            ↪ "text/xml;charset=\"utf-8\"";
 8        webRequest.Accept = "text/xml";
 9        webRequest.Method = "POST";
10
11        XmlDocument soapEnvelopeXml = new XmlDocument();
12        String stg = "<?xml version=\"1.0\" ←
            ↪ encoding=\"utf-8\"?>" + Environment.NewLine ←
            ↪ +
13          "<soap:Envelope ←
              ↪ xmlns:soap=\"http://schemas.xmlsoap.org/ ←
              ↪ soap/envelope/\" ←
              ↪ xmlns:xsi=\"http://www.w3.org/ ←
              ↪ 2001/XMLSchema-instance\" ←
              ↪ xmlns:xsd=\"http://www.w3.org/ ←
              ↪ 2001/XMLSchema\">" + Environment.NewLine +
14          "<soap:Body>" + Environment.NewLine +
15          "    <GetEmployee ←
              ↪ xmlns=\"http://tempuri.org/\">" + ←
              ↪ Environment.NewLine +
16          "        <employeeID>" + empId + ←
              ↪ "</employeeID>" + Environment.NewLine +
17          "    </GetEmployee>" + Environment.NewLine +
18          "</soap:Body>" + Environment.NewLine +
19          "</soap:Envelope>";
20
21        Log.Info("stg: " + stg);
22
23        soapEnvelopeXml.LoadXml(stg);
24
25        using (Stream stream = ←
            ↪ webRequest.GetRequestStream())
26        {
27            soapEnvelopeXml.Save(stream);
28        }
29
30        string soapResult;
31
32        using (WebResponse response = ←
            ↪ webRequest.GetResponse())
33        {
34            using (StreamReader rd = new ←
                ↪ StreamReader(response.GetResponseStream()))
35            {
```

```
36                      soapResult = rd.ReadToEnd();
37                      Log.Info(soapResult);
38                  }
39              }
40
41          XmlDocument xml = new XmlDocument();
42          xml.LoadXml(soapResult);
43
44          return xml;
45      }
46      catch (Exception exception)
47      {
48          Utility.Log.Error("exception" + ↵
              ↪ exception.ToString());
49          throw exception;
50      }
51  }
52
53  public static void VerifyEmployeeWithDB(String empId, ↵
      ↪ XmlDocument xml)
54  {
55      string stringSQL = "SELECT [EmployeeID], [Title], ↵
          ↪ [Name], [Gender], [DateOfBirth], [ContractJob]" ↵
          ↪ + "\r\n";
56      stringSQL = stringSQL + "FROM [dbo].[Employees] where ↵
          ↪ EmployeeID = '" + empId + "'";
57
58      Utility.Log.Info("SQL is: " + stringSQL);
59
60      String actEmpId = "", actTitle = "", actName = "", ↵
          ↪ actGender = "", actDob = "", actContract = "";
61
62      using (SqlConnection con = new ↵
          ↪ SqlConnection(Config.connectionString))
63      {
64          con.Open();
65
66          using (SqlCommand command = new ↵
              ↪ SqlCommand(stringSQL, con))
67          using (SqlDataReader reader = ↵
              ↪ command.ExecuteReader())
68          {
69              while (reader.Read())
70              {
71                  actEmpId = reader.GetString(0);
```

```
72              actTitle = reader.GetString(1);
73              actName = reader.GetString(2);
74              actGender = reader.GetString(3);
75              actDob = reader.GetDateTime(4).ToString();
76              actContract = reader.GetString(5);
77            }
78          }
79        }
80
81        ReportExpectedVsActual(actEmpId, ↵
           ↪ (xml.GetElementsByTagName("EmpID"))[0].InnerXml);
82        ReportExpectedVsActual(actTitle, ↵
           ↪ xml.GetElementsByTagName("Title").Item(0). ↵
           ↪ InnerXml);
83        ReportExpectedVsActual(actName, ↵
           ↪ xml.GetElementsByTagName("Name").Item(0).InnerXml);
84        ReportExpectedVsActual(DecodeGender(actGender), ↵
           ↪ xml.GetElementsByTagName("Gender").Item(0). ↵
           ↪ InnerXml);
85        ReportExpectedVsActual(actDob.Substring(0, 10), ↵
           ↪ (xml.GetElementsByTagName("BirthDate").Item(0). ↵
           ↪ InnerXml).Substring(0, 10));
86        ReportExpectedVsActual(actContract, ↵
           ↪ xml.GetElementsByTagName("Contract").Item(0). ↵
           ↪ InnerXml);
87 }
```

◈ Line 5: Initialises a new `WebRequest` instance for the specified URI. Please change the port number (50380) to the value you see in your workstation's browser window.

◈ Line 6: Adds a header with the name and value separated by a colon i.e. "`SOAP:Action`".

◈ Line 7: Sets the `ContentType` property of the `WebRequest`.

◈ Line 8: Sets the `Accept` property to accept "text/xml".

◈ Line 9: Sets the `Method` property to "POST" to post data to the URI.

◈ Line 11: Initialises a new instance of the `XmlDocument`.

◈ Line 12: Constructs the SOAP Envelope.

◈ Line 16: Inserts the Employee ID in the SOAP Envelope.

◈ Line 23: Loads the XML document from the specified string.

◈ Line 25: Gets the stream to use to write request data.

◈ Line 27: Saves the XML document to the specified stream.

◈ Line 32: Gets the response from the web service.

◈ Line 34: Initialises a new instance of the `StreamReader` class for the specified stream.

◈ Line 36: Reads all characters from the current position to the end of the stream.

◈ Line 42: Loads the SOAP result into XML document.

◈ Line 44: Returns the XML document.

◈ Lines 55 - 56: Construct the SQL Query to fetch data.

⬦ Lines 71 - 76: Store data from the database into temporary variables.

⬦ Lines 81 - 86: Compare data fetched from the database with values from the web service and report the outcome.

8.3.2   Creating Test

Add Listing 8.5 code to the 'WebServicesTests.cs' file.

Listing 8.5: 'WebServicesTests.cs' - Code for WebServicesHttpWebRequest

```
1  [TestMethod]
2  public void WebServicesHttpWebRequest()
3  {
4      Utility.Log.Info("Starting Test ***** " + ↵
           ↪ Utility.TestName + " *****");
5
6      try
7      {
8          XmlDocument xmlRec = ↵
               ↪ Utility.GetEmployeeByHttpWebRequest("10004");
9
10         Utility.VerifyEmployeeWithDB("10004", xmlRec);
11
12         Utility.ReportResult();
13     }
14     catch (Exception exception)
15     {
16         Utility.ReportExpectedVsActual(Utility.TestName, ↵
               ↪ "Exception occurred");
17         Utility.Log.Error("Exception: " + ↵
               ↪ exception.ToString());
18         throw exception;
19     }
20 }
```

⬦ Line 8: Gets the employee detail by the `HttpWebRequest` method for employee id "10004".

⬦ Line 10: Verifies the employee detail with database values for employee id "10004".

8.3.3   Executing Tests

Ensure that 'IIS Express' is running as shown in Figure 8.11. The output is shown in Figure 8.16 for a successful execution.

Test Name: WebServicesHttpWebRequest

Test Outcome: ● Passed

```
Standard Output
2017-04-08 10:14:38.752 INFO  CodedUITesting.Utility - SetupSummaryFile
2017-04-08 10:14:38.818 INFO  CodedUITesting.Utility - Starting Test ***** WebServicesHttpWebRequest *****
2017-04-08 10:14:38.857 INFO  CodedUITesting.Utility - stg: <?xml version="1.0" encoding="utf-8"?>
<soap:Envelope xmlns:soap="http://schemas.xmlsoap.org/soap/envelope/" xmlns:xsi="http://www.w3.org/2001/XMLSchema
<soap:Body>
   <GetEmployee xmlns="http://tempuri.org/">
      <employeeID>10004</employeeID>
   </GetEmployee>
</soap:Body>
</soap:Envelope>
2017-04-08 10:14:38.884 INFO  CodedUITesting.Utility - <?xml version="1.0" encoding="utf-8"?><soap:Envelope xmlns:soap
2017-04-08 10:14:38.888 INFO  CodedUITesting.Utility - SQL is: SELECT [EmployeeID], [Title], [Name], [Gender], [DateOfBirth],
FROM [dbo].[Employees] where EmployeeID = '10004'
2017-04-08 10:14:39.149 INFO  CodedUITesting.Utility - [Expected:] 10004    [Actual:] 10004    [Step Passed]
2017-04-08 10:14:39.150 INFO  CodedUITesting.Utility - [Expected:] Miss     [Actual:] Miss     [Step Passed]
2017-04-08 10:14:39.151 INFO  CodedUITesting.Utility - [Expected:] Sarah Smith    [Actual:] Sarah Smith    [Step Passed]
2017-04-08 10:14:39.153 INFO  CodedUITesting.Utility - [Expected:] Female   [Actual:] Female   [Step Passed]
2017-04-08 10:14:39.154 INFO  CodedUITesting.Utility - [Expected:] 25/12/1982    [Actual:] 25/12/1982    [Step Passed]
2017-04-08 10:14:39.155 INFO  CodedUITesting.Utility - [Expected:] No    [Actual:] No    [Step Passed]
2017-04-08 10:14:39.156 INFO  CodedUITesting.Utility - Reporting Result......
2017-04-08 10:14:39.157 INFO  CodedUITesting.Utility - Test Passed
```

Figure 8.16: Web Services HttpWebRequest Output

8.4   Testing The Web Service via Service Reference

Let's perform the following Test Scenario to demonstrate the process of accessing our web service via the *Service Reference* method:

- Call the demo web service via the *Service Reference* method with the Employee ID = 10004 to get the *actual result* values.

- Read the *expected result* values from an Excel source.

- Compare both the *expected* and the *actual result* values and report the outcome.

8.4.1   Adding Service Reference

Add the web service reference as follows:

- In the *Solution Explorer*, right click on the *References* in *CodedUITesting* project and select *Add Service Reference...* as shown in Figure 8.17.

- Type the URL in the *Address* box. Please change the port number (59362) to the value you see in your workstation's browser window.

- Click on the *Go* button. After a successful connection, you should be able to see **EmployeeWebService** in the *Services* box.

- Type the *Namespace* as 'EmployeeWebService'.

- Press the *OK* button.

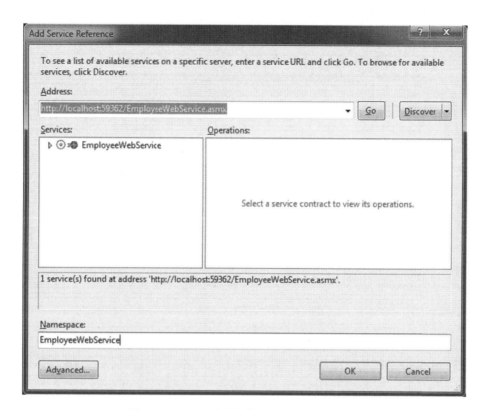

Figure 8.17: Add Service Reference

- Right click on the 'App.config' file in the *CodedUITesting* project and select *Properties*.

- Ensure that the settings are as shown in Figure 8.18

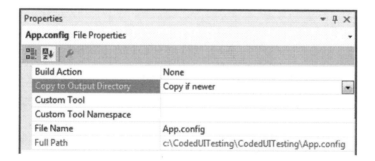

Figure 8.18: App Config File Properties

8.4.2   Utility Functions

Let's define two new Utility functions as follows:

GetEmployeeByServiceReference - Gets an employee's detail by the Service Reference method		
Input Parameters	*empId*	Employee ID
Return Value	*empRec*	Returns the employee record

VerifyEmployeeWithXLSData - Compares an employee's record with the data from an XLS source and reports the outcome		
Input Parameters	*empID*	Employee Id
	empRec	Employee record
Return Value	*void*	Returns nothing

Add Listing 8.6 code to the 'Utility.cs' file.

Listing 8.6: 'Utility.cs' - Additional code

```
1  public static EmployeeWebService.Employee ↵
      ↪ GetEmployeeByServiceReference(String empId)
2  {
3    try
4    {
5      EmployeeWebService.EmployeeWebServiceSoapClient ↵
         ↪ ser1 = new ↵
         ↪ EmployeeWebService.EmployeeWebServiceSoapClient();
6      EmployeeWebService.Employee empRec = ↵
         ↪ ser1.GetEmployee(empId);
7      return empRec;
8    }
9    catch (Exception exception)
10   {
11     Utility.Log.Error("exception" + exception.ToString());
12     throw exception;
13   }
14 }
15
16 public static void VerifyEmployeeWithXLSData(String ↵
      ↪ empID, EmployeeWebService.Employee empRec)
17 {
18   String[][] data = Utility.GetSpreadSheetXLS( ↵
        ↪ @"C:\CodedUITesting\CodedUITesting\TestData\ ↵
        ↪ UserData.xls", 1);
19
20   ReportExpectedVsActual(empID, empRec.EmpID);
21   ReportExpectedVsActual(data[1][0], empRec.Title);
```

```
22      ReportExpectedVsActual(data[1][1], empRec.Name);
23      ReportExpectedVsActual(data[1][2], empRec.Gender);
24      ReportExpectedVsActual(ExcelDateParse(data[1][3]). ↵
            ↪ Substring(0, 10), empRec.BirthDate);
25      ReportExpectedVsActual(data[1][5], empRec.Contract);
26   }
```

◈ Line 5: Initialises a new instance of the `EmployeeWebServiceSoapClient` class.

◈ Line 6: Gets the employee record for the specified employee id.

◈ Line 7: Returns the `Employee` record.

◈ Line 18: Reads data in the XLS file into an array-of-arrays.

◈ Line 20: Note that we are comparing the employee id with the supplied id as the XLS file doesn't store the Employee ID.

◈ Lines 21 - 25: Compare the XLS data with the data fetched via the web service.

8.4.3   Creating Test

Add Listing 8.7 code to the 'WebServicesTests.cs' file.

Listing 8.7: 'WebServicesTests.cs' - Code for WebServicesServiceReference

```
1    [TestMethod]
2    public void WebServicesServiceReference()
3    {
4       Utility.Log.Info("Starting Test ***** " + ↵
            ↪ Utility.TestName + " *****");
5
6       try
7       {
8          String empId = "10004";
9
10         EmployeeWebService.Employee empRec = ↵
               ↪ Utility.GetEmployeeByServiceReference(empId);
11
12         Utility.VerifyEmployeeWithXLSData(empId, empRec);
13
14         Utility.ReportResult();
15      }
16      catch (Exception exception)
17      {
18         Utility.ReportExpectedVsActual(Utility.TestName, ↵
               ↪ "Exception occurred");
19         Utility.Log.Error("Exception: " + ↵
               ↪ exception.ToString());
```

```
20        throw exception;
21    }
22  }
```

◈ Line 10: Calls the Utility function `GetEmployeeByServiceReference` with Employee ID "10004".

◈ Line 12: Verifies the employee detail with the data in the XLS file.

8.4.4 Executing Tests

Ensure that 'IIS Express' is running as shown in Figure 8.11. The output is shown in Figure 8.19 for a successful execution.

Test Name: WebServicesServiceReference

Test Outcome: Passed

┌─ Standard Output ───
│ 2017-04-08 10:07:20.554 INFO CodedUITesting.Utility - SetupSummaryFile
│ 2017-04-08 10:07:20.624 INFO CodedUITesting.Utility - Starting Test ***** WebServicesServiceReference *****
│ 2017-04-08 10:07:20.910 INFO CodedUITesting.Utility - GetSpreadSheetXLS...... File: C:\CodedUITesting\CodedU
│ 2017-04-08 10:07:21.237 INFO CodedUITesting.Utility - SHEET Name: EmployeeData
│ 2017-04-08 10:07:21.239 INFO CodedUITesting.Utility - SHEET LastRowNum: 1
│ 2017-04-08 10:07:21.246 INFO CodedUITesting.Utility - SHEET ColumnCount: 7
│ 2017-04-08 10:07:21.250 INFO CodedUITesting.Utility - CellType: String
│ 2017-04-08 10:07:21.253 INFO CodedUITesting.Utility - Row: 0   Col: 0 Title
│ 2017-04-08 10:07:21.254 INFO CodedUITesting.Utility - CellType: String
│ 2017-04-08 10:07:21.255 INFO CodedUITesting.Utility - Row: 0   Col: 1 Name
│ 2017-04-08 10:07:21.257 INFO CodedUITesting.Utility - CellType: String
│ 2017-04-08 10:07:21.258 INFO CodedUITesting.Utility - Row: 0   Col: 2 Gender
│ 2017-04-08 10:07:21.259 INFO CodedUITesting.Utility - CellType: String
│ 2017-04-08 10:07:21.262 INFO CodedUITesting.Utility - Row: 0   Col: 3 DateOfBirth
│ 2017-04-08 10:07:21.264 INFO CodedUITesting.Utility - CellType: String
│ 2017-04-08 10:07:21.265 INFO CodedUITesting.Utility - Row: 0   Col: 4 Email
│ 2017-04-08 10:07:21.266 INFO CodedUITesting.Utility - CellType: String
│ 2017-04-08 10:07:21.268 INFO CodedUITesting.Utility - Row: 0   Col: 5 Contract
│ 2017-04-08 10:07:21.269 INFO CodedUITesting.Utility - CellType: String
│ 2017-04-08 10:07:21.270 INFO CodedUITesting.Utility - Row: 0   Col: 6 Postcode
│ 2017-04-08 10:07:21.271 INFO CodedUITesting.Utility - CellType: String
│ 2017-04-08 10:07:21.272 INFO CodedUITesting.Utility - Row: 1   Col: 0 Miss
```

Figure 8.19: Web Services Service Reference Output
```

Chapter 9

Windows Forms Application - WinControls

Windows Forms Application - WinControls

In this chapter, we will learn about how to perform:

- *Login tasks on Windows Forms Applications*

- *Data entry and verification tasks on Windows Forms Applications*

- *Drag-and-drop tasks on Windows Forms Applications*

- *Verification tasks using data fetched from Excel® files and database tables*

So let's get on with it...

A Windows-based Application is a stand-alone software that runs locally on your computer. A Web Application, on the other hand, runs on a browser using a Web Server. A Web Application can be accessed from any computer via internet whereas a Windows-based Application can only be accessed from a computer on which it is installed. So far we have been learning how to automate the testing of a Web Application and a Web Service using Coded UI. Now let's learn how to automate the testing of Windows-based Applications using Coded UI.

We will explore two type of Windows-based Applications for the purposes of automation namely Windows Forms Applications and Windows Presentation Foundation (WPF) Applications. In this chapter we will cover Windows Forms Applications and the next chapter will cover Windows Presentation Foundation (WPF) Applications.

9.1 Demo Windows Forms Application

A demo Windows Forms Application has been developed for you to carry out the Test Scenarios listed in this chapter. Here are the steps to download and compile the demo project.

- In your chosen browser, navigate to `http://www.arkenstone-ltd.com/`.

- Click on the *Downloads* link.

- Click on the *Download Windows Forms Application* link and save the compressed file on your local workstation.

- Extract the files to the 'C:\' folder. You can select a different location; however this book assumes you have chosen 'C:\'.

- Navigate to the 'C:\WindowsFormsApplication' folder and double click on the 'WindowsFormsApplication.sln' file. The project will open in Visual Studio®.

- In Visual Studio's Toolbar, select the *'Release' Solution Configuration* as shown in Figure 9.1.

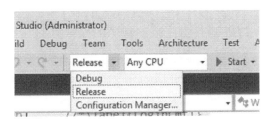

Figure 9.1: Selecting Solution Configuration

- In the *Solution Explorer*, right click on the *WindowsFormsApplication* and select *Rebuild*. On successful compilation, 'WindowsFormsApplication.exe' will be generated in the 'C:\WindowsFormsApplication\bin\Release' folder.

There are two types of users that exist for the demo Windows Forms Application:

- A general or normal user whose credentials are:

  User: Tester

  Password: Tester123

- An administrator user whose credentials are:

  Admin User: Admin

  Password: Admin123

Please note that the credentials are case-sensitive.

9.2 WinControls - Login

We will perform the following Test Scenario to demonstrate the use of `WinControls` in the *Login* functionality:

- Launch the demo Windows Forms Application.

- Click the menu item *File* ⇒ *Login*.

- Login with the user 'Tester'.

- Click the menu item *File* ⇒ *Logout*.

- Click the menu item *File* ⇒ *Exit*.

9.2.1 Configuration Parameters

First of all, let's add some configuration variables which we will need throughout our Automation Framework. Double click the 'Config.cs' file in the *Solution Explorer* and add Listing 9.1 code to it.

Listing 9.1: 'Config.cs' - Parameters for WinControls

```
1  public const string WIN_APP = ↵
       ↪ "C:\\WindowsFormsApplication\\bin\\Release\\ ↵
       ↪ WindowsFormsApplication.exe";
2
3  public const string WIN_MENU_ITEM = ↵
       ↪ "Microsoft.VisualStudio.TestTools.UITesting. ↵
       ↪ WinControls.WinMenuItem";
4  public const string WIN_EDIT = ↵
       ↪ "Microsoft.VisualStudio.TestTools.UITesting. ↵
       ↪ WinControls.WinEdit";
5  public const string WIN_BUTTON = ↵
       ↪ "Microsoft.VisualStudio.TestTools.UITesting. ↵
       ↪ WinControls.WinButton";
```

◈ Line 1: Defines the path of Windows Forms Application's executable.
◈ Lines 3 - 5: Define string constants for `WinMenuItem`, `WinEdit` and `WinButton` controls.

9.2.2 Object Repository

Ok, let's start building the repository of our demo Windows Forms Application.

9.2.2.1   AUT - Home Window

Launch the Windows Forms Application and using *UI Spy*, note down the following elements:

Windows Forms Application - Home Page Controls			
Control	*Type*	*Property*	*Value*
Main Menu Bar	Menu Bar	TechnologyName ControlType Name	MSAA MenuBar menuStripMain
File	Menu Item	TechnologyName ControlType Name	MSAA MenuItem File
File ⇒ Login	Menu Item	TechnologyName ControlType Name	MSAA MenuItem Login

Before we start writing the repository code, there is something else we need to learn. In web testing, all the controls can be defined as having the web browser as the parent. However, in Windows Applications we need to be very meticulous in defining the parental hierarchy otherwise you may have difficulties in identifying the controls. This may result in either failing to identify the control or may take very long time to identify the control using the *smart match* algorithm. So let's see what this hierarchy is and how to identify it. Figure 9.2 is a pictorial representation of the controls (identified above) on the main window of our demo Windows Forms Application.

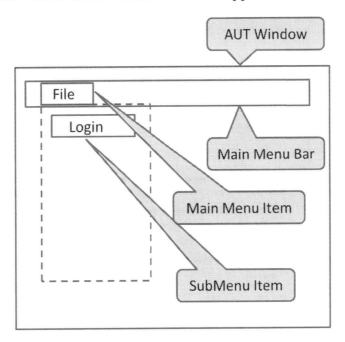

Figure 9.2: WinControls Parental Hierarchy

It can be seen that:

- The top level window is the Application Under Test (AUT) itself i.e. *Coded UI Testing - Windows Application* window.

- Next we have the *Main Menu Bar* which lists the *Main Menu* items like *File, Edit, Tools and Help*. The *Parent* of the *Main Menu Bar* is the demo application i.e. *Coded UI Testing - Windows Application* window.

- The *Parent* of the *Main Menu* items *File, Edit, Tools and Help* is the *Main Menu Bar*.

- Each *Main Menu* item has a SubMenu e.g. *File* has SubMenu items *Login, Logout, Exit* etc. The *Parent* of each SubMenu item is its corresponding *Main Menu* item e.g. *Parent* of *Login, Logout* and *Exit* is *File*.

So let's see how to identify this hierarchy in Coded UI. In the demo Windows Forms Application, hover onto the *Login* SubMenu item and press [Shift] + [Ctrl] + [I] . In the *Control Properties* window, click on the left chevron icon [«] on its top left corner and it will display a *UI Control Map* window as shown in Figure 9.3. It will display a number of controls in the hierarchical order. The hierarchy displayed in here matches what we have seen in Figure 9.2 i.e. *Coded UI Testing - Windows Application* window (the AUT Window) at the top, followed by the *Main Menu Bar* and then the *Main Menu* item *File* and finally the *Login* SubMenu item. You can click on individual controls in the *UI Control Map* to view their properties.

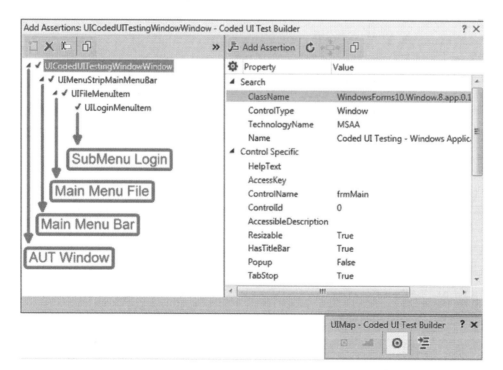

Figure 9.3: WinMenu Hierarchy

So let's revisit our repository table and add the *Parent* of each control as shown in the following table. Note that this book has only defined the controls that we will use for demonstration purposes.

Windows Forms Application - Home Page Controls			
Control	*Type*	*Property*	*Value*
Main Menu Bar *Parent: AUT Window*	Menu Bar	TechnologyName ControlType Name	MSAA MenuBar menuStripMain
File *Parent: Main Menu Bar*	Menu Item	TechnologyName ControlType Name	MSAA MenuItem File
File ⇒ Login *Parent: File*	Menu Item	TechnologyName ControlType Name	MSAA MenuItem Login
File ⇒ Logout *Parent: File*	Menu Item	TechnologyName ControlType Name	MSAA MenuItem Logout
File ⇒ Exit *Parent: File*	Menu Item	TechnologyName ControlType Name	MSAA MenuItem Exit
Tester *Parent: Main Menu Bar*	Menu Item	TechnologyName ControlType Name	MSAA MenuItem Tester
Tester ⇒ Add Employee *Parent: Tester*	Menu Item	TechnologyName ControlType Name	MSAA MenuItem Add Employee
Tester ⇒ View Employee *Parent: Tester*	Menu Item	TechnologyName ControlType Name	MSAA MenuItem View Employee
Tester ⇒ Other *Parent: Tester*	Menu Item	TechnologyName ControlType Name	MSAA MenuItem Other
Admin *Parent: Main Menu Bar*	Menu Item	TechnologyName ControlType Name	MSAA MenuItem Admin
Admin ⇒ Employee List *Parent: Admin*	Menu Item	TechnologyName ControlType Name	MSAA MenuItem Employee List

We need to be mindful of this hierarchy when defining the repository of each control in our code. We will also setup a *Base Window Scope* procedure when defining the repository of each page or window in our demo application. This will essentially set the scene to identify the current main window - controls on which we are planning to interact with. For example, for the *Home* page repository, the *Base Window Scope* will be set to the *Main Menu Bar*. We will call this function `SetBaseWindowScope` in each repository page. Don't worry if the things aren't clear at this stage. We will have a better understanding as we move through this chapter.

Add a new class 'repWinHome.cs' to the *Repository* folder and add Listing 9.2 code to it.

 After adding the code, you will see an error on the `Utility.WinAUT` variable. Don't worry about this as we will define it soon.

Listing 9.2: 'repWinHome.cs' - Repository for the Home window

```
1  /************************************************************
2   * All rights reserved. Copyright 2017 Arkenstone-ltd.com *
3   ***********************************************************/
4  using
      ↪ Microsoft.VisualStudio.TestTools.UITesting.WinControls;
5
6  namespace CodedUITesting
7  {
8      public static class repWinHome
9      {
10         private static WinMenuBar mMenuBarWindow;
11
12         private static WinMenuItem mMenuItem_File;
13         private static WinMenuItem mMenuItem_FileLogin;
14         private static WinMenuItem mMenuItem_FileLogout;
15         private static WinMenuItem mMenuItem_FileExit;
16
17         private static WinMenuItem mMenuItem_Tester;
18         private static WinMenuItem mMenuItem_TesterAddEmp;
19         private static WinMenuItem mMenuItem_TesterViewEmp;
20         private static WinMenuItem
               ↪ mMenuItem_TesterOther;
21
22         private static WinMenuItem mMenuItem_Admin;
23         private static WinMenuItem
               ↪ mMenuItem_AdminEmpList;
24
25         public static WinMenuBar SetBaseWindowScope()
```

5,884.94

333-89-3903

CE 6087

Jobview Issues

1) ~~Launch~~ Jobview
   - => Create Walls
   - -> Frame Walls : Labels are shown in Jobview
   - -> Erase Walls : ~~Labels~~ Nothing is in Jobview   OK
   - -> Undo : Walls are back but Labels in Jobview are not
     * It works now

TRs:

✓ #231 Enter a ticket when changing location of
          Rate Fascia. Audit happens
* This only happens with an old drawing. When I create a
  drawing from scratch I don't get the Audit. No ticket needed.

8   ~~5754~~

6 | TT 34472 | about Manual Connections ✓

Planning Meeting Steel Engine
   1) Talk about whet not ticket related fixes do to
      the scope of testing.

084

* Add a ticket for undo on two manually added actions.

```
26              {
27                  mMenuBarWindow = new ↵
                        ↪ WinMenuBar(Utility.WinAUT);
28
29                  mMenuBarWindow.SearchProperties.Add(WinMenuBar. ↵
                        ↪ PropertyNames.Name, "menuStripMain");
30
31                  return mMenuBarWindow;
32              }
33
34          public static WinMenuItem MenuItem_File
35          {
36              get
37              {
38                  if (mMenuItem_File == null)
39                  {
40                      mMenuItem_File = new ↵
                            ↪ WinMenuItem(mMenuBarWindow);
41                      mMenuItem_File.SearchProperties.Add( ↵
                            ↪ WinMenuItem.PropertyNames.Name, ↵
                            ↪ "File");
42                  }
43
44                  return mMenuItem_File;
45              }
46          }
47
48          public static WinMenuItem MenuItem_FileLogin
49          {
50              get
51              {
52                  if (mMenuItem_FileLogin == null)
53                  {
54                      mMenuItem_FileLogin = new ↵
                            ↪ WinMenuItem(mMenuItem_File);
55                      mMenuItem_FileLogin.SearchProperties. ↵
                            ↪ Add(WinMenuItem.PropertyNames. ↵
                            ↪ Name, "Login");
56                  }
57
58                  return mMenuItem_FileLogin;
59              }
60          }
61
62          public static WinMenuItem MenuItem_FileLogout
```

```
63              {
64                  get
65                  {
66                      if (mMenuItem_FileLogout == null)
67                      {
68                          mMenuItem_FileLogout = new ↵
                               ↪ WinMenuItem(mMenuItem_File);
69                          mMenuItem_FileLogout.SearchProperties. ↵
                               ↪ Add(WinMenuItem.PropertyNames. ↵
                               ↪ Name, "Logout");
70                      }
71
72                      return mMenuItem_FileLogout;
73                  }
74              }
75
76          public static WinMenuItem MenuItem_FileExit
77          {
78              get
79              {
80                  if (mMenuItem_FileExit == null)
81                  {
82                      mMenuItem_FileExit = new ↵
                           ↪ WinMenuItem(mMenuItem_File);
83                      mMenuItem_FileExit.SearchProperties.Add( ↵
                           ↪ WinMenuItem.PropertyNames.Name, ↵
                           ↪ "Exit");
84                  }
85
86                  return mMenuItem_FileExit;
87              }
88          }
89
90          public static WinMenuItem MenuItem_Tester
91          {
92              get
93              {
94                  if (mMenuItem_Tester == null)
95                  {
96                      mMenuItem_Tester = new ↵
                           ↪ WinMenuItem(mMenuBarWindow);
97                      mMenuItem_Tester.SearchProperties.Add( ↵
                           ↪ WinMenuItem.PropertyNames.Name, ↵
                           ↪ "Tester");
98                  }
```

```
 99
100                     return mMenuItem_Tester;
101             }
102         }
103
104     public static WinMenuItem MenuItem_TesterAddEmp
105     {
106         get
107         {
108             if (mMenuItem_TesterAddEmp == null)
109             {
110                 mMenuItem_TesterAddEmp = new ↵
                        ↪ WinMenuItem(mMenuItem_Tester);
111                 mMenuItem_TesterAddEmp. ↵
                        ↪ SearchProperties.Add( ↵
                        ↪ WinMenuItem.PropertyNames.Name, ↵
                        ↪ "Add Employee");
112             }
113
114             return mMenuItem_TesterAddEmp;
115         }
116     }
117
118     public static WinMenuItem MenuItem_TesterViewEmp
119     {
120         get
121         {
122             if (mMenuItem_TesterViewEmp == null)
123             {
124                 mMenuItem_TesterViewEmp = new ↵
                        ↪ WinMenuItem(mMenuItem_Tester);
125                 mMenuItem_TesterViewEmp. ↵
                        ↪ SearchProperties.Add( ↵
                        ↪ WinMenuItem.PropertyNames.Name, ↵
                        ↪ "View Employee");
126             }
127
128             return mMenuItem_TesterViewEmp;
129         }
130     }
131
132     public static WinMenuItem MenuItem_TesterOther
133     {
134         get
135         {
```

```
136                    if (mMenuItem_TesterOther == null)
137                    {
138                        mMenuItem_TesterOther = new ↵
                              ↪ WinMenuItem(mMenuItem_Tester);
139                        mMenuItem_TesterOther.SearchProperties. ↵
                              ↪ Add(WinMenuItem.PropertyNames. ↵
                              ↪ Name, "Other");
140                    }
141
142                    return mMenuItem_TesterOther;
143                }
144            }
145
146        public static WinMenuItem MenuItem_Admin
147        {
148            get
149            {
150
151                if (mMenuItem_Admin == null)
152                {
153                    mMenuItem_Admin = new ↵
                          ↪ WinMenuItem(mMenuBarWindow);
154                    mMenuItem_Admin.SearchProperties.Add( ↵
                          ↪ WinMenuItem.PropertyNames.Name, ↵
                          ↪ "Admin");
155                }
156
157                return mMenuItem_Admin;
158            }
159        }
160
161        public static WinMenuItem MenuItem_AdminEmpList
162        {
163            get
164            {
165                if (mMenuItem_AdminEmpList == null)
166                {
167                    mMenuItem_AdminEmpList = new ↵
                          ↪ WinMenuItem(mMenuItem_Admin);
168                    mMenuItem_AdminEmpList.SearchProperties. ↵
                          ↪ Add(WinMenuItem.PropertyNames.Name, ↵
                          ↪ "Employee List");
169                }
170
171                return mMenuItem_AdminEmpList;
```

```
172                    }
173                }
174            }
175 }
```

◈ Line 10: Defines a `private` member variable for the Menu Bar.

◈ Lines 12 - 15: Define `private` member variables for the `File` menu item and its SubMenu items.

◈ Lines 17 - 20: Define `private` member variables for the `Tester` menu item and its SubMenu items.

◈ Lines 22 - 23: Define `private` member variables for the `Admin` menu item and its SubMenu items.

◈ Line 25: Defines a `public` function `SetBaseWindowScope` to set the base window scope and returns `mMenuBarWindow` - a control of type `WinMenuBar`.

◈ Line 27: Initialises a new instance of the `WinMenuBar` class whose *Parent* is `Utility.WinAUT` which is our demo application.

◈ Line 29: Sets the base window scope to the *Main Menu Bar* for this repository.

◈ Lines 40, 96 and 153: Initialise a new instance of the `WinMenuItem` class whose *Parent* is `mMenuBarWindow`.

◈ Lines 54, 68 and 82: Initialise a new instance of the `WinMenuItem` class whose *Parent* is `mMenuItem_File`.

◈ Lines 110, 124 and 138: Initialise a new instance of the `WinMenuItem` class whose *Parent* is `mMenuItem_Tester`.

◈ Line 167: Initialises a new instance of the `WinMenuItem` class whose *Parent* is `mMenuItem_Admin`.

☞ Since we have defined the Menu Bar control as `WinMenuBar` therefore, `TechnologyName = "MSAA"` and `ControlType = "MenuBar"` is implicit so there is no need to specify these properties while defining the repository. The same is true for other `WinControls`.

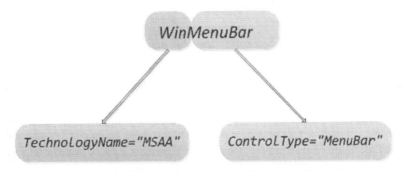

Figure 9.4: WinMenuBar Control

9.2.2.2 AUT - Login Window

Let's start building the object repository of our *Login* window. Similar to what we did in the previous subsection, let me show you the hierarchy of the *User ID* edit box in the *Login* window. Hover onto the *User ID* control and press ⟨Shift⟩ + ⟨Ctrl⟩ + ⟨I⟩ . In the *Control Properties* window, click on the left chevron icon `«` on its top left corner and it will display a *UI Control Map* window as shown in Figure 9.5.

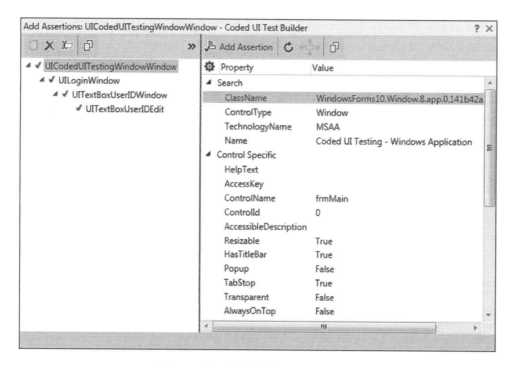

Figure 9.5: WinEdit Hierarchy

It can be seen that:

- The top level window is the Application Under Test (AUT) itself i.e. *Coded UI Testing - Windows Application* window.

- At the next level is the *Login* window.

- At the next level in the hierarchy, what we expect to see is the *User ID* edit box. However, before we see that, there is another window! The *User ID* edit box is encapsulated in the *User ID* window.

This hierarchy is illustrated in Figure 9.6. We need to be mindful of this hierarchy while defining the object repository in our code.

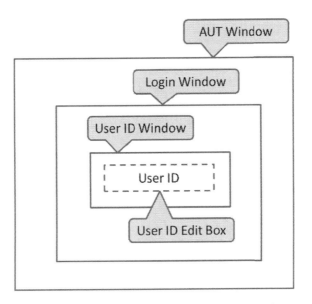

Figure 9.6: WinEdit Parental Hierarchy

Let's note down all the controls on the *Login* window as follows:

Windows Forms Application - Login Window Controls			
Control	*Type*	*Property*	*Value*
Login Window *Parent: AUT Window*	Window	TechnologyName ControlType ControlName	MSAA Window frmLogin
User ID Window *Parent: Login Window*	Window	TechnologyName ControlType ControlName	MSAA Window textBoxUserID
User ID Edit Box *Parent: User ID Window*	Edit Box	TechnologyName ControlType	MSAA Edit
Password Window *Parent: Login Window*	Window	TechnologyName ControlType ControlName	MSAA Window textBoxPassword
Password Edit Box *Parent: Password Window*	Edit Box	TechnologyName ControlType	MSAA Edit
Login Button Window *Parent: Login Window*	Window	TechnologyName ControlType ControlName	MSAA Window btnLogin
Login Button *Parent: Login Button Window*	Button	TechnologyName ControlType	MSAA Button

Add a new class 'repWinLogin.cs' to the *Repository* folder and add Listing 9.3 code to it.

Listing 9.3: 'repWinLogin.cs' - Repository for the Login window

```
1   /*******************************************************
2    * All rights reserved. Copyright 2017 Arkenstone-ltd.com *
3    *******************************************************/
4   using ↵
        ↪ Microsoft.VisualStudio.TestTools.UITesting.WinControls;
5
6   namespace CodedUITesting
7   {
8       public static class repWinLogin
9       {
10          private static WinWindow mLoginWindow;
11
12          private static WinWindow mUserIDWindow;
13          private static WinEdit mUserID;
14
15          private static WinWindow mPasswordWindow;
16          private static WinEdit mPassword;
17
18          private static WinWindow mLoginButtonWindow;
19          private static WinButton mLoginButton;
20
21          public static WinWindow SetBaseWindowScope()
22          {
23              mLoginWindow = new ↵
                    ↪ WinWindow(Utility.WinAUT);
24
25              mLoginWindow.SearchProperties[WinWindow. ↵
                    ↪ PropertyNames.ControlName] = "frmLogin";
26
27              return mLoginWindow;
28          }
29
30          public static WinEdit UserID
31          {
32              get
33              {
34                  if (mUserIDWindow == null)
35                  {
36                      mUserIDWindow = new ↵
                            ↪ WinWindow(mLoginWindow);
37                      mUserIDWindow.SearchProperties[WinWindow. ↵
                            ↪ PropertyNames.ControlName] = ↵
```

```
                              ↪ "textBoxUserID";
38                    }
39
40                    if (mUserID == null)
41                    {
42                        mUserID = new ↩
                            ↪ WinEdit(mUserIDWindow);
43                    }
44
45                    return mUserID;
46            }
47        }
48
49        public static WinEdit Password
50        {
51            get
52            {
53                if (mPasswordWindow == null)
54                {
55                    mPasswordWindow = new ↩
                        ↪ WinWindow(mLoginWindow);
56                    mPasswordWindow.SearchProperties[ ↩
                        ↪ WinWindow.PropertyNames. ↩
                        ↪ ControlName] = "textBoxPassword";
57                }
58
59                if (mPassword == null)
60                {
61                    mPassword = new ↩
                        ↪ WinEdit(mPasswordWindow);
62                }
63
64                return mPassword;
65            }
66        }
67
68        public static WinButton LoginButton
69        {
70            get
71            {
72                if (mLoginButtonWindow == null)
73                {
74                    mLoginButtonWindow = new ↩
                        ↪ WinWindow(mLoginWindow);
75                    mLoginButtonWindow.SearchProperties[ ↩
```

```
                        ↪ WinWindow.PropertyNames.ControlName]  ↵
                        ↪ = "btnLogin";
76              }
77
78              if (mLoginButton == null)
79              {
80                  mLoginButton = new ↵
                        ↪ WinButton(mLoginButtonWindow);
81              }
82
83              return mLoginButton;
84          }
85      }
86    }
87  }
```

◈ Line 21: Sets the *Login* window as the base window scope for this repository.

◈ Line 23: Initialises a new instance of the `WinWindow` class whose *Parent* is `Utility.WinAUT`, which is our demo application.

◈ Lines 36, 55 and 74: Initialise a new instance of the `WinWindow` class whose *Parent* is `mLoginWindow`.

◈ Line 42: Initialises a new instance of the `WinEdit` class whose *Parent* is `mUserIDWindow`.

◈ Line 61: Initialises a new instance of the `WinEdit` class whose *Parent* is `mPasswordWindow`.

◈ Line 80: Initialises a new instance of the `WinButton` class whose *Parent* is `mLoginButtonWindow`.

9.2.3 Utility Functions

Let's define some additional generic functions as follows:

LaunchWinApp - Launches the Windows Forms Application		
Input Parameters	*none*	No arguments
Return Value	*void*	Returns nothing

CloseWinApp - Closes the Windows Forms Application		
Input Parameters	*none*	No arguments
Return Value	*void*	Returns nothing

KillProcess - Kills a process		
Input Parameters	*task*	Task name to be killed
Return Value	*void*	Returns nothing

Update the 'Utility.cs' file as shown in Listing 9.4.

 Note that the listing shows the changes only and not the complete 'Utility.cs' file.

Listing 9.4: 'Utility.cs' - Additional changes

```
1  using ↵
      ↪ Microsoft.VisualStudio.TestTools.UITesting.WinControls;
2  using System.Diagnostics;
3
4  namespace CodedUITesting
5  {
6      public static class Utility
7      {
8          public static ApplicationUnderTest WinAUT;
9
10         public static void LaunchWinApp()
11         {
12             WinAUT = ↵
                   ↪ ApplicationUnderTest.Launch(Config.WIN_APP);
13         }
14
15         public static void CloseWinApp()
16         {
17             string taskName = Path. ↵
                   ↪ GetFileNameWithoutExtension(Config.WIN_APP);
18             KillProcess(taskName);
19         }
20
21         public static void KillProcess(string task)
22         {
23             foreach (var process in ↵
                   ↪ Process.GetProcessesByName(task))
24             {
25                 Log.Info("Cleaning... " + ↵
                       ↪ process.ProcessName);
26                 process.Kill();
27                 process.WaitForExit();
28             }
29         }
30     }
31 }
```

◈ Line 8: Defines a `public static WinAUT` object representing the Windows Forms Application Under Test.

◈ Line 12: `ApplicationUnderTest.Launch` returns the application that was started.

◈ Line 27: The Kill method runs asynchronously i.e. it may return before the respective process has actually been killed so use `WaitForExit`.

We need to update our existing `Click()` function as per Listing 9.5.

Listing 9.5: 'Utility.cs' - Extra case statements in the Click function

```
1  case Config.WIN_MENU_ITEM:
2      Log.Info("Click WinMenuItem: ControlName - " + ↵
           ↳ ((WinMenuItem)obj).ControlName + " (DisplayText ↵
           ↳ - " + ((WinMenuItem)obj).DisplayText + ")");
3      Mouse.Click((WinMenuItem)obj);
4      break;
5
6  case Config.WIN_BUTTON:
7      Log.Info("Click WinButton: ControlName - " + ↵
           ↳ ((WinButton)obj).ControlName + " (DisplayText - ↵
           ↳ " + ((WinButton)obj).DisplayText + ")");
8      Mouse.Click((WinButton)obj);
9      break;
```

◈ Line 3: Note the casting to type `WinMenuItem`.

◈ Line 8: Note the casting to type `WinButton`.

Similarly, we need to update our existing `SetValue()` function as per Listing 9.6

Listing 9.6: 'Utility.cs' - Extra case statement in the SetValue function

```
1  case Config.WIN_EDIT:
2      Log.Info("SetValue WinEdit: ControlName - " + ↵
           ↳ ((WinEdit)obj).ControlName + " (Name - " + ↵
           ↳ ((WinEdit)obj).Name + ")" + " Value: " + val);
3      if (((WinEdit)obj).IsPassword)
4          Keyboard.SendKeys((WinEdit)obj, val, true);
5      else
6          ((WinEdit)obj).Text = val;
7      break;
```

◈ Line 3: If it is a password control then uses `SendKeys` to enter a value in the control. Note the third argument `true` in the `SendKeys` function signifies that the value being passed is encrypted.

◈ Line 5: Otherwise uses the `.Text` property to enter a value in the control.

9.2.4   Page Logic

The *Home* page will have the following actions:

Action	Description
ClickMenuItemFileLogin()	This action will click the *File* ⇒ *Login* menu option.
ClickMenuItemFileLogout()	This action will click the *File* ⇒ *Logout* menu option.
ClickMenuItemFileExit()	This action will click the *File* ⇒ *Exit* menu option.
ClickMenuItemTesterAddEmployee()	This action will click the *Tester* ⇒ *Add Employee* menu option.
ClickMenuItemTesterViewEmployee()	This action will click the *Tester* ⇒ *View Employee* menu option.
ClickMenuItemTesterOther()	This action will click the *Tester* ⇒ *Other* menu option.
ClickMenuItemAdminEmployeeList()	This action will click the *Admin* ⇒ *Employee List* menu option.

Add a new class 'pageWinHome.cs' to the *Pages* folder and insert the code as shown in Listing 9.7.

Listing 9.7: 'pageWinHome.cs' - Page logic for the Home window

```
 1  /*****************************************************
 2   * All rights reserved. Copyright 2017 Arkenstone-ltd.com *
 3   *****************************************************/
 4
 5  namespace CodedUITesting
 6  {
 7      class pageWinHome
 8      {
 9          public pageWinHome()
10          {
11              repWinHome.SetBaseWindowScope();
12          }
13
```

```
14          public void ClickMenuItemFileLogin()
15          {
16              Utility.Click(repWinHome.MenuItem_File);
17              Utility.Click(repWinHome.MenuItem_FileLogin);
18          }
19
20          public void ClickMenuItemFileLogout()
21          {
22              Utility.Click(repWinHome.MenuItem_File);
23              Utility.Click(repWinHome.MenuItem_FileLogout);
24          }
25
26          public void ClickMenuItemFileExit()
27          {
28              Utility.Click(repWinHome.MenuItem_File);
29              Utility.Click(repWinHome.MenuItem_FileExit);
30          }
31
32          public void ClickMenuItemTesterAddEmployee()
33          {
34              Utility.Click(repWinHome.MenuItem_Tester);
35              Utility.Click(repWinHome.MenuItem_TesterAddEmp);
36          }
37
38          public void ClickMenuItemTesterViewEmployee()
39          {
40              Utility.Click(repWinHome.MenuItem_Tester);
41              Utility.Click(repWinHome.MenuItem_TesterViewEmp);
42          }
43
44          public void ClickMenuItemTesterOther()
45          {
46              Utility.Click(repWinHome.MenuItem_Tester);
47              Utility.Click(repWinHome.MenuItem_TesterOther);
48          }
49
50          public void ClickMenuItemAdminEmployeeList()
51          {
52              Utility.Click(repWinHome.MenuItem_Admin);
53              Utility.Click(repWinHome.MenuItem_AdminEmpList);
54          }
55      }
56 }
```

◈ Line 11: Sets the base window scope by calling SetBaseWindowScope in the class constructor.

Let's define the business logic for the *Login* window which will have the following action:

Action	Description
LoginUser()	Action for the user login with given credentials.

Add a new class 'pageWinLogin.cs' to the *Pages* folder and insert the code as shown in Listing 9.8.

Listing 9.8: 'pageWinLogin.cs' - Page logic for the Login window

```
1  /*****************************************************
2   * All rights reserved. Copyright 2017 Arkenstone-ltd.com *
3   *****************************************************/
4
5  namespace CodedUITesting
6  {
7      class pageWinLogin
8      {
9          public pageWinLogin()
10         {
11             repWinLogin.SetBaseWindowScope();
12         }
13
14         public void LoginUser(string uid, string pwd)
15         {
16             Utility.SetValue(repWinLogin.UserID, uid);
17             Utility.SetValue(repWinLogin.Password, pwd);
18             Utility.Click(repWinLogin.LoginButton);
19         }
20     }
21 }
```

◈ Line 11: Sets the base window scope by calling `SetBaseWindowScope` in the class constructor.

9.2.5 Creating Tests

Add a new class 'WinTests.cs' to the *CodedUITesting* project with the code as shown in Listing 9.9.

```
1  /*************************************************
2   * All rights reserved. Copyright 2017 Arkenstone-ltd.com *
3   *************************************************/
4  using System;
5  using Microsoft.VisualStudio.TestTools.UITesting;
6  using Microsoft.VisualStudio.TestTools.UnitTesting;
7  using System.IO;
8
9  namespace CodedUITesting
10 {
11     [CodedUITest]
12     public class WinTests
13     {
14         public WinTests()
15         {
16         }
17
18         [TestInitialize()]
19         public void Initialize()
20         {
21             Utility.TestResult = Config.PASS;
22             Utility.TestName = TestContext.TestName;
23             Utility.TestResultFolder = ↵
                   ↪ TestContext.TestResultsDirectory;
24             Utility.TestRunFolder = ↵
                   ↪ TestContext.TestRunDirectory;
25
26             log4net.Config.XmlConfigurator.ConfigureAndWatch( ↵
                   ↪ new FileInfo(Config.PROJECT_FOLDER + ↵
                   ↪ "log4net.config"));
27             Utility.SetupSummaryFile();
28         }
29
30         [TestCleanup()]
31         public void Cleanup()
32         {
33             Utility.MoveScreenshots();
34
35             string logFile = Utility.SaveLogFile();
36
37             Utility.CreateSummaryFileEntry(DateTime.Now. ↵
                   ↪ ToString() + "," + TestContext.TestName ↵
```

```
                     ↪ + "," + Utility.TestResult + "," + ↵
                     ↪ logFile);
38
39             Utility.CreateShortcut("TestSummary", ↵
                     ↪ Utility.TestResultFolder, ↵
                     ↪ Config.SUMMARY_PATHFILENAME);
40
41             Utility.CloseWinApp();
42
43             Playback.Cleanup();
44         }
45
46         [TestMethod]
47         public void WinTesterLogin()
48         {
49             Utility.Log.Info("Starting Test ***** " + ↵
                     ↪ Utility.TestName + " *****");
50
51             try
52             {
53                 Utility.LaunchWinApp();
54
55                 pageWinHome wph = new pageWinHome();
56                 wph.ClickMenuItemFileLogin();
57
58                 pageWinLogin wpl = new pageWinLogin();
59                 wpl.LoginUser("Tester", ↵
                         ↪ "YUvYOM5Wj5zuFhaWOfT/NWW5dVsOpKIO");
60
61                 wph.ClickMenuItemFileLogout();
62
63                 wph.ClickMenuItemFileExit();
64
65                 Utility.ReportResult();
66             }
67             catch (Exception exception)
68             {
69                 Utility.ReportExpectedVsActual(Utility. ↵
                         ↪ TestName, "Exception: " + ↵
                         ↪ exception.ToString());
70                 Utility.Log.Error("Exception: " + ↵
                         ↪ exception.ToString());
71                 throw exception;
72             }
73         }
```

```
74
75        public TestContext TestContext
76        {
77            get
78            {
79                return testContextInstance;
80            }
81            set
82            {
83                testContextInstance = value;
84            }
85        }
86        private TestContext testContextInstance;
87    }
88 }
```

◈ Line 59: Note that the *Password* field in the demo Windows Forms Application is encrypted. Coded UI can't key in or fetch the *Clear Text* (i.e. the real password Tester123) in such fields. If you use the value Tester123 in the test, it will fail with the *Bad Data* exception. I recorded the password entry action and used the generated code (which gave me the encrypted password) for the password parameter.

9.2.6 Executing Tests

Execute the test WinTesterLogin and you will see an output as shown in Figure 9.7. The test should execute successfully.

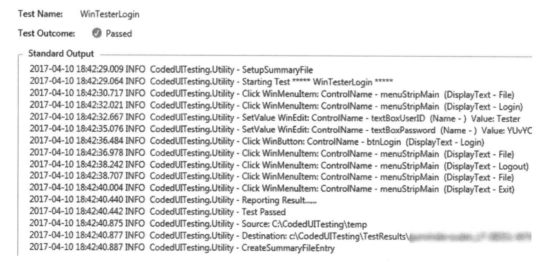

Figure 9.7: Windows Forms Application Login

9.3 WinControls - Add Employee

We will perform the following Test Scenario to demonstrate the use of `WinControls` in the *Add Employee* functionality:

- Launch the demo Windows Forms Application.

- Click the menu item *File* ⇒ *Login*.

- Login with the user 'Tester'.

- Click the menu item *Tester* ⇒ *Add Employee*.

- Add an employee.

- Handle the dialog message box.

- Click the menu item *File* ⇒ *Logout*.

- Click the menu item *File* ⇒ *Exit*.

9.3.1 Configuration Parameters

Double click the 'Config.cs' file in the *Solution Explorer* and add Listing 9.10 code to it.

Listing 9.10: 'Config.cs' - Additional parameters

```
1 public const string WIN_COMBOBOX = ↵
     ↳ "Microsoft.VisualStudio.TestTools.UITesting. ↵
     ↳ WinControls.WinComboBox";
2 public const string WIN_RADIOBUTTON = ↵
     ↳ "Microsoft.VisualStudio.TestTools.UITesting. ↵
     ↳ WinControls.WinRadioButton";
3 public const string WIN_CHECKBOX = ↵
     ↳ "Microsoft.VisualStudio.TestTools.UITesting. ↵
     ↳ WinControls.WinCheckBox";
4 public const string WIN_DATE_PICKER = ↵
     ↳ "Microsoft.VisualStudio.TestTools.UITesting. ↵
     ↳ WinControls.WinDateTimePicker";
```

9.3.2 Object Repository

9.3.2.1 Add Employee Window

Let's note down all the controls on the *Add Employee* window as follows:

Windows Forms Application - Add Employee Controls

Control	Type	Property	Value
Add Employee Window *Parent: AUT Window*	Window	TechnologyName ControlType ControlName	MSAA Window frmEmployee
Title Window *Parent: Add Employee Window*	Window	TechnologyName ControlType ControlName	MSAA Window cmbTitle
Title *Parent: Title Window*	ComboBox	TechnologyName ControlType Name	MSAA ComboBox Title:
Emp Name Window *Parent: Add Employee Window*	Window	TechnologyName ControlType ControlName	MSAA Window txtName
Emp Name *Parent: Emp Name Window*	Edit Box	TechnologyName ControlType	MSAA Edit
Male Window *Parent: Add Employee Window*	Window	TechnologyName ControlType ControlName	MSAA Window rbMale
Male *Parent: Male Window*	Radio Button	TechnologyName ControlType Name	MSAA RadioButton Male
Female Window *Parent: Add Employee Window*	Window	TechnologyName ControlType ControlName	MSAA Window rbFemale
Female *Parent: Female Window*	Radio Button	TechnologyName ControlType Name	MSAA RadioButton Female
DOB Window *Parent: Add Employee Window*	Window	TechnologyName ControlType ControlName	MSAA Window dtDOB
DOB *Parent: DOB Window*	Date	TechnologyName ControlType	MSAA DateTimePicker
Email Window *Parent: Add Employee Window*	Window	TechnologyName ControlType ControlName	MSAA Window txtEmail
Email *Parent: Email Window*	Edit Box	TechnologyName ControlType	MSAA Edit

Windows Forms Application - Add Employee Controls Contd...			
Control	*Type*	*Property*	*Value*
Contract Window *Parent: Add Employee Window*	Window	TechnologyName ControlType ControlName	MSAA Window cbContract
Contract *Parent: Contract Window*	CheckBox	TechnologyName ControlType Name	MSAA CheckBox Contract Job?
Postcode Window *Parent: Add Employee Window*	Window	TechnologyName ControlType ControlName	MSAA Window txtPostcode
Postcode *Parent: Postcode Window*	Edit Box	TechnologyName ControlType	MSAA Edit
OK Window *Parent: Add Employee Window*	Window	TechnologyName ControlType ControlName	MSAA Window btnOk
OK *Parent: OK Window*	Button	TechnologyName ControlType	MSAA Button
Cancel Window *Parent: Add Employee Window*	Window	TechnologyName ControlType ControlName	MSAA Window btnCancel
Cancel *Parent: Cancel Window*	Button	TechnologyName ControlType	MSAA Button

Add a new class 'repWinTesterEmployee.cs' to the *Repository* folder and add Listing 9.11 code to it.

Listing 9.11: 'repWinTesterEmployee.cs' - Repository for Tester's Add Employee

```
1  /*******************************************************
2   * All rights reserved. Copyright 2017 Arkenstone-ltd.com *
3   *******************************************************/
4
5  using ↵
      ↪ Microsoft.VisualStudio.TestTools.UITesting.WinControls;
6
7  namespace CodedUITesting
8  {
9      public static class repWinTesterEmployee
10     {
11         private static WinWindow mEmployeeWindow;
```

```
12
13        private static WinWindow mTitleWindow;
14        private static WinComboBox mTitle;
15
16        private static WinWindow mEmpNameWindow;
17        private static WinEdit mEmpName;
18
19        private static WinWindow mMaleWindow;
20        private static WinRadioButton mMale;
21
22        private static WinWindow mFemaleWindow;
23        private static WinRadioButton mFemale;
24
25        private static WinWindow mDOBWindow;
26        private static WinDateTimePicker mDOB;
27
28        private static WinWindow mEmailWindow;
29        private static WinEdit mEmail;
30
31        private static WinWindow mContractWindow;
32        private static WinCheckBox mContract;
33
34        private static WinWindow mPostcodeWindow;
35        private static WinEdit mPostcode;
36
37        private static WinWindow mOkButtonWindow;
38        private static WinButton mOkButton;
39
40        private static WinWindow mCancelButtonWindow;
41        private static WinButton mCancelButton;
42
43        public static WinWindow SetBaseWindowScope()
44        {
45            mEmployeeWindow = new ↵
                 ↪ WinWindow(Utility.WinAUT);
46            mEmployeeWindow.SearchProperties[WinWindow. ↵
                 ↪ PropertyNames.ControlName] = "frmEmployee";
47
48            return mEmployeeWindow;
49        }
50
51        public static WinComboBox Title
52        {
53            get
54            {
```

```
55            if (mTitleWindow == null)
56            {
57                mTitleWindow = new ↵
                     ↪ WinWindow(mEmployeeWindow);
58                mTitleWindow.SearchProperties[WinWindow. ↵
                     ↪ PropertyNames.ControlName] = ↵
                     ↪ "cmbTitle";
59            }
60
61            if (mTitle == null)
62            {
63                mTitle = new WinComboBox(mTitleWindow);
64                mTitle.SearchProperties[WinComboBox. ↵
                     ↪ PropertyNames.Name] = "Title:";
65            }
66
67            return mTitle;
68        }
69    }
70
71    public static WinEdit EmpName
72    {
73        get
74        {
75            if (mEmpNameWindow == null)
76            {
77                mEmpNameWindow = new ↵
                     ↪ WinWindow(mEmployeeWindow);
78                mEmpNameWindow.SearchProperties[ ↵
                     ↪ WinWindow.PropertyNames. ↵
                     ↪ ControlName] = "txtName";
79            }
80
81            if (mEmpName == null)
82            {
83                mEmpName = new WinEdit(mEmpNameWindow);
84            }
85
86            return mEmpName;
87        }
88    }
89
90    public static WinRadioButton Male
91    {
92        get
```

```
 93                    {
 94                        if (mMaleWindow == null)
 95                        {
 96                            mMaleWindow = new ↵
                                 ↪ WinWindow(mEmployeeWindow);
 97                            mMaleWindow.SearchProperties[WinWindow. ↵
                                 ↪ PropertyNames.ControlName] = ↵
                                 ↪ "rbMale";
 98                        }
 99
100                        if (mMale == null)
101                        {
102                            mMale = new WinRadioButton(mMaleWindow);
103                            mMale.SearchProperties[WinRadioButton. ↵
                                 ↪ PropertyNames.Name] = "Male";
104                        }
105
106                        return mMale;
107                    }
108                }
109
110                public static WinRadioButton Female
111                {
112                    get
113                    {
114                        if (mFemaleWindow == null)
115                        {
116                            mFemaleWindow = new ↵
                                 ↪ WinWindow(mEmployeeWindow);
117                            mFemaleWindow.SearchProperties[WinWindow. ↵
                                 ↪ PropertyNames.ControlName] = ↵
                                 ↪ "rbFemale";
118                        }
119
120                        if (mFemale == null)
121                        {
122                            mFemale = new ↵
                                 ↪ WinRadioButton(mFemaleWindow);
123                            mFemale.SearchProperties[WinRadioButton. ↵
                                 ↪ PropertyNames.Name] = "Female";
124                        }
125
126                        return mFemale;
127                    }
128                }
```

```
129
130          public static WinDateTimePicker DOB
131          {
132              get
133              {
134                  if (mDOBWindow == null)
135                  {
136                      mDOBWindow = new ↵
                         ↪ WinWindow(mEmployeeWindow);
137                      mDOBWindow.SearchProperties[WinWindow. ↵
                         ↪ PropertyNames.ControlName] = ↵
                         ↪ "dtDOB";
138                  }
139
140                  if (mDOB == null)
141                  {
142                      mDOB = new ↵
                         ↪ WinDateTimePicker(mDOBWindow);
143                  }
144
145                  return mDOB;
146              }
147          }
148
149          public static WinEdit Email
150          {
151              get
152              {
153                  if (mEmailWindow == null)
154                  {
155                      mEmailWindow = new ↵
                         ↪ WinWindow(mEmployeeWindow);
156                      mEmailWindow.SearchProperties[WinWindow. ↵
                         ↪ PropertyNames.ControlName] = ↵
                         ↪ "txtEmail";
157                  }
158
159                  if (mEmail == null)
160                  {
161                      mEmail = new WinEdit(mEmailWindow);
162                  }
163
164                  return mEmail;
165              }
166          }
```

```
167
168        public static WinCheckBox Contract
169        {
170            get
171            {
172                if (mContractWindow == null)
173                {
174                    mContractWindow = new ↵
                        ↳ WinWindow(mEmployeeWindow);
175                    mContractWindow.SearchProperties[ ↵
                        ↳ WinWindow.PropertyNames. ↵
                        ↳ ControlName] = "cbContract";
176                }
177
178                if (mContract == null)
179                {
180                    mContract = new ↵
                        ↳ WinCheckBox(mContractWindow);
181                    mContract.SearchProperties[WinCheckBox. ↵
                        ↳ PropertyNames.Name] = "Contract ↵
                        ↳ Job?";
182                }
183
184                return mContract;
185            }
186        }
187
188        public static WinEdit Postcode
189        {
190            get
191            {
192                if (mPostcodeWindow == null)
193                {
194                    mPostcodeWindow = new ↵
                        ↳ WinWindow(mEmployeeWindow);
195                    mPostcodeWindow.SearchProperties[ ↵
                        ↳ WinWindow.PropertyNames.ControlName] ↵
                        ↳ = "txtPostcode";
196                }
197
198                if (mPostcode == null)
199                {
200                    mPostcode = new ↵
                        ↳ WinEdit(mPostcodeWindow);
201                }
```

```
202
203              return mPostcode;
204          }
205      }
206
207      public static WinButton OKButton
208      {
209          get
210          {
211              if (mOkButtonWindow == null)
212              {
213                  mOkButtonWindow = new ↵
                        ↪ WinWindow(mEmployeeWindow);
214                  mOkButtonWindow.SearchProperties[ ↵
                        ↪ WinWindow.PropertyNames. ↵
                        ↪ ControlName] = "btnOk";
215              }
216
217              if (mOkButton == null)
218              {
219                  mOkButton = new ↵
                        ↪ WinButton(mOkButtonWindow);
220              }
221
222              return mOkButton;
223          }
224      }
225
226      public static WinButton CancelButton
227      {
228          get
229          {
230              if (mCancelButtonWindow == null)
231              {
232                  mCancelButtonWindow = new ↵
                        ↪ WinWindow(mEmployeeWindow);
233                  mCancelButtonWindow.SearchProperties[ ↵
                        ↪ WinWindow.PropertyNames. ↵
                        ↪ ControlName] = "btnCancel";
234              }
235
236              if (mCancelButton == null)
237              {
238                  mCancelButton = new ↵
                        ↪ WinButton(mCancelButtonWindow);
```

```
239                    }
240
241                    return mCancelButton;
242                }
243            }
244        }
245  }
```

◈ Line 45: Sets the base window scope with *Parent* as `Utility.WinAUT`.

9.3.2.2   Message Box Window

Let's have a look at the controls on the *Message Box* window. In the demo Windows Forms Application, hover onto the *OK* control on the *Message Box* window and press `Shift` + `Ctrl` + `I` . In the *Control Properties* window, click on the left chevron icon 《 on its top left corner and it will display a *UI Control Map* window as shown in Figure 9.8.

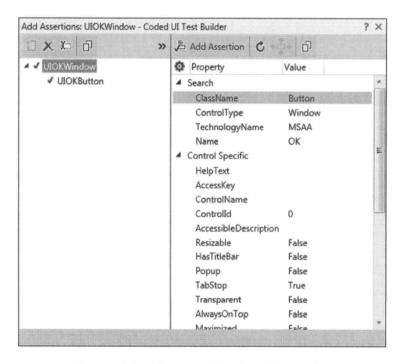

Figure 9.8: Message Window Hierarchy

Figure 9.9 shows its parental hierarchy which we need to keep in mind while writing the repository code. Note that the *Message Box* window doesn't have the *AUT* window as its *Parent*.

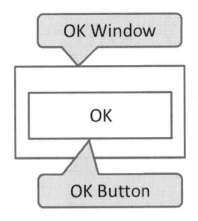

Figure 9.9: Message Box Window Parental Hierarchy

Let's note down all the controls on the *Message Box* window as follows:

Message Box Window Controls			
Control	*Type*	*Property*	*Value*
OK Window Parent: NA	Window	TechnologyName ControlType Name	MSAA Window OK
OK Parent: OK Window	Button	TechnologyName ControlType Name	MSAA Button OK

Add a new class 'repWinMessageBox.cs' to the *Repository* folder and add Listing 9.12 code to it.

Listing 9.12: 'repWinMessageBox.cs' - Message box repository

```
1  /************************************************************
2   * All rights reserved. Copyright 2017 Arkenstone-ltd.com *
3   ************************************************************/
4
5  using ↵
     ↪ Microsoft.VisualStudio.TestTools.UITesting.WinControls;
6
7  namespace CodedUITesting
8  {
9      public static class repWinMessageBox
10     {
11         private static WinWindow mOKWindow;
12
13         private static WinButton mOKButton;
```

```
14
15    public static WinWindow SetBaseWindowScope()
16    {
17        mOKWindow = new WinWindow();
18        mOKWindow.SearchProperties[WinWindow. ←
            ↪ PropertyNames.Name] = "OK";
19
20        return mOKWindow;
21    }
22
23    public static WinButton OkButton
24    {
25        get
26        {
27            if (mOKButton == null)
28            {
29                mOKButton = new WinButton(mOKWindow);
30                mOKButton.SearchProperties[WinButton. ←
                    ↪ PropertyNames.Name] = "OK";
31            }
32
33            return mOKButton;
34        }
35    }
36    }
37 }
```

◈ Line 17: Sets the base window scope with no *Parent*.

9.3.3 Utility Functions

We need to update our existing `Click()` function as per Listing 9.13.

Listing 9.13: 'Utility.cs' - Updates to the Click function

```
1 case Config.WIN_RADIOBUTTON:
2     Log.Info("SetValue WinRadioButton: ControlName - " + ←
          ↪ ((WinRadioButton)obj).ControlName + " (Name - " ←
          ↪ + ((WinRadioButton)obj).Name + ")");
3
4     ((WinRadioButton)obj).Selected = true;
5
6     break;
```

Similarly, we need to update our existing SetValue() function as per Listing 9.14

```
1  case Config.WIN_COMBOBOX:
2      Log.Info("SetValue WinComboBox: ControlName - " + ↵
           ↪ ((WinComboBox)obj).ControlName + "  (Name - " + ↵
           ↪ ((WinComboBox)obj).Name + ")" + "  Value: " + val);
3
4      ((WinComboBox)obj).SelectedItem = val;
5
6      break;
7
8  case Config.WIN_DATE_PICKER:
9      Log.Info("SetValue WinDateTimePicker: ControlName - " ↵
           ↪ + ((WinDateTimePicker)obj).ControlName + "  ↵
           ↪ (Name - " + ((WinDateTimePicker)obj).Name + ")" ↵
           ↪ + "  Value: " + val);
10
11     ((WinDateTimePicker)obj).DateTimeAsString = val;
12
13     break;
14
15 case Config.WIN_CHECKBOX:
16     Log.Info("SetValue WinCheckBox: ControlName - " + ↵
           ↪ ((WinCheckBox)obj).ControlName + "  (Name - " + ↵
           ↪ ((WinCheckBox)obj).Name + ")");
17
18     if (val.Equals(Config.TRUE))
19         ((WinCheckBox)obj).Checked = true;
20     else if (val.Equals(Config.FALSE))
21         ((WinCheckBox)obj).Checked = false;
22     else
23         ReportExpectedVsActual("WinCheckBox Error", ↵
               ↪ "Unknown value");
24
25     break;
```

9.3.4 Page Logic

The *Add Employee* page of our demo Windows Forms Application will have the following action:

Action	Description
AddEmployee()	This action will add an employee.

Add a new class 'pageWinTesterEmployee.cs' to the *Pages* folder and add Listing 9.15 code to it.

Listing 9.15: 'pageWinTesterEmployee.cs' - Add an employee

```
1   /***********************************************************
2    * All rights reserved. Copyright 2017 Arkenstone-ltd.com *
3    ***********************************************************/
4
5   namespace CodedUITesting
6   {
7       class pageWinTesterEmployee
8       {
9           public pageWinTesterEmployee()
10          {
11              repWinTesterEmployee.SetBaseWindowScope();
12          }
13
14          public void AddEmployee()
15          {
16              Utility.SetValue(repWinTesterEmployee.Title, ↵
                    ↪ "Miss");
17
18              Utility.SetValue(repWinTesterEmployee.EmpName, ↵
                    ↪ "Nicola Smith");
19
20              Utility.Click(repWinTesterEmployee.Female);
21
22              Utility.SetValue(repWinTesterEmployee.DOB, ↵
                    ↪ "11-Jul-1995");
23
24              Utility.SetValue(repWinTesterEmployee.Email, ↵
                    ↪ "Nicola.Smith@arkenstone-ltd.com");
25
26              Utility.SetValue(repWinTesterEmployee.Contract, ↵
                    ↪ Config.TRUE);
27
28              Utility.SetValue(repWinTesterEmployee.Postcode, ↵
                    ↪ "SN1 5GS");
29
```

```
30                Utility.Click(repWinTesterEmployee.OKButton);
31          }
32      }
33 }
```

◈ Line 11: Sets the base window scope by calling `SetBaseWindowScope` in the class constructor.

Add a new class 'pageWinMessageBox.cs' to the *Pages* folder and add Listing 9.16 code to it.

Listing 9.16: 'pageWinMessageBox.cs' - Handle message box

```
1  /******************************************************
2   * All rights reserved. Copyright 2017 Arkenstone-ltd.com *
3   ******************************************************/
4
5  namespace CodedUITesting
6  {
7      class pageWinMessageBox
8      {
9          public pageWinMessageBox()
10         {
11             repWinMessageBox.SetBaseWindowScope();
12         }
13
14         public void ClickOkButton()
15         {
16             Utility.Click(repWinMessageBox.OkButton);
17         }
18     }
19 }
```

◈ Line 11: Sets the base window scope by calling `SetBaseWindowScope` in the class constructor.

9.3.5   Creating Tests

Add a new test to the 'WinTests.cs' file as shown in Listing 9.17.

Listing 9.17: 'WinTests.cs' - WinTesterAddEmployee

```
1  [TestMethod]
2  public void WinTesterAddEmployee()
3  {
```

```
 4        Utility.Log.Info("Starting Test ***** " + ↩
              ↪ Utility.TestName + " *****");
 5
 6     try
 7     {
 8         Utility.LaunchWinApp();
 9
10         pageWinHome wph = new pageWinHome();
11         wph.ClickMenuItemFileLogin();
12
13         pageWinLogin wpl = new pageWinLogin();
14         wpl.LoginUser("Tester", ↩
              ↪ "YUvYOM5Wj5zuFhaWOfT/NWW5dVsOpKIO");
15
16         wph.ClickMenuItemTesterAddEmployee();
17
18         pageWinTesterEmployee wpe = new ↩
              ↪ pageWinTesterEmployee();
19         wpe.AddEmployee();
20
21         pageWinMessageBox winpmb = new pageWinMessageBox();
22         winpmb.ClickOkButton();
23
24         wph.ClickMenuItemFileLogout();
25
26         wph.ClickMenuItemFileExit();
27
28         Utility.ReportResult();
29     }
30     catch (Exception exception)
31     {
32         Utility.ReportExpectedVsActual(Utility.TestName, ↩
              ↪ "Exception: " + exception.ToString());
33         Utility.Log.Error("Exception: " + ↩
              ↪ exception.ToString());
34         throw exception;
35     }
36 }
```

9.3.6 Executing Tests

Execute the test WinTesterAddEmployee and you will see an output as shown in Figure 9.10. The test should execute successfully.

Test Name: WinTesterAddEmployee

Test Outcome: ✅ Passed

```
Standard Output
2017-04-11 17:56:08.130 INFO  CodedUITesting.Utility - SetupSummaryFile
2017-04-11 17:56:08.175 INFO  CodedUITesting.Utility - Starting Test ***** WinTesterAddEmployee *****
2017-04-11 17:56:09.803 INFO  CodedUITesting.Utility - Click WinMenuItem: ControlName - menuStripMain  (DisplayText - File)
2017-04-11 17:56:10.461 INFO  CodedUITesting.Utility - Click WinMenuItem: ControlName - menuStripMain  (DisplayText - Login)
2017-04-11 17:56:10.878 INFO  CodedUITesting.Utility - SetValue WinEdit: ControlName - textBoxUserID  (Name - ) Value: Tester
2017-04-11 17:56:12.282 INFO  CodedUITesting.Utility - SetValue WinEdit: ControlName - textBoxPassword  (Name - ) Value: YUvYOM5Wj5
2017-04-11 17:56:13.153 INFO  CodedUITesting.Utility - Click WinButton: ControlName - btnLogin  (DisplayText - Login)
2017-04-11 17:56:13.658 INFO  CodedUITesting.Utility - Click WinMenuItem: ControlName - menuStripMain  (DisplayText - Tester)
2017-04-11 17:56:14.265 INFO  CodedUITesting.Utility - Click WinMenuItem: ControlName - menuStripMain  (DisplayText - Add Employee)
2017-04-11 17:56:14.699 INFO  CodedUITesting.Utility - SetValue WinComboBox: ControlName - cmbTitle  (Name - Title:) Value: Miss
2017-04-11 17:56:16.304 INFO  CodedUITesting.Utility - SetValue WinEdit: ControlName - txtName  (Name - Name:) Value: Nicola Smith
2017-04-11 17:56:17.838 INFO  CodedUITesting.Utility - SetValue WinRadioButton: ControlName - rbFemale  (Name - Female)
2017-04-11 17:56:18.434 INFO  CodedUITesting.Utility - SetValue WinDateTimePicker: ControlName - dtDOB  (Name - ) Value: 11-Jul-1995
2017-04-11 17:56:20.164 INFO  CodedUITesting.Utility - SetValue WinEdit: ControlName - txtEmail  (Name - Email:) Value: Nicola.Smith@arl
2017-04-11 17:56:22.057 INFO  CodedUITesting.Utility - SetValue WinCheckBox: ControlName - cbContract  (Name - Contract Job?)
2017-04-11 17:56:22.690 INFO  CodedUITesting.Utility - SetValue WinEdit: ControlName - txtPostcode  (Name - Postcode) Value: SN1 5GS
2017-04-11 17:56:24.111 INFO  CodedUITesting.Utility - Click WinButton: ControlName - btnOk  (DisplayText - OK)
2017-04-11 17:56:25.162 INFO  CodedUITesting.Utility - Click WinButton: ControlName -   (DisplayText - OK)
2017-04-11 17:56:25.480 INFO  CodedUITesting.Utility - Click WinMenuItem: ControlName - menuStripMain  (DisplayText - File)
2017-04-11 17:56:26.069 INFO  CodedUITesting.Utility - Click WinMenuItem: ControlName - menuStripMain  (DisplayText - Logout)
2017-04-11 17:56:26.396 INFO  CodedUITesting.Utility - Click WinMenuItem: ControlName - menuStripMain  (DisplayText - File)
2017-04-11 17:56:27.057 INFO  CodedUITesting.Utility - Click WinMenuItem: ControlName - menuStripMain  (DisplayText - Exit)
2017-04-11 17:56:27.541 INFO  CodedUITesting.Utility - Reporting Result......
2017-04-11 17:56:27.541 INFO  CodedUITesting.Utility - Test Passed
2017-04-11 17:56:27.946 INFO  CodedUITesting.Utility - Source: C:\CodedUITesting\temp
2017-04-11 17:56:27.946 INFO  CodedUITesting.Utility - Destination: c:\CodedUITesting\TestResults\
2017-04-11 17:56:27.950 INFO  CodedUITesting.Utility - CreateSummaryFileEntry
```

Figure 9.10: Windows Forms Application - Add Employee Output

9.4   WinControls - Verify Employee

We will perform the following Test Scenario to demonstrate the use of `WinControls` in the *Verify Employee* functionality:

- Launch the demo Windows Forms Application.
- Click the menu item *File ⇒ Login*.
- Login with the user 'Tester'.
- Click the menu item *Tester ⇒ Verify Employee*.
- Verify employee's detail.
- Click the menu item *File ⇒ Logout*.
- Click the menu item *File ⇒ Exit*.

9.4.1   Utility Functions

We need to update our existing `GetValue()` function in the 'Utility.cs' file as per Listing 9.18.

```
1   case Config.WIN_COMBOBOX:
2       Log.Info("GetValue WinComboBox: ControlName - " + ↵
            ↳ ((WinComboBox)obj).ControlName + "  (Name - " + ↵
            ↳ ((WinComboBox)obj).Name + ")");
3       retValue = ((WinComboBox)obj).SelectedItem;
4       break;
5
6   case Config.WIN_EDIT:
7       Log.Info("GetValue WinEdit: ControlNamed - " + ↵
            ↳ ((WinEdit)obj).ControlName + "  (Name - " + ↵
            ↳ ((WinEdit)obj).Name + ")");
8       retValue = ((WinEdit)obj).Text;
9       break;
10
11  case Config.WIN_RADIOBUTTON:
12      Log.Info("GetValue WinRadioButton: ControlNamed - " + ↵
            ↳ ((WinRadioButton)obj).ControlName + "  ↵
            ↳ (FriendlyName - " + ↵
            ↳ ((WinRadioButton)obj).FriendlyName + ")");
13      retValue = ((WinRadioButton)obj).Selected.ToString();
14      break;
15
16  case Config.WIN_DATE_PICKER:
17      Log.Info("GetValue WinDateTimePicker: ControlName - " ↵
            ↳ + ((WinDateTimePicker)obj).ControlName + "  ↵
            ↳ (Name - " + ((WinDateTimePicker)obj).Name + ")");
18
19      DateTime date = ((WinDateTimePicker)obj).DateTime;
20
21      retValue = date.ToString("dd-MMM-yyyy");
22      break;
23
24  case Config.WIN_CHECKBOX:
25      Log.Info("GetValue WinCheckBox: ControlName - " + ↵
            ↳ ((WinCheckBox)obj).ControlName + "  (Name - " + ↵
            ↳ ((WinCheckBox)obj).Name + ")");
26
27      if (((WinCheckBox)obj).Checked.ToString() == ↵
            ↳ Config.TRUE)
28          retValue = Config.TRUE;
29      else if (((WinCheckBox)obj).Checked.ToString() == ↵
            ↳ Config.FALSE)
```

```
30        retValue = Config.FALSE;
31    else
32        ReportExpectedVsActual("WinCheckBox Error", ←
              ↪ "Unknown value");
33
34    break;
```

9.4.2 Page Logic

We need to add an additional action in the page logic as follows:

Action	Description
VerifyEmployee()	This action will verify an employee.

Add Listing 9.19 code to the 'pageWinTesterEmployee.cs' file.

Listing 9.19: 'pageWinTesterEmployee.cs' - Code for VerifyEmployee

```
1  public void VerifyEmployee()
2  {
3      Utility.ReportExpectedVsActual("Miss", ←
          ↪ Utility.GetValue(repWinTesterEmployee.Title));
4      Utility.ReportExpectedVsActual("Sharon Smith", ←
          ↪ Utility.GetValue(repWinTesterEmployee.EmpName));
5      Utility.ReportExpectedVsActual(Config.TRUE, ←
          ↪ Utility.GetValue(repWinTesterEmployee.Female));
6      Utility.ReportExpectedVsActual("01-Oct-1970", ←
          ↪ Utility.GetValue(repWinTesterEmployee.DOB));
7      Utility.ReportExpectedVsActual( ←
          ↪ "Sharon.Smith@arkenstone-ltd.com", ←
          ↪ Utility.GetValue(repWinTesterEmployee.Email));
8      Utility.ReportExpectedVsActual(Config.TRUE, ←
          ↪ Utility.GetValue(repWinTesterEmployee.Contract));
9      Utility.ReportExpectedVsActual("SN1 5BS", ←
          ↪ Utility.GetValue(repWinTesterEmployee.Postcode));
10
11     Utility.Click(repWinTesterEmployee.CancelButton);
12 }
```

9.4.3 Creating Tests

Add an additional test to the 'WinTests.cs' file as shown in Listing 9.20.

```
1  [TestMethod]
2  public void WinTesterVerifyEmployee()
3  {
4      Utility.Log.Info("Starting Test ***** " + ↵
          ↪ Utility.TestName + " *****");
5
6      try
7      {
8          Utility.LaunchWinApp();
9
10         pageWinHome wph = new pageWinHome();
11         wph.ClickMenuItemFileLogin();
12
13         pageWinLogin wpl = new pageWinLogin();
14         wpl.LoginUser("Tester", ↵
              ↪ "YUvYOM5Wj5zuFhaWOfT/NWW5dVsOpKIO");
15
16         wph.ClickMenuItemTesterViewEmployee();
17
18         pageWinTesterEmployee wpe = new ↵
              ↪ pageWinTesterEmployee();
19         wpe.VerifyEmployee();
20
21         wph.ClickMenuItemFileLogout();
22
23         wph.ClickMenuItemFileExit();
24
25         Utility.ReportResult();
26     }
27     catch (Exception exception)
28     {
29         Utility.ReportExpectedVsActual(Utility.TestName, ↵
              ↪ "Exception: " + exception.ToString());
30         Utility.Log.Error("Exception: " + ↵
              ↪ exception.ToString());
31         throw exception;
32     }
33 }
```

9.4.4 Executing Tests

Execute the test `WinTesterVerifyEmployee` and you will see an output as shown in Figure 9.11. The test should execute successfully.

Test Name: WinTesterVerifyEmployee

Test Outcome: ⊘ Passed

```
Standard Output
2017-04-11 17:59:45.557 INFO  CodedUITesting.Utility - SetupSummaryFile
2017-04-11 17:59:45.598 INFO  CodedUITesting.Utility - Starting Test ***** WinTesterVerifyEmployee *****
2017-04-11 17:59:46.629 INFO  CodedUITesting.Utility - Click WinMenuItem: ControlName - menuStripMain  (DisplayText - File)
2017-04-11 17:59:47.259 INFO  CodedUITesting.Utility - Click WinMenuItem: ControlName - menuStripMain  (DisplayText - Login)
2017-04-11 17:59:47.658 INFO  CodedUITesting.Utility - SetValue WinEdit: ControlName - textBoxUserID  (Name - )  Value: Tester
2017-04-11 17:59:48.858 INFO  CodedUITesting.Utility - SetValue WinEdit: ControlName - textBoxPassword  (Name - )  Value: YUvYOM5Wj5z
2017-04-11 17:59:49.608 INFO  CodedUITesting.Utility - Click WinButton: ControlName - btnLogin  (DisplayText - Login)
2017-04-11 17:59:50.082 INFO  CodedUITesting.Utility - Click WinMenuItem: ControlName - menuStripMain  (DisplayText - Tester)
2017-04-11 17:59:50.667 INFO  CodedUITesting.Utility - Click WinMenuItem: ControlName - menuStripMain  (DisplayText - View Employee)
2017-04-11 17:59:51.067 INFO  CodedUITesting.Utility - GetValue WinComboBox: ControlName - cmbTitle  (Name - Title:)
2017-04-11 17:59:51.078 INFO  CodedUITesting.Utility - [Expected:] Miss      [Actual:] Miss      [Step Passed]
2017-04-11 17:59:51.165 INFO  CodedUITesting.Utility - GetValue WinEdit: ControlNamed - txtName  (Name - Name:)
2017-04-11 17:59:51.171 INFO  CodedUITesting.Utility - [Expected:] Sharon Smith      [Actual:] Sharon Smith      [Step Passed]
2017-04-11 17:59:51.256 INFO  CodedUITesting.Utility - GetValue WinRadioButton: ControlNamed - rbFemale  (FriendlyName - Female)
2017-04-11 17:59:51.273 INFO  CodedUITesting.Utility - [Expected:] True      [Actual:] True      [Step Passed]
2017-04-11 17:59:51.356 INFO  CodedUITesting.Utility - GetValue WinDateTimePicker: ControlName - dtDOB  (Name - )
2017-04-11 17:59:51.369 INFO  CodedUITesting.Utility - [Expected:] 01-Oct-1970      [Actual:] 01-Oct-1970      [Step Passed]
2017-04-11 17:59:51.448 INFO  CodedUITesting.Utility - GetValue WinEdit: ControlNamed - txtEmail  (Name - Email:)
2017-04-11 17:59:51.454 INFO  CodedUITesting.Utility - [Expected:] Sharon.Smith@arkenstone-ltd.com      [Actual:] Sharon.Smith@arkenston
2017-04-11 17:59:51.543 INFO  CodedUITesting.Utility - GetValue WinCheckBox: ControlName - cbContract  (Name - Contract Job?)
2017-04-11 17:59:51.577 INFO  CodedUITesting.Utility - [Expected:] True      [Actual:] True      [Step Passed]
2017-04-11 17:59:51.664 INFO  CodedUITesting.Utility - GetValue WinEdit: ControlNamed - txtPostcode  (Name - Postcode)
2017-04-11 17:59:51.671 INFO  CodedUITesting.Utility - [Expected:] SN1 5BS      [Actual:] SN1 5BS      [Step Passed]
2017-04-11 17:59:51.754 INFO  CodedUITesting.Utility - Click WinButton: ControlName - btnCancel  (DisplayText - Close)
2017-04-11 17:59:52.102 INFO  CodedUITesting.Utility - Click WinMenuItem: ControlName - menuStripMain  (DisplayText - File)
2017-04-11 17:59:52.703 INFO  CodedUITesting.Utility - Click WinMenuItem: ControlName - menuStripMain  (DisplayText - Logout)
2017-04-11 17:59:53.028 INFO  CodedUITesting.Utility - Click WinMenuItem: ControlName - menuStripMain  (DisplayText - File)
2017-04-11 17:59:53.608 INFO  CodedUITesting.Utility - Click WinMenuItem: ControlName - menuStripMain  (DisplayText - Exit)
2017-04-11 17:59:53.919 INFO  CodedUITesting.Utility - Reporting Result......
2017-04-11 17:59:53.919 INFO  CodedUITesting.Utility - Test Passed
```

Figure 9.11: Windows Forms Application - View Employee Output

9.5 WinControls - Drag and Drop

We will perform the following Test Scenario to demonstrate the use of `WinControls` in the *Drag and Drop* functionality:

- Launch the demo Windows Forms Application.

- Click the menu item *File ⇒ Login*.

- Login with the user 'Tester'.

- Click the menu item *Tester ⇒ Other*.

- Drag the image and drop it to the canvas area.

- Click the menu item *File ⇒ Logout*.

- Click the menu item *File ⇒ Exit*.

9.5.1   Object Repository

Let's note down all the controls on the *Drag-n-Drop* window as follow:

Windows Forms Application - Add Employee Controls			
Control	*Type*	*Property*	*Value*
Drag-n-Drop Window *Parent: AUT Window*	Window	TechnologyName ControlType ControlName	MSAA Window frmOther
PictureBox1 Window *Parent: Drag-n-Drop Window*	Window	TechnologyName ControlType ControlName	MSAA Window pictureBox1
PictureBox1 *Parent: PictureBox1 Window*	Client	TechnologyName ControlType	MSAA Client
PictureBox2 Window *Parent: Drag-n-Drop Window*	Window	TechnologyName ControlType ControlName	MSAA Window pictureBox2
PictureBox2 *Parent: PictureBox2 Window*	Client	TechnologyName ControlType	MSAA Client
Reset Window *Parent: Drag-n-Drop Window*	Window	TechnologyName ControlType ControlName	MSAA Window btnReset
Reset *Parent: Reset Window*	Button	TechnologyName ControlType	MSAA Button
Close Window *Parent: Drag-n-Drop Window*	Window	TechnologyName ControlType ControlName	MSAA Window btnClose
Close *Parent: Close Window*	Button	TechnologyName ControlType	MSAA Button

Add a new class 'repWinTesterOther.cs' to the *Repository* folder and insert the code as shown in Listing 9.21.

Listing 9.21: 'repWinTesterOther.cs' - Repository for the Other window

```
1  /*************************************************
2   * All rights reserved. Copyright 2017 Arkenstone-ltd.com *
3   *************************************************/
4
5  using Microsoft.VisualStudio.TestTools.UITesting;
6  using ↵
```

```
       ↪ Microsoft.VisualStudio.TestTools.UITesting.WinControls;
 7
 8  namespace CodedUITesting
 9  {
10      public static class repWinTesterOther
11      {
12          private static WinWindow mDragDropWindow;
13
14          private static UITestControl mPictureBox1Window;
15          private static WinClient mPictureBox1;
16
17          private static UITestControl mPictureBox2Window;
18          private static WinClient mPictureBox2;
19
20          private static WinWindow mResetButtonWindow;
21          private static WinButton mResetButton;
22
23          private static WinWindow mCloseButtonWindow;
24          private static WinButton mCloseButton;
25
26
27          public static WinWindow SetBaseWindowScope()
28          {
29              mDragDropWindow = new WinWindow(Utility.WinAUT);
30              mDragDropWindow.SearchProperties[WinWindow. ↵
                  ↪ PropertyNames.ControlName] = "frmOther";
31
32              return mDragDropWindow;
33          }
34
35          public static WinClient PictureBox1
36          {
37              get
38              {
39                  if (mPictureBox1Window == null)
40                  {
41                      mPictureBox1Window = new ↵
                          ↪ WinWindow(mDragDropWindow);
42                      mPictureBox1Window.SearchProperties[ ↵
                          ↪ WinWindow.PropertyNames. ↵
                          ↪ ControlName] = "pictureBox1";
43                  }
44
45                  if (mPictureBox1 == null)
46                  {
```

```
47                       mPictureBox1 = new ↵
                           ↪ WinClient(mPictureBox1Window);
48                   }
49
50               return mPictureBox1;
51           }
52       }
53
54       public static WinClient PictureBox2
55       {
56           get
57           {
58               if (mPictureBox2Window == null)
59               {
60                   mPictureBox2Window = new ↵
                       ↪ WinWindow(mDragDropWindow);
61                   mPictureBox2Window.SearchProperties[ ↵
                       ↪ WinWindow.PropertyNames. ↵
                       ↪ ControlName] = "pictureBox2";
62               }
63
64               if (mPictureBox2 == null)
65               {
66                   mPictureBox2 = new ↵
                       ↪ WinClient(mPictureBox2Window);
67               }
68
69               return mPictureBox2;
70           }
71       }
72
73       public static WinButton ResetButton
74       {
75           get
76           {
77               if (mResetButtonWindow == null)
78               {
79                   mResetButtonWindow = new ↵
                       ↪ WinWindow(mDragDropWindow);
80                   mResetButtonWindow.SearchProperties[ ↵
                       ↪ WinWindow.PropertyNames. ↵
                       ↪ ControlName] = "btnReset";
81               }
82
83               if (mResetButton == null)
```

```
84                      {
85                          mResetButton = new ↵
                                ↪ WinButton(mResetButtonWindow);
86                      }
87
88                      return mResetButton;
89                  }
90              }
91
92          public static WinButton CloseButton
93          {
94              get
95              {
96                  if (mCloseButtonWindow == null)
97                  {
98                      mCloseButtonWindow = new ↵
                            ↪ WinWindow(mDragDropWindow);
99                      mCloseButtonWindow.SearchProperties[ ↵
                            ↪ WinWindow.PropertyNames. ↵
                            ↪ ControlName] = "btnClose";
100                 }
101
102                 if (mCloseButton == null)
103                 {
104                     mCloseButton = new ↵
                            ↪ WinButton(mCloseButtonWindow);
105                 }
106
107                 return mCloseButton;
108             }
109         }
110     }
111 }
```

9.5.2 Page Logic

The Tester's *Other* page will have the following action:

Action	Description
DragDrop()	This action will perform the Drag and Drop operation.

Add a new class 'pageWinTesterOther.cs' to the *Pages* folder and insert the code as shown in Listing 9.22.

Listing 9.22: 'pageWinTesterOther.cs' - Page logic for the Drag and Drop operation

```
 1  /*******************************************************
 2   * All rights reserved. Copyright 2017 Arkenstone-ltd.com *
 3   *******************************************************/
 4
 5  using Microsoft.VisualStudio.TestTools.UITesting;
 6  using System.Drawing;
 7
 8  namespace CodedUITesting
 9  {
10      class pageWinTesterOther
11      {
12          public pageWinTesterOther()
13          {
14              repWinTesterOther.SetBaseWindowScope();
15          }
16
17          public void DragDrop()
18          {
19              int waitForReadyTimeOut = ↵
                    ↪ Playback.PlaybackSettings.WaitForReadyTimeout;
20
21              Utility.Log.Info("Original value of ↵
                    ↪ WaitForReadyTimeout: " + ↵
                    ↪ waitForReadyTimeOut);
22
23              Playback.PlaybackSettings.WaitForReadyTimeout ↵
                    ↪ = 0;
24
25              int xx = repWinTesterOther.PictureBox1. ↵
                    ↪ GetClickablePoint().X;
26
27              int yy = repWinTesterOther.PictureBox1. ↵
                    ↪ GetClickablePoint().Y;
28
29              Point finalLoc = new ↵
                    ↪ Point(repWinTesterOther.PictureBox2. ↵
                    ↪ BoundingRectangle.Location.X + xx, ↵
                    ↪ repWinTesterOther.PictureBox2. ↵
                    ↪ BoundingRectangle.Location.Y + yy);
30
```

```
31          repWinTesterOther.PictureBox2.EnsureClickable();
32
33          Mouse.StartDragging( ↵
              ↪ repWinTesterOther.PictureBox1, ↵
              ↪ repWinTesterOther.PictureBox1. ↵
              ↪ GetClickablePoint());
34
35          Mouse.Move(finalLoc);
36
37          Mouse.StopDragging( ↵
              ↪ repWinTesterOther.PictureBox2, ↵
              ↪ finalLoc);
38
39          Playback.PlaybackSettings.WaitForReadyTimeout ↵
              ↪ = waitForReadyTimeOut;
40
41          Utility.Click(repWinTesterOther.CloseButton);
42        }
43      }
44 }
```

◈ Line 14: Sets the base window scope by calling **SetBaseWindowScope** in the class constructor.

◈ Line 19: Saves the original value of **WaitForReadyTimeout** for later restore.

◈ Line 23: Disables the wait for ready of user interface thread so that we can move the mouse a bit and initiate the drag and drop operation.

◈ Line 25: Gets the **X** coordinate of a clickable point on the **PictureBox1**.

◈ Line 27: Gets the **Y** coordinate of a clickable point on the **PictureBox1**.

◈ Line 29: Initialises a new instance of the **Point** class with the specified coordinates on the **PictureBox2**.

◈ Line 31: Ensures **PictureBox2** is clickable.

◈ Line 33: Starts the dragging process on **PictureBox1**.

◈ Line 35: Moves the mouse to the final location.

◈ Line 37: Stops the dragging at the final location.

◈ Line 19: Restores the original value of **WaitForReadyTimeout**.

9.5.3 Creating Tests

Add an additional test to the 'WinTests.cs' file as shown in Listing 9.23.

Listing 9.23: 'WinTests.cs' - WinTesterDragnDrop

```
1 [TestMethod]
2 public void WinTesterDragnDrop()
```

```
3    {
4        Utility.Log.Info("Starting Test ***** " + ↵
             ↪ Utility.TestName + " *****");
5
6        try
7        {
8            Utility.LaunchWinApp();
9
10           pageWinHome wph = new pageWinHome();
11           wph.ClickMenuItemFileLogin();
12
13           pageWinLogin wpl = new pageWinLogin();
14           wpl.LoginUser("Tester", ↵
                 ↪ "YUvYOM5Wj5zuFhaWOfT/NWW5dVsOpKIO");
15
16           wph.ClickMenuItemTesterOther();
17
18           pageWinTesterOther wpo = new pageWinTesterOther();
19           wpo.DragDrop();
20
21           wph.ClickMenuItemFileLogout();
22
23           wph.ClickMenuItemFileExit();
24
25           Utility.ReportResult();
26       }
27       catch (Exception exception)
28       {
29           Utility.ReportExpectedVsActual(Utility.TestName, ↵
                 ↪ "Exception: " + exception.ToString());
30           Utility.Log.Error("Exception: " + ↵
                 ↪ exception.ToString());
31           throw exception;
32       }
33   }
```

◈ Line 19: Calls the `DragDrop` method in the page logic.

9.5.4   Executing Tests

Execute the test `WinTesterDragnDrop` and you will see an output as shown in Figure 9.12. The test should execute successfully.

```
Test Name:     WinTesterDragnDrop

Test Outcome:  ⊘ Passed

┌─ Standard Output ──────────────────────────────────────────────────────────────
│  2017-04-11 18:05:32.897 INFO  CodedUITesting.Utility - SetupSummaryFile
│  2017-04-11 18:05:32.958 INFO  CodedUITesting.Utility - Starting Test ***** WinTesterDragnDrop *****
│  2017-04-11 18:05:34.309 INFO  CodedUITesting.Utility - Click WinMenuItem: ControlName - menuStripMain  (DisplayText - File)
│  2017-04-11 18:05:35.477 INFO  CodedUITesting.Utility - Click WinMenuItem: ControlName - menuStripMain  (DisplayText - Login)
│  2017-04-11 18:05:36.048 INFO  CodedUITesting.Utility - SetValue WinEdit: ControlName - textBoxUserID  (Name - )  Value: Tester
│  2017-04-11 18:05:37.931 INFO  CodedUITesting.Utility - SetValue WinEdit: ControlName - textBoxPassword  (Name - )  Value: YUvY(
│  2017-04-11 18:05:38.996 INFO  CodedUITesting.Utility - Click WinButton: ControlName - btnLogin  (DisplayText - Login)
│  2017-04-11 18:05:39.933 INFO  CodedUITesting.Utility - Click WinMenuItem: ControlName - menuStripMain  (DisplayText - Tester)
│  2017-04-11 18:05:41.180 INFO  CodedUITesting.Utility - Click WinMenuItem: ControlName - menuStripMain  (DisplayText - Other)
│  2017-04-11 18:05:41.612 INFO  CodedUITesting.Utility - Original value of WaitForReadyTimeout: 60000
│  2017-04-11 18:05:52.490 INFO  CodedUITesting.Utility - Click WinButton: ControlName - btnClose  (DisplayText - Close)
│  2017-04-11 18:05:52.973 INFO  CodedUITesting.Utility - Click WinMenuItem: ControlName - menuStripMain  (DisplayText - File)
│  2017-04-11 18:05:54.204 INFO  CodedUITesting.Utility - Click WinMenuItem: ControlName - menuStripMain  (DisplayText - Logout)
│  2017-04-11 18:05:54.645 INFO  CodedUITesting.Utility - Click WinMenuItem: ControlName - menuStripMain  (DisplayText - File)
│  2017-04-11 18:05:55.950 INFO  CodedUITesting.Utility - Click WinMenuItem: ControlName - menuStripMain  (DisplayText - Exit)
│  2017-04-11 18:05:56.369 INFO  CodedUITesting.Utility - Reporting Result......
│  2017-04-11 18:05:56.385 INFO  CodedUITesting.Utility - Test Passed
│  2017-04-11 18:05:56.792 INFO  CodedUITesting.Utility - Source: C:\CodedUITesting\temp
│  2017-04-11 18:05:56.794 INFO  CodedUITesting.Utility - Destination: c:\CodedUITesting\TestResults\
│  2017-04-11 18:05:56.800 INFO  CodedUITesting.Utility - CreateSummaryFileEntry
```

Figure 9.12: Windows Forms Application - Drag And Drop Output

9.6   WinControls - Verify Employee List With Excel Data

We will perform the following Test Scenario to demonstrate the use of `WinControls` in the *Employee List* functionality:

- Launch the demo Windows Forms Application.

- Click the menu item *File ⇒ Login*.

- Login with the user 'Admin'.

- Click the menu item *Admin ⇒ Employee List*.

- Verify the employee list with the data read from a file in XLSX format.

- Click the menu item *File ⇒ Logout*.

- Click the menu item *File ⇒ Exit*.

9.6.1   Configuration Parameters

Double click on the 'Config.cs' file in the *Solution Explorer* and add Listing 9.24 code to it.

Listing 9.24: 'Config.cs' - Additional parameter

```
1  public const string WIN_LIST = ↵
   ↪ "Microsoft.VisualStudio.TestTools.UITesting. ↵
   ↪ WinControls.WinList";
```

9.6.2 Object Repository

Let's note down all the controls on the *Employee List* window as follow:

Windows Forms Application - Employee List Controls			
Control	**Type**	**Property**	**Value**
Employees Window *Parent: AUT Window*	Window	TechnologyName ControlType ControlName	MSAA Window frmEmployeeList
Employees List Window *Parent: Employees Window*	Window	TechnologyName ControlType ControlName	MSAA Window lvEmployeeList
Employees List *Parent: Employees List Window*	List	TechnologyName ControlType	MSAA List
View Window *Parent: Employees Window*	Window	TechnologyName ControlType ControlName	MSAA Window btnView
View *Parent: View Window*	Button	TechnologyName ControlType	MSAA Button
Close Window *Parent: Employees Window*	Window	TechnologyName ControlType ControlName	MSAA Window btnClose
Close *Parent: Close Window*	Button	TechnologyName ControlType	MSAA Button

Add a new class 'repWinAdminEmpList.cs' to the *Repository* folder and insert the code as shown in Listing 9.25.

Listing 9.25: 'repWinAdminEmpList.cs' - Repository for Employee List

```
1  /*******************************************************
2   * All rights reserved. Copyright 2017 Arkenstone-ltd.com *
3   *******************************************************/
4  using ↵
   ↪ Microsoft.VisualStudio.TestTools.UITesting.WinControls;
5
```

```
 6  namespace CodedUITesting
 7  {
 8      public static class repWinAdminEmpList
 9      {
10          private static WinWindow mEmployeesWindow;
11
12          private static WinWindow mEmployeesListWindow;
13          private static WinList mEmployeesList;
14
15          private static WinWindow mViewButtonWindow;
16          private static WinButton mViewButton;
17
18          private static WinWindow mCloseButtonWindow;
19          private static WinButton mCloseButton;
20
21          public static WinWindow SetBaseWindowScope()
22          {
23              mEmployeesWindow = new ↵
                    ↪ WinWindow(Utility.WinAUT);
24
25              mEmployeesWindow.SearchProperties[WinWindow. ↵
                    ↪ PropertyNames.ControlName] = ↵
                    ↪ "frmEmployeeList";
26
27              return mEmployeesWindow;
28          }
29
30          public static WinList EmployeesList
31          {
32              get
33              {
34                  if (mEmployeesListWindow == null)
35                  {
36                      mEmployeesListWindow = new ↵
                            ↪ WinWindow(mEmployeesWindow);
37                      mEmployeesListWindow.SearchProperties[ ↵
                            ↪ WinWindow.PropertyNames. ↵
                            ↪ ControlName] = "lvEmployeeList";
38                  }
39
40                  if (mEmployeesList == null)
41                  {
42                      mEmployeesList = new ↵
                            ↪ WinList(mEmployeesListWindow);
43                  }
```

```
44
45                    return mEmployeesList;
46              }
47        }
48
49        public static WinButton ViewButton
50        {
51             get
52             {
53                  if (mViewButtonWindow == null)
54                  {
55                       mViewButtonWindow = new ←
                            ↪ WinWindow(mEmployeesWindow);
56                       mViewButtonWindow.SearchProperties[ ←
                            ↪ WinWindow.PropertyNames. ←
                            ↪ ControlName] = "btnView";
57                  }
58
59                  if (mViewButton == null)
60                  {
61                       mViewButton = new ←
                            ↪ WinButton(mViewButtonWindow);
62                  }
63
64                  return mViewButton;
65             }
66        }
67
68        public static WinButton CloseButton
69        {
70             get
71             {
72                  if (mCloseButtonWindow == null)
73                  {
74                       mCloseButtonWindow = new ←
                            ↪ WinWindow(mEmployeesWindow);
75                       mCloseButtonWindow.SearchProperties[ ←
                            ↪ WinWindow.PropertyNames. ←
                            ↪ ControlName] = "btnClose";
76                  }
77
78                  if (mCloseButton == null)
79                  {
80                       mCloseButton = new ←
                            ↪ WinButton(mCloseButtonWindow);
```

```
81                         }
82
83                         return mCloseButton;
84                     }
85                 }
86         }
87 }
```

9.6.3 Utility Functions

Add an additional case statement in the `GetTableData` function in the 'Utility.cs' file as shown in Listing 9.26.

```
1  using System.Linq;
2
3  case Config.WIN_LIST:
4      Log.Info("GetTableData WinList: ControlName - " + ↵
           ↪ ((WinList)obj).ControlName + "  (Name - " + ↵
           ↪ ((WinList)obj).Name + ")");
5
6      rowCount = ((WinList)obj).Items.Count;
7      Array.Resize(ref tblData, rowCount);
8
9      int ii = 0;
10
11     foreach (WinListItem item in ((WinList)obj).Items)
12     {
13         string[] subItems = item.GetColumnValues();
14         int colCount = subItems.Count();
15
16         Array.Resize(ref tblData[ii], colCount);
17
18         for (int j = 0; j < colCount; j++)
19         {
20             tblData[ii][j] = subItems[j];
21
22             Log.Info("Row: " + ii + "  Col: " + j + "  ↵
                   ↪ Value: " + tblData[ii][j]);
23         }
24
25         ii++;
```

```
26        }
27
28      break;
```

◈ Line 1: Additional import required to support the functionality.

9.6.4   Page Logic

The *Employee List* window of our demo application will have the following action:

Action	Description
VerifyEmployeeListXLSXData()	This action will verify the employee list with the data read from a file in XLSX format.

Add a new class 'pageWinAdminEmpList.cs' to the *Pages* folder and insert the code as shown in Listing 9.27.

Listing 9.27: 'pageWinAdminEmpList.cs' - Logic for the Employee List

```
1  /**********************************************************
2   * All rights reserved. Copyright 2017 Arkenstone-ltd.com *
3   **********************************************************/
4  using System;
5
6  namespace CodedUITesting
7  {
8      class pageWinAdminEmpList
9      {
10         public pageWinAdminEmpList()
11         {
12             repWinAdminEmpList.SetBaseWindowScope();
13         }
14
15         public void VerifyEmployeeListXLSXData()
16         {
17             String[][] empList = ↵
                   ↪ Utility.GetTableData(repWinAdminEmpList. ↵
                   ↪ EmployeesList);
18
19             String[][] xlsxData = ↵
                   ↪ Utility.GetSpreadSheetXLSX( ↵
                   ↪ @"C:\CodedUITesting\CodedUITesting\ ↵
                   ↪ TestData\UserData.xlsx", 1);
```

```
20
21          for (int ii = 0; ii < empList.Length; ii++)
22          {
23              Utility.ReportExpectedVsActual( ↵
                  ↪ empList[ii][0], xlsxData[ii + 1][0]);
24
25              Utility.ReportExpectedVsActual( ↵
                  ↪ empList[ii][1], xlsxData[ii + 1][1]);
26
27              Utility.ReportExpectedVsActual( ↵
                  ↪ empList[ii][2], xlsxData[ii + 1][2]);
28
29              Utility.ReportExpectedVsActual( ↵
                  ↪ empList[ii][3], xlsxData[ii + 1][3]);
30
31              Utility.ReportExpectedVsActual( ↵
                  ↪ empList[ii][4], ↵
                  ↪ Utility.ExcelDateParse(xlsxData[ii + ↵
                  ↪ 1][4]).Substring(0, 10));
32
33              Utility.ReportExpectedVsActual( ↵
                  ↪ empList[ii][5], xlsxData[ii + 1][5]);
34          }
35
36          Utility.Click(repWinAdminEmpList.CloseButton);
37      }
38    }
39 }
```

◈ Line 12: Sets the base window scope by calling SetBaseWindowScope in the class constructor.

9.6.5 Creating Tests

Add a new test to the 'WinTests.cs' file as shown in Listing 9.28.

Listing 9.28: 'WinTests.cs' - WinAdminVerifyEmployeeListXLSXData

```
1 [TestMethod]
2 public void WinAdminVerifyEmployeeListXLSXData()
3 {
4     Utility.Log.Info("Starting Test ***** " + ↵
          ↪ Utility.TestName + " *****");
5
6     try
```

```
 7      {
 8              Utility.LaunchWinApp();
 9
10              pageWinHome wph = new pageWinHome();
11              wph.ClickMenuItemFileLogin();
12
13              pageWinLogin wpl = new pageWinLogin();
14              wpl.LoginUser("Admin", ↵
                    ↪ "+rvVFpEB1/R9sAhRQ12knU/Vax4Vmtqs");
15
16              wph.ClickMenuItemAdminEmployeeList();
17
18              pageWinAdminEmpList wpe = new pageWinAdminEmpList();
19              wpe.VerifyEmployeeListXLSXData();
20
21              wph.ClickMenuItemFileLogout();
22
23              wph.ClickMenuItemFileExit();
24
25              Utility.ReportResult();
26      }
27      catch (Exception exception)
28      {
29              Utility.ReportExpectedVsActual(Utility.TestName, ↵
                    ↪ "Exception: " + exception.ToString());
30              Utility.Log.Error("Exception: " + ↵
                    ↪ exception.ToString());
31              throw exception;
32      }
33 }
```

◈ Line 14: Recorded the password entry action and used the generated code for the password parameter.

9.6.6 Executing Tests

Execute the test WinAdminVerifyEmployeeListXLSXData and you will see an output as shown in Figure 9.13. The test should execute successfully.

Test Name: WinAdminVerifyEmployeeListXLSXData

Test Outcome: ⊘ Passed

Standard Output

```
2017-04-12 20:33:21.163 INFO  CodedUITesting.Utility - SetupSummaryFile
2017-04-12 20:33:21.209 INFO  CodedUITesting.Utility - Starting Test ***** WinAdminVerifyEmployeeListXLSXData *****
2017-04-12 20:33:22.520 INFO  CodedUITesting.Utility - Click WinMenuItem: ControlName - menuStripMain  (DisplayText - File)
2017-04-12 20:33:23.210 INFO  CodedUITesting.Utility - Click WinMenuItem: ControlName - menuStripMain  (DisplayText - Login)
2017-04-12 20:33:23.665 INFO  CodedUITesting.Utility - SetValue WinEdit: ControlName - textBoxUserID  (Name - )  Value: Admin
2017-04-12 20:33:24.977 INFO  CodedUITesting.Utility - SetValue WinEdit: ControlName - textBoxPassword  (Name - )  Value: +rvVFpE
2017-04-12 20:33:26.824 INFO  CodedUITesting.Utility - Click WinButton: ControlName - btnLogin  (DisplayText - Login)
2017-04-12 20:33:28.076 INFO  CodedUITesting.Utility - Click WinMenuItem: ControlName - menuStripMain  (DisplayText - Admin)
2017-04-12 20:33:29.321 INFO  CodedUITesting.Utility - Click WinMenuItem: ControlName - menuStripMain  (DisplayText - Employee
2017-04-12 20:33:29.976 INFO  CodedUITesting.Utility - GetTableData WinList: ControlName - lvEmployeeList  (Name - )
2017-04-12 20:33:31.737 INFO  CodedUITesting.Utility - Row: 0  Col: 0   Value: 10001
2017-04-12 20:33:31.739 INFO  CodedUITesting.Utility - Row: 0  Col: 1   Value: Mrs
2017-04-12 20:33:31.740 INFO  CodedUITesting.Utility - Row: 0  Col: 2   Value: Carla Brown
2017-04-12 20:33:31.741 INFO  CodedUITesting.Utility - Row: 0  Col: 3   Value: Female
2017-04-12 20:33:31.742 INFO  CodedUITesting.Utility - Row: 0  Col: 4   Value: 02/05/1965
2017-04-12 20:33:31.743 INFO  CodedUITesting.Utility - Row: 0  Col: 5   Value: Yes
2017-04-12 20:33:32.520 INFO  CodedUITesting.Utility - Row: 1  Col: 0   Value: 10002
2017-04-12 20:33:32.521 INFO  CodedUITesting.Utility - Row: 1  Col: 1   Value: Mr
2017-04-12 20:33:32.522 INFO  CodedUITesting.Utility - Row: 1  Col: 2   Value: James Jones
```

Figure 9.13: Windows Forms Application - Employee List Output

9.7   WinControls - Verify Employee With Database

We will perform the following Test Scenario to demonstrate the use of `WinControls` in the *Verify Employee* functionality:

- Launch the demo Windows Forms Application.

- Click the menu item *File ⇒ Login.*

- Login with the user 'Admin'.

- Click the menu item *Admin ⇒ Employee List.*

- Verify the details of employee id "10002" with the data fetched from the database.

- Click the menu item *File ⇒ Logout.*

- Click the menu item *File ⇒ Exit.*

9.7.1   Utility Functions

Add an additional case statement in the `ClickCellWithValue` function in the 'Utility.cs' file as shown in Listing 9.29.

Listing 9.29: 'Utility.cs' - Updates to the ClickCellWithValue function

```
1  case Config.WIN_LIST:
2      ((WinList)obj).SelectedItemsAsString = val;
3      break;
```

We also need to define a new function as follows:

FormatDate - Formats a date to the "dd-MMM-yyyy" format		
Input Parameters	*stg*	Date in the string format
Return Value	*string*	Returns the formatted date

Add the additional function to the 'Utility.cs' file as shown in Listing 9.30.

Listing 9.30: 'Utility.cs' - Additional function FormatDate

```
1  public static string FormatDate(string stg)
2  {
3      DateTime dt = DateTime.ParseExact(stg.Substring(0, ↵
         ↪ 10), "dd/MM/yyyy", System.Globalization. ↵
         ↪ CultureInfo.GetCultureInfo("en-GB"));
4      return dt.ToString("dd-MMM-yyyy");
5  }
```

◈ Line 4: Returns the formatted date.

9.7.2 Object Repository

Note down the following controls on the *View Employee* window:

Windows Forms Application - View Employee Controls			
Control	*Type*	*Property*	*Value*
View Employee Window *Parent: NA*	Window	TechnologyName ControlType ControlName	MSAA Window frmEmployee
Title Window *Parent: View Employee Window*	Window	TechnologyName ControlType ControlName	MSAA Window cmbTitle
Title *Parent: Title Window*	ComboBox	TechnologyName ControlType Name	MSAA ComboBox Title:
Emp Name Window *Parent: View Employee Window*	Window	TechnologyName ControlType ControlName	MSAA Window txtName
Emp Name *Parent: Emp Name Window*	Edit Box	TechnologyName ControlType	MSAA Edit

Windows Forms Application - View Employee Controls Contd...			
Control	**Type**	**Property**	**Value**
Male Window *Parent: View Employee Window*	Window	TechnologyName ControlType ControlName	MSAA Window rbMale
Male *Parent: Male Window*	Radio Button	TechnologyName ControlType Name	MSAA RadioButton Male
Female Window *Parent: View Employee Window*	Window	TechnologyName ControlType ControlName	MSAA Window rbFemale
Female *Parent: Female Window*	Radio Button	TechnologyName ControlType Name	MSAA RadioButton Female
DOB Window *Parent: View Employee Window*	Window	TechnologyName ControlType ControlName	MSAA Window dtDOB
DOB *Parent: DOB Window*	Date	TechnologyName ControlType	MSAA DateTimePicker
Email Window *Parent: View Employee Window*	Window	TechnologyName ControlType ControlName	MSAA Window txtEmail
Email *Parent: Email Window*	Edit Box	TechnologyName ControlType	MSAA Edit
Contract Window *Parent: View Employee Window*	Window	TechnologyName ControlType ControlName	MSAA Window cbContract
Contract *Parent: Contract Window*	CheckBox	TechnologyName ControlType Name	MSAA CheckBox Contract Job?
Postcode Window *Parent: View Employee Window*	Window	TechnologyName ControlType ControlName	MSAA Window txtPostcode
Postcode *Parent: Postcode Window*	Edit Box	TechnologyName ControlType	MSAA Edit
Cancel Window *Parent: View Employee Window*	Window	TechnologyName ControlType ControlName	MSAA Window btnCancel

Windows Forms Application - View Employee Controls Contd...			
Control	*Type*	*Property*	*Value*
Cancel	Button	TechnologyName	MSAA
Parent: Cancel Window		ControlType	Button

Add a new class 'repWinAdminEmployee.cs' to the *Repository* folder and add Listing 9.31 code to it.

Listing 9.31: 'repWinAdminEmployee.cs' - Repository for Admin's View Employee

```
/*****************************************************
 * All rights reserved. Copyright 2017 Arkenstone-ltd.com *
 *****************************************************/

using ↵
    ↪ Microsoft.VisualStudio.TestTools.UITesting.WinControls;

namespace CodedUITesting
{
    public static class repWinAdminEmployee
    {
        private static WinWindow mEmployeeWindow;

        private static WinWindow mTitleWindow;
        private static WinComboBox mTitle;

        private static WinWindow mEmpNameWindow;
        private static WinEdit mEmpName;

        private static WinWindow mMaleWindow;
        private static WinRadioButton mMale;

        private static WinWindow mFemaleWindow;
        private static WinRadioButton mFemale;

        private static WinWindow mDOBWindow;
        private static WinDateTimePicker mDOB;

        private static WinWindow mEmailWindow;
        private static WinEdit mEmail;

        private static WinWindow mContractWindow;
        private static WinCheckBox mContract;

```

```
34        private static WinWindow mPostcodeWindow;
35        private static WinEdit mPostcode;
36
37        private static WinWindow mCloseButtonWindow;
38        private static WinButton mCloseButton;
39
40        public static WinWindow SetBaseWindowScope()
41        {
42            mEmployeeWindow = new WinWindow();
43            mEmployeeWindow.SearchProperties[WinWindow. ↵
                  ↪ PropertyNames.ControlName] = "frmEmployee";
44
45            return mEmployeeWindow;
46        }
47
48        public static WinComboBox Title
49        {
50            get
51            {
52
53                if (mTitleWindow == null)
54                {
55                    mTitleWindow = new ↵
                          ↪ WinWindow(mEmployeeWindow);
56                    mTitleWindow.SearchProperties[ ↵
                          ↪ WinWindow.PropertyNames. ↵
                          ↪ ControlName] = "cmbTitle";
57                }
58
59                if (mTitle == null)
60                {
61                    mTitle = new WinComboBox(mTitleWindow);
62                    mTitle.SearchProperties[WinComboBox. ↵
                          ↪ PropertyNames.Name] = "Title:";
63                }
64
65                return mTitle;
66            }
67        }
68
69        public static WinEdit EmpName
70        {
71            get
72            {
73
```

```
74              if (mEmpNameWindow == null)
75              {
76                  mEmpNameWindow = new ↵
                        ↪ WinWindow(mEmployeeWindow);
77                  mEmpNameWindow.SearchProperties[ ↵
                        ↪ WinWindow.PropertyNames. ↵
                        ↪ ControlName] = "txtName";
78              }
79
80              if (mEmpName == null)
81              {
82                  mEmpName = new WinEdit(mEmpNameWindow);
83              }
84
85              return mEmpName;
86          }
87      }
88
89      public static WinRadioButton Male
90      {
91          get
92          {
93              if (mMaleWindow == null)
94              {
95                  mMaleWindow = new ↵
                        ↪ WinWindow(mEmployeeWindow);
96                  mMaleWindow.SearchProperties[WinWindow. ↵
                        ↪ PropertyNames.ControlName] = ↵
                        ↪ "rbMale";
97              }
98
99              if (mMale == null)
100             {
101                 mMale = new WinRadioButton(mMaleWindow);
102                 mMale.SearchProperties[WinRadioButton. ↵
                        ↪ PropertyNames.Name] = "Male";
103             }
104
105             return mMale;
106         }
107     }
108
109     public static WinRadioButton Female
110     {
111         get
```

```
112              {
113
114                  if (mFemaleWindow == null)
115                  {
116                      mFemaleWindow = new ↵
                            ↪ WinWindow(mEmployeeWindow);
117                      mFemaleWindow.SearchProperties[ ↵
                            ↪ WinWindow.PropertyNames. ↵
                            ↪ ControlName] = "rbFemale";
118                  }
119
120                  if (mFemale == null)
121                  {
122                      mFemale = new ↵
                            ↪ WinRadioButton(mFemaleWindow);
123                      mFemale.SearchProperties[ ↵
                            ↪ WinRadioButton.PropertyNames. ↵
                            ↪ Name] = "Female";
124                  }
125
126                  return mFemale;
127              }
128          }
129
130          public static WinDateTimePicker DOB
131          {
132              get
133              {
134
135                  if (mDOBWindow == null)
136                  {
137                      mDOBWindow = new ↵
                            ↪ WinWindow(mEmployeeWindow);
138                      mDOBWindow.SearchProperties[WinWindow. ↵
                            ↪ PropertyNames.ControlName] = ↵
                            ↪ "dtDOB";
139                  }
140
141                  if (mDOB == null)
142                  {
143                      mDOB = new ↵
                            ↪ WinDateTimePicker(mDOBWindow);
144                  }
145
146                  return mDOB;
```

```
147                    }
148                }

150            public static WinEdit Email
151            {
152                get
153                {

155                    if (mEmailWindow == null)
156                    {
157                        mEmailWindow = new ↵
                              ↪ WinWindow(mEmployeeWindow);
158                        mEmailWindow.SearchProperties[WinWindow. ↵
                              ↪ PropertyNames.ControlName] = ↵
                              ↪ "txtEmail";
159                    }

161                    if (mEmail == null)
162                    {
163                        mEmail = new WinEdit(mEmailWindow);
164                    }

166                    return mEmail;
167                }
168            }
169            public static WinCheckBox Contract
170            {
171                get
172                {

174                    if (mContractWindow == null)
175                    {
176                        mContractWindow = new ↵
                              ↪ WinWindow(mEmployeeWindow);
177                        mContractWindow.SearchProperties[ ↵
                              ↪ WinWindow.PropertyNames. ↵
                              ↪ ControlName] = "cbContract";
178                    }

180                    if (mContract == null)
181                    {
182                        mContract = new ↵
                              ↪ WinCheckBox(mContractWindow);
183                        mContract.SearchProperties[WinCheckBox. ↵
                              ↪ PropertyNames.Name] = "Contract ↵
```

```
                                    ↪ Job?";
184                      }
185
186                  return mContract;
187              }
188          }
189
190      public static WinEdit Postcode
191      {
192          get
193          {
194
195              if (mPostcodeWindow == null)
196              {
197                  mPostcodeWindow = new ↩
                         ↪ WinWindow(mEmployeeWindow);
198                  mPostcodeWindow.SearchProperties[ ↩
                         ↪ WinWindow.PropertyNames. ↩
                         ↪ ControlName] = "txtPostcode";
199              }
200
201              if (mPostcode == null)
202              {
203                  mPostcode = new ↩
                         ↪ WinEdit(mPostcodeWindow);
204              }
205
206              return mPostcode;
207          }
208      }
209
210      public static WinButton CloseButton
211      {
212          get
213          {
214              if (mCloseButtonWindow == null)
215              {
216                  mCloseButtonWindow = new ↩
                         ↪ WinWindow(mEmployeeWindow);
217                  mCloseButtonWindow.SearchProperties[ ↩
                         ↪ WinWindow.PropertyNames. ↩
                         ↪ ControlName] = "btnCancel";
218              }
219
220              if (mCloseButton == null)
```

```
221                          {
222                              mCloseButton = new ↵
                               ↪ WinButton(mCloseButtonWindow);
223                          }
224
225                          return mCloseButton;
226                      }
227                  }
228              }
229  }
```

◈ Line 42: Note that there is no parent.

9.7.3   Page Logic

We need to define some additional actions as follows:

Action	Description
SelectEmployeeById()	This action will select an individual employee by its id from the list.
VerifyEmployeeById()	This action will verify an employee's detail with the values in the database.

Add the additional action to the 'pageWinAdminEmpList.cs' file as shown in Listing 9.32.

Listing 9.32: 'pageWinAdminEmpList.cs' - SelectEmployeeById

```
1  public void SelectEmployeeById(string empId)
2  {
3      Utility.ClickCellWithValue(repWinAdminEmpList. ↵
           ↪ EmployeesList, empId);
4
5      Utility.Click(repWinAdminEmpList.ViewButton);
6  }
```

◈ Line 3: Clicks the cell with the specified `empId`.
◈ Line 5: Clicks the *View* button to display details.

Add a new class 'pageWinAdminEmployee.cs' to the *Pages* folder and insert the code as shown in Listing 9.33.

Listing 9.33: 'pageWinAdminEmployee.cs' - Logic for VerifyEmployeeById

```
1   /******************************************************
2    * All rights reserved. Copyright 2017 Arkenstone-ltd.com *
3    ******************************************************/
4   using System;
5   using System.Data.SqlClient;
6
7   namespace CodedUITesting
8   {
9       class pageWinAdminEmployee
10      {
11          public pageWinAdminEmployee()
12          {
13              repWinAdminEmployee.SetBaseWindowScope();
14          }
15
16          public void VerifyEmployeeById(string empId)
17          {
18              string stringSQL = "SELECT [EmployeeID], ↵
                    ↪ [Title], [Name], [Gender], ↵
                    ↪ [DateOfBirth], [Email], [ContractJob], ↵
                    ↪ [Postcode]" + "\r\n";
19              stringSQL = stringSQL + "FROM ↵
                    ↪ [dbo].[Employees] where EmployeeID = '" ↵
                    ↪ + empId + "'";
20
21              Utility.Log.Info("SQL is: " + stringSQL);
22
23              String expEmpId = "", expTitle = "", expName ↵
                    ↪ = "", expGender = "", expDob = "", ↵
                    ↪ expEmail = "", expContract = "", ↵
                    ↪ expPostcode = "";
24
25              using (SqlConnection con = new ↵
                    ↪ SqlConnection(Config.connectionString))
26              {
27                  con.Open();
28
29                  using (SqlCommand command = new ↵
                        ↪ SqlCommand(stringSQL, con))
30
31                  using (SqlDataReader reader = ↵
                        ↪ command.ExecuteReader())
```

```
32                  {
33                      while (reader.Read())
34                      {
35                          expEmpId = reader.GetString(0);
36                          expTitle = reader.GetString(1);
37                          expName = reader.GetString(2);
38                          expGender = reader.GetString(3);
39                          expDob = ↵
                              ↪ reader.GetDateTime(4).ToString();
40                          expEmail = reader.GetString(5);
41                          expContract = reader.GetString(6);
42                          expPostcode = ↵
                              ↪ reader.GetString(7);
43                      }
44                  }
45              }
46
47              Utility.ReportExpectedVsActual(expTitle, ↵
                  ↪ Utility.GetValue(repWinAdminEmployee.Title));
48
49              Utility.ReportExpectedVsActual(expName, ↵
                  ↪ Utility.GetValue(repWinAdminEmployee. ↵
                  ↪ EmpName));
50
51              if (Utility.DecodeGender(expGender) == ↵
                  ↪ Config.MALE_TEXT)
52              {
53                  Utility.Log.Info("Verifying... " + ↵
                      ↪ Config.MALE_TEXT);
54                  Utility.ReportExpectedVsActual(Config.TRUE, ↵
                      ↪ Utility.GetValue(repWinAdminEmployee. ↵
                      ↪ Male));
55              }
56              else if (Utility.DecodeGender(expGender) == ↵
                  ↪ Config.FEMALE_TEXT)
57              {
58                  Utility.Log.Info("Verifying... " + ↵
                      ↪ Config.FEMALE_TEXT);
59                  Utility.ReportExpectedVsActual(Config.TRUE, ↵
                      ↪ Utility.GetValue(repWinAdminEmployee. ↵
                      ↪ Female));
60              }
61              else
62                  Utility.ReportExpectedVsActual("Invalid ↵
                      ↪ Value*** ", ↵
```

```
                        ↪ Utility.DecodeGender(expGender));
63
64
65              Utility.ReportExpectedVsActual( ↵
                    ↪ Utility.FormatDate(expDob), ↵
                    ↪ Utility.GetValue(repWinAdminEmployee.DOB));
66
67              Utility.ReportExpectedVsActual( ↵
                    ↪ expEmail.ToLower(), ↵
                    ↪ Utility.GetValue(repWinAdminEmployee. ↵
                    ↪ Email).ToLower());
68
69              Utility.ReportExpectedVsActual( ↵
                    ↪ Utility.DecodeContract(expContract), ↵
                    ↪ Utility.GetValue(repWinAdminEmployee. ↵
                    ↪ Contract));
70
71              Utility.ReportExpectedVsActual(expPostcode, ↵
                    ↪ Utility.GetValue(repWinAdminEmployee. ↵
                    ↪ Postcode));
72
73              Utility.Click(repWinAdminEmployee.CloseButton);
74          }
75      }
76 }
```

◈ Line 13: Sets the base window scope by calling **SetBaseWindowScope** in the class constructor.

9.7.4   Creating Tests

Add an additional test to the 'WinTests.cs' file as shown in Listing 9.34.

Listing 9.34: 'WinTests.cs' - WinAdminVerifyEmployeeByIdWithDatabase

```
1 [TestMethod]
2 public void WinAdminVerifyEmployeeByIdWithDatabase()
3 {
4     Utility.Log.Info("Starting Test ***** " + ↵
          ↪ Utility.TestName + " *****");
5
6     try
7     {
8         string empID = "10002";
9
```

```
10        Utility.LaunchWinApp();
11
12        pageWinHome wph = new pageWinHome();
13        wph.ClickMenuItemFileLogin();
14
15        pageWinLogin wpl = new pageWinLogin();
16        wpl.LoginUser("Admin", ↵
              ↪ "+rvVFpEB1/R9sAhRQ12knU/Vax4Vmtqs");
17
18        wph.ClickMenuItemAdminEmployeeList();
19
20        pageWinAdminEmpList wpel = new ↵
              ↪ pageWinAdminEmpList();
21        wpel.SelectEmployeeById(empID);
22
23        pageWinAdminEmployee wped = new ↵
              ↪ pageWinAdminEmployee();
24        wped.VerifyEmployeeById(empID);
25
26        wph.ClickMenuItemFileLogout();
27
28        wph.ClickMenuItemFileExit();
29
30        Utility.ReportResult();
31    }
32    catch (Exception exception)
33    {
34        Utility.ReportExpectedVsActual(Utility.TestName, ↵
              ↪ "Exception: " + exception.ToString());
35        Utility.Log.Error("Exception: " + ↵
              ↪ exception.ToString());
36        throw exception;
37    }
38 }
```

◈ Line 8: Sets the employee id to be verified.

9.7.5 Executing Tests

Execute the test `WinAdminVerifyEmployeeByIdWithDatabase` and you will see an output as shown in Figure 9.14. The test should execute successfully.

Test Name: WinAdminVerifyEmployeeByIdWithDatabase

Test Outcome: ⊘ Passed

Standard Output

```
2017-04-12 20:38:32.900 INFO  CodedUITesting.Utility - SetupSummaryFile
2017-04-12 20:38:32.936 INFO  CodedUITesting.Utility - Starting Test ***** WinAdminVerifyEmployeeByIdWithDatabase *****
2017-04-12 20:38:34.101 INFO  CodedUITesting.Utility - Click WinMenuItem: ControlName - menuStripMain  (DisplayText - File)
2017-04-12 20:38:34.725 INFO  CodedUITesting.Utility - Click WinMenuItem: ControlName - menuStripMain  (DisplayText - Login)
2017-04-12 20:38:35.144 INFO  CodedUITesting.Utility - SetValue WinEdit: ControlName - textBoxUserID  (Name - }  Value: Admin
2017-04-12 20:38:36.434 INFO  CodedUITesting.Utility - SetValue WinEdit: ControlName - textBoxPassword  (Name - )  Value: +rvVF
2017-04-12 20:38:37.883 INFO  CodedUITesting.Utility - Click WinButton: ControlName - btnLogin  (DisplayText - Login)
2017-04-12 20:38:38.775 INFO  CodedUITesting.Utility - Click WinMenuItem: ControlName - menuStripMain  (DisplayText - Admin)
2017-04-12 20:38:39.884 INFO  CodedUITesting.Utility - Click WinMenuItem: ControlName - menuStripMain  (DisplayText - Employe
2017-04-12 20:38:42.844 INFO  CodedUITesting.Utility - Click WinButton: ControlName - btnView  (DisplayText - View)
2017-04-12 20:38:43.327 INFO  CodedUITesting.Utility - SQL is: SELECT [EmployeeID], [Title], [Name], [Gender], [DateOfBirth], [Email]
FROM [dbo].[Employees] where EmployeeID = '10002'
2017-04-12 20:38:44.109 INFO  CodedUITesting.Utility - GetValue WinComboBox: ControlName - cmbTitle  (Name - Title:)
2017-04-12 20:38:44.140 INFO  CodedUITesting.Utility - [Expected:] Mr     [Actual:] Mr     [Step Passed]
2017-04-12 20:38:44.304 INFO  CodedUITesting.Utility - GetValue WinEdit: ControlNamed - txtName  (Name - Name:)
2017-04-12 20:38:44.318 INFO  CodedUITesting.Utility - [Expected:] James Jones     [Actual:] James Jones     [Step Passed]
2017-04-12 20:38:44.320 INFO  CodedUITesting.Utility - Verifying... Male
2017-04-12 20:38:44.510 INFO  CodedUITesting.Utility - GetValue WinRadioButton: ControlNamed - rbMale  (FriendlyName - Male)
2017-04-12 20:38:44.547 INFO  CodedUITesting.Utility - [Expected:] True     [Actual:] True     [Step Passed]
2017-04-12 20:38:44.778 INFO  CodedUITesting.Utility - GetValue WinDateTimePicker: ControlName - dtDOB  (Name - )
2017-04-12 20:38:44.796 INFO  CodedUITesting.Utility - [Expected:] 03-Dec-1978     [Actual:] 03-Dec-1978     [Step Passed]
```

Figure 9.14: Windows Forms Application - Verify Employee Output

Chapter 10

Windows Presentation Foundation (WPF) Application - WpfControls

Windows Presentation Foundation (WPF) Application - WpfControls

In this chapter, we will learn about how to perform:

- *Login tasks on Windows Presentation Foundation (WPF) Applications*

- *Verification tasks on WPF Applications using data fetched from Excel® files*

- *Verification tasks on WPF Applications using data fetched from database tables*

So let's get on with it...

I N the previous chapter we learnt about how to use Coded UI to automate the testing of Windows Forms Applications using a demo application. In this chapter, we will concentrate on another type of Windows-based Application namely Windows Presentation Foundation (WPF) Application, which is a newer and more flexible approach to the application development.

10.1 Demo Windows Presentation Foundation (WPF) Application

A demo WPF Application has been developed for you to carry out the Test Scenarios listed in this chapter. Here are the steps to download and compile the demo project.

- In your chosen browser, navigate to `http://www.arkenstone-ltd.com/`.

- Click on the *Downloads* link.

- Click on the *Download Windows Presentation Foundation (WPF) Application* link and save the compressed file on your local workstation.

- Extract the files to the 'C:\' folder. You can select a different location; however this book assumes you have chosen 'C:\'.

- Navigate to the 'C:\WpfApplication' folder and double click on the 'WpfApplication.sln' file. The project will open in Visual Studio®.

- Ensure that the *Solution Configuration 'Release'* is selected in Visual Studio's Toolbar as shown in Figure 9.1.

- In the *Solution Explorer*, right click on the *WpfApplication* and select *Rebuild*. On successful compilation, 'WpfApplication.exe' will be generated in the 'C:\WpfApplication\bin\Release' folder.

There are two types of users that exist for the demo WPF Application:

- A general or normal user whose credentials are:

    User: Tester

    Password: Tester123

- An administrator user whose credentials are:

    Admin User: Admin

    Password: Admin123

Please note that the credentials are case-sensitive.

10.2   WpfControls - Login

We will perform the following Test Scenario to demonstrate the use of `WpfControls` in the *Login* functionality:

- Launch the demo WPF Application.

- Click the menu item *File* ⇒ *Login*.

- Login with the user 'Tester'.

- Click the menu item *File* ⇒ *Logout*.

- Click the menu item *File* ⇒ *Exit*.

10.2.1 Configuration Parameters

Double click the 'Config.cs' file in the *Solution Explorer* and add Listing 10.1 code to it.

Listing 10.1: 'Config.cs' - Parameters for WPF controls

```
1  public const string WPF_APP = ↵
       ↪ "C:\\WpfApplication\\bin\\Release\\WpfApplication.exe";
2
3  public const string WPF_MENU_ITEM = ↵
       ↪ "Microsoft.VisualStudio.TestTools.UITesting. ↵
       ↪ WpfControls.WpfMenuItem";
4
5  public const string WPF_EDIT = ↵
       ↪ "Microsoft.VisualStudio.TestTools.UITesting. ↵
       ↪ WpfControls.WpfEdit";
6
7  public const string WPF_BUTTON = ↵
       ↪ "Microsoft.VisualStudio.TestTools.UITesting. ↵
       ↪ WpfControls.WpfButton";
```

◈ Line 1: Defines the path of the WPF Application's executable.

10.2.2 Object Repository

Let's start building the repository of our demo WPF Application.

10.2.2.1 WPF - Home Window

Launch the WPF Application and using *UI Spy*, note down the following elements on the main window. Note that this book has only defined the controls that we will use for demonstration purposes.

WPF Application - Home Page Controls			
Control	*Type*	*Property*	*Value*
Main Menu Parent: AUT Window	Menu	TechnologyName ControlType	UIA Menu
File Parent: Main Menu	Menu Item	TechnologyName ControlType Name	UIA MenuItem File
File ⇒ Login Parent: AUT Window	Menu Item	TechnologyName ControlType Name	UIA MenuItem Login

WPF Application - Home Page Controls Contd...			
Control	**Type**	**Property**	**Value**
File ⇒ Logout *Parent: AUT Window*	Menu Item	TechnologyName ControlType Name	UIA MenuItem Logout
File ⇒ Exit *Parent: AUT Window*	Menu Item	TechnologyName ControlType Name	UIA MenuItem Exit
Admin *Parent: Main Menu*	Menu Item	TechnologyName ControlType Name	UIA MenuItem Admin
Admin ⇒ Employee List *Parent: AUT Window*	Menu Item	TechnologyName ControlType Name	UIA MenuItem Employee List

The *Main Menu* parental hierarchy is depicted in Figure 10.1.

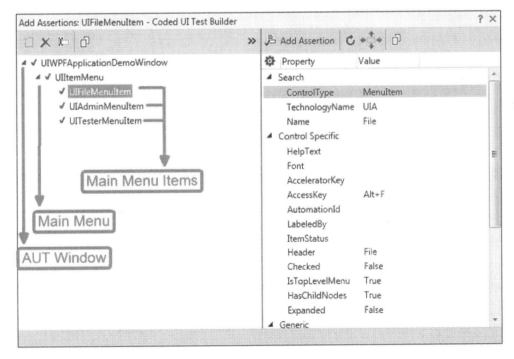

Figure 10.1: Menu Hierarchy

The *SubMenu* parental hierarchy is depicted in Figure 10.2.

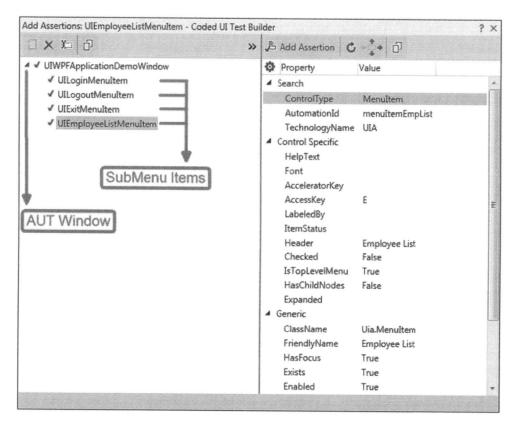

Figure 10.2: SubMenu Hierarchy

Add a new class 'repWpfHome.cs' to the *Repository* folder and add Listing 10.2 code to it.

 After adding the code, you will see errors on the `Utility.WpfAUT` variable. Don't worry about this as we will define it soon.

Listing 10.2: 'repWpfHome.cs' - Repository for WPF Home window

```
1  /*************************************************************
2   * All rights reserved. Copyright 2017 Arkenstone-ltd.com *
3   *************************************************************/
4  using ↵
      ↪ Microsoft.VisualStudio.TestTools.UITesting.WpfControls;
5
6  namespace CodedUITesting
7  {
8      public static class repWpfHome
9      {
10         private static WpfMenu mMenuWpf;
11
```

```
12          private static WpfMenuItem mMenuItem_File;
13          private static WpfMenuItem mMenuItem_FileLogin;
14          private static WpfMenuItem mMenuItem_FileLogout;
15          private static WpfMenuItem mMenuItem_FileExit;
16
17          private static WpfMenuItem mMenuItem_Admin;
18          private static WpfMenuItem ←
                ↪ mMenuItem_AdminEmployeeList;
19
20          public static WpfMenu SetBaseWindowScope()
21          {
22              mMenuWpf = new WpfMenu(Utility.WpfAUT);
23              mMenuWpf.SearchProperties.Add(WpfMenu. ←
                    ↪ PropertyNames.ControlType, "Menu");
24
25              return mMenuWpf;
26          }
27
28          public static WpfMenuItem MenuItem_File
29          {
30              get
31              {
32                  if (mMenuItem_File == null)
33                  {
34                      mMenuItem_File = new ←
                            ↪ WpfMenuItem(mMenuWpf);
35                      mMenuItem_File.SearchProperties. ←
                            ↪ Add(WpfMenuItem.PropertyNames. ←
                            ↪ Name, "File");
36                  }
37
38                  return mMenuItem_File;
39              }
40          }
41
42          public static WpfMenuItem MenuItem_FileLogin
43          {
44              get
45              {
46                  if (mMenuItem_FileLogin == null)
47                  {
48                      mMenuItem_FileLogin = new ←
                            ↪ WpfMenuItem(Utility.WpfAUT);
49                      mMenuItem_FileLogin.SearchProperties. ←
                            ↪ Add(WpfMenuItem.PropertyNames ←
```

```
                              ↪ .Name, "Login");
50                    }
51
52                    return mMenuItem_FileLogin;
53              }
54        }
55
56        public static WpfMenuItem MenuItem_FileLogout
57        {
58            get
59            {
60                if (mMenuItem_FileLogout == null)
61                {
62                    mMenuItem_FileLogout = new ↵
                          ↪ WpfMenuItem(Utility.WpfAUT);
63                    mMenuItem_FileLogout.SearchProperties. ↵
                          ↪ Add(WpfMenuItem.PropertyNames. ↵
                          ↪ Name, "Logout");
64                }
65
66                return mMenuItem_FileLogout;
67            }
68        }
69
70        public static WpfMenuItem MenuItem_FileExit
71        {
72            get
73            {
74                if (mMenuItem_FileExit == null)
75                {
76                    mMenuItem_FileExit = new ↵
                          ↪ WpfMenuItem(Utility.WpfAUT);
77                    mMenuItem_FileExit.SearchProperties. ↵
                          ↪ Add(WpfMenuItem.PropertyNames. ↵
                          ↪ Name, "Exit");
78                }
79
80                return mMenuItem_FileExit;
81            }
82        }
83
84        public static WpfMenuItem MenuItem_Admin
85        {
86            get
87            {
```

```
88
89              if (mMenuItem_Admin == null)
90              {
91                  mMenuItem_Admin = new ↵
                        ↪ WpfMenuItem(mMenuWpf);
92                  mMenuItem_Admin.SearchProperties. ↵
                        ↪ Add(WpfMenuItem.PropertyNames. ↵
                        ↪ Name, "Admin");
93              }
94
95              return mMenuItem_Admin;
96          }
97      }
98
99      public static WpfMenuItem MenuItem_AdminEmployeeList
100     {
101         get
102         {
103             if (mMenuItem_AdminEmployeeList == null)
104             {
105                 mMenuItem_AdminEmployeeList = new ↵
                        ↪ WpfMenuItem(Utility.WpfAUT);
106                 mMenuItem_AdminEmployeeList. ↵
                        ↪ SearchProperties. ↵
                        ↪ Add(WpfMenuItem.PropertyNames. ↵
                        ↪ Name, "Employee List");
107             }
108
109             return mMenuItem_AdminEmployeeList;
110         }
111     }
112 }
113 }
```

◈ Lines 22, 48, 62, 76 and 105: Initialise a new instance whose `Parent` is `Utility.WpfAUT` which is our demo application.

10.2.2.2   WPF - Login Window

Let's note down all the controls on the *Login* window as follows:

WPF Application - Login Window Controls			
Control	**Type**	**Property**	**Value**
Login Window Parent: NA	Window	TechnologyName ControlType Name	UIA Window Login
User ID Edit Box Parent: Login Window	Edit Box	TechnologyName ControlType AutomationId	UIA Edit txtLogin
Password Edit Box Parent: Login Window	Edit Box	TechnologyName ControlType AutomationId	UIA Edit txtPassword
Login Button Parent: Login Window	Button	TechnologyName ControlType AutomationId	UIA Button button

The *Login* window's controls' hierarchy is depicted in Figure 10.3.

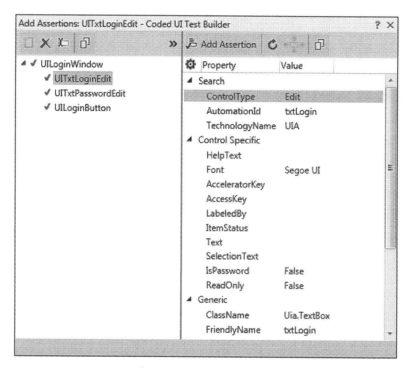

Figure 10.3: Login Window Controls Hierarchy

Add a new class 'repWpfLogin.cs' to the *Repository* folder and add Listing 10.3 code.

Listing 10.3: 'repWpfLogin.cs' - Repository for the Login window

```
1  /*********************************************************
```

```
 2   * All rights reserved. Copyright 2017 Arkenstone-ltd.com *
 3   **********************************************************/
 4   using ↵
         ↪ Microsoft.VisualStudio.TestTools.UITesting.WpfControls;
 5
 6   namespace CodedUITesting
 7   {
 8       public static class repWpfLogin
 9       {
10           private static WpfWindow mLoginWindow;
11
12           private static WpfEdit mUserID;
13           private static WpfEdit mPassword;
14           private static WpfButton mLoginButton;
15
16           public static WpfWindow SetBaseWindowScope()
17           {
18               mLoginWindow = new WpfWindow();
19               mLoginWindow.SearchProperties[WpfWindow. ↵
                     ↪ PropertyNames.Name] = "Login";
20               return mLoginWindow;
21           }
22
23           public static WpfEdit UserID
24           {
25               get
26               {
27                   if (mUserID == null)
28                   {
29                       mUserID = new WpfEdit(mLoginWindow);
30                       mUserID.SearchProperties[WpfEdit. ↵
                             ↪ PropertyNames.AutomationId] = ↵
                             ↪ "txtLogin";
31                   }
32                   return mUserID;
33               }
34           }
35
36           public static WpfEdit Password
37           {
38               get
39               {
40                   if (mPassword == null)
41                   {
42                       mPassword = new WpfEdit(mLoginWindow);
```

```
43                          mPassword.SearchProperties[WpfEdit. ↵
                              ↪ PropertyNames.AutomationId] = ↵
                              ↪ "txtPassword";
44                  }
45              return mPassword;
46          }
47      }
48
49      public static WpfButton LoginButton
50      {
51          get
52          {
53              if (mLoginButton == null)
54              {
55                  mLoginButton = new ↵
                      ↪ WpfButton(mLoginWindow);
56                  mLoginButton.SearchProperties[ ↵
                      ↪ WpfButton.PropertyNames. ↵
                      ↪ AutomationId] = "button";
57              }
58              return mLoginButton;
59          }
60      }
61  }
62 }
```

◈ Line 18: Initialises a new instance of the `WpfWindow` class with no *Parent*.

☞ As you would have already noticed that we have defined the edit box as `WpfEdit` therefore, `TechnologyName = "UIA"` and `ControlType = "Edit"` is implicit so there is no need to specify these properties while defining the repository. The same is true for other `WpfControls`.

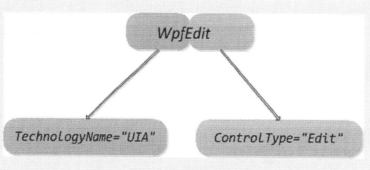

Figure 10.4: WpfEdit Control

10.2.3 Utility Functions

Let's define some additional generic functions as follows:

LaunchWpfApp - Launches the WPF Application		
Input Parameters	*none*	No arguments
Return Value	*void*	Returns nothing

CloseWpfApp - Closes the WPF Application		
Input Parameters	*none*	No arguments
Return Value	*void*	Returns nothing

Update the 'Utility.cs' file as shown in Listing 10.4.

 Note that the listing only shows the changes and not the complete 'Utility.cs' file.

Listing 10.4: 'Utility.cs' - Additional changes

```
1  using ↵
      ↳ Microsoft.VisualStudio.TestTools.UITesting.WpfControls;
2
3  namespace CodedUITesting
4  {
5      public static class Utility
6      {
7          public static ApplicationUnderTest WpfAUT;
8
9          public static void LaunchWpfApp()
10         {
11             WpfAUT = ↵
                  ↳ ApplicationUnderTest.Launch(Config.WPF_APP);
12         }
13
14         public static void CloseWpfApp()
15         {
16             string taskName = Path. ↵
                  ↳ GetFileNameWithoutExtension(Config.WPF_APP);
17             KillProcess(taskName);
18         }
19     }
20 }
```

◈ Line 7: Defines a `public static WpfAUT` object representing the WPF Application Under Test.

◈ Line 11: `ApplicationUnderTest.Launch` returns the application that was started.

We need to update our existing `Click()` function as per Listing 10.5.

Listing 10.5: 'Utility.cs' - Additional case statements in the Click function

```
1  case Config.WPF_MENU_ITEM:
2      Log.Info("Click WpfMenuItem: Id - " + ↵
           ↪ ((WpfMenuItem)obj).AutomationId + "  ↵
           ↪ (DisplayText - " + ↵
           ↪ ((WpfMenuItem)obj).FriendlyName + ")");
3      Mouse.Click((WpfMenuItem)obj);
4      break;
5
6  case Config.WPF_BUTTON:
7      Log.Info("Click WpfButton: Id - " + ↵
           ↪ ((WpfButton)obj).AutomationId + "  (DisplayText ↵
           ↪ - " + ((WpfButton)obj).FriendlyName + ")");
8      Mouse.Click((WpfButton)obj);
9      break;
```

◈ Line 3: Note the casting to type `WpfMenuItem`.
◈ Line 8: Note the casting to type `WpfButton`.

Similarly, we need to update our existing `SetValue()` function as per Listing 10.6

Listing 10.6: 'Utility.cs' - Additional case statement in the SetValue function

```
1  case Config.WPF_EDIT:
2      Log.Info("SetValue WpfEdit: Id - " + ↵
           ↪ ((WpfEdit)obj).AutomationId + "  (Name - " + ↵
           ↪ ((WpfEdit)obj).Name + ")" + "  Value: " + val);
3      ((WpfEdit)obj).Text = val;
4      break;
```

◈ Line 3: Note the casting to type `WpfEdit`.

10.2.4   Page Logic

10.2.4.1   WPF - Home Window

The *Home* page will have the following actions:

Action	Description
ClickMenuItemFileLogin()	This action will click the *File ⇒ Login* menu option.
ClickMenuItemFileLogout()	This action will click the *File ⇒ Logout* menu option.
ClickMenuItemFileExit()	This action will click the *File ⇒ Exit* menu option.
ClickMenuItemAdminEmployeeList()	This action will click the *Admin ⇒ Employee List* menu option.

Add a new class 'pageWpfHome.cs' to the *Pages* folder and insert the code as shown in Listing 10.7.

Listing 10.7: 'pageWpfHome.cs' - Page logic for the WPF Home window

```
1   /*******************************************************
2    * All rights reserved. Copyright 2017 Arkenstone-ltd.com *
3    *******************************************************/
4   namespace CodedUITesting
5   {
6       class pageWpfHome
7       {
8           public pageWpfHome()
9           {
10              repWpfHome.SetBaseWindowScope();
11          }
12
13          public void ClickMenuItemFileLogin()
14          {
15              Utility.Click(repWpfHome.MenuItem_File);
16              Utility.Click(repWpfHome.MenuItem_FileLogin);
17          }
18
19          public void ClickMenuItemFileLogout()
20          {
21              Utility.Click(repWpfHome.MenuItem_File);
22              Utility.Click(repWpfHome.MenuItem_FileLogout);
23          }
24
25          public void ClickMenuItemFileExit()
26          {
```

```
27              Utility.Click(repWpfHome.MenuItem_File);
28              Utility.Click(repWpfHome.MenuItem_FileExit);
29          }
30
31          public void ClickMenuItemAdminEmployeeList()
32          {
33              Utility.Click(repWpfHome.MenuItem_Admin);
34              Utility.Click(repWpfHome. ←
                 ↪ MenuItem_AdminEmployeeList);
35          }
36      }
37 }
```

◈ Line 10: Sets the base window scope by calling `SetBaseWindowScope` in the class constructor.

10.2.4.2 WPF - Login Window

Let's define the business logic for the *Login* window which will have the following action:

Action	Description
LoginUser()	Action for the user login with given credentials.

Add a new class 'pageWpfLogin.cs' to the *Pages* folder and insert the code as shown in Listing 10.8.

Listing 10.8: 'pageWpfLogin.cs' - Page logic for the WPF Login window

```
1  /******************************************************
2   * All rights reserved. Copyright 2017 Arkenstone-ltd.com *
3   ******************************************************/
4  namespace CodedUITesting
5  {
6      class pageWpfLogin
7      {
8          public pageWpfLogin()
9          {
10             repWpfLogin.SetBaseWindowScope();
11         }
12
13         public void LoginUser(string uid, string pwd)
14         {
15             Utility.SetValue(repWpfLogin.UserID, uid);
```

```
16                Utility.SetValue(repWpfLogin.Password, pwd);
17                Utility.Click(repWpfLogin.LoginButton);
18            }
19        }
20  }
```

◈ Line 10: Sets the base window scope by calling SetBaseWindowScope in the class constructor.

10.2.5 Creating Tests

Add a new class 'WpfTests.cs' to the *CodedUITesting* project folder and insert the code as shown in Listing 10.9.

Listing 10.9: 'WpfTests.cs' - WpfTesterLogin and WpfAdminLogin

```
1   /**********************************************************
2    * All rights reserved. Copyright 2017 Arkenstone-ltd.com *
3    **********************************************************/
4   using System;
5   using Microsoft.VisualStudio.TestTools.UITesting;
6   using Microsoft.VisualStudio.TestTools.UnitTesting;
7   using System.IO;
8
9   namespace CodedUITesting
10  {
11      [CodedUITest]
12      public class WpfTests
13      {
14          public WpfTests()
15          {
16          }
17
18          [TestInitialize()]
19          public void Initialize()
20          {
21              Utility.TestResult = Config.PASS;
22              Utility.TestName = TestContext.TestName;
23              Utility.TestResultFolder = ↵
                    ↪ TestContext.TestResultsDirectory;
24              Utility.TestRunFolder = ↵
                    ↪ TestContext.TestRunDirectory;
25
26              log4net.Config.XmlConfigurator. ↵
                    ↪ ConfigureAndWatch(new FileInfo( ↵
```

```
                            ↪ Config.PROJECT_FOLDER + "log4net.config"));
27              Utility.SetupSummaryFile();
28          }
29
30      [TestCleanup()]
31      public void Cleanup()
32      {
33          Utility.MoveScreenshots();
34          string logFile = Utility.SaveLogFile();
35          Utility.CreateSummaryFileEntry(DateTime.Now. ↩
                ↪ ToString() + "," + TestContext.TestName ↩
                ↪ + "," + Utility.TestResult + "," + ↩
                ↪ logFile);
36          Utility.CreateShortcut("TestSummary", ↩
                ↪ Utility.TestResultFolder, ↩
                ↪ Config.SUMMARY_PATHFILENAME);
37          Utility.CloseWpfApp();
38          Playback.Cleanup();
39      }
40
41      [TestMethod]
42      public void WpfTesterLogin()
43      {
44          Utility.Log.Info("Starting Test ***** " + ↩
                ↪ Utility.TestName + " *****");
45
46          try
47          {
48              Utility.LaunchWpfApp();
49
50              pageWpfHome wpfph = new pageWpfHome();
51              wpfph.ClickMenuItemFileLogin();
52
53              pageWpfLogin wpfpl = new pageWpfLogin();
54              wpfpl.LoginUser("Tester", "Tester123");
55
56              pageWinMessageBox winmb = new ↩
                    ↪ pageWinMessageBox();
57              winmb.ClickOkButton();
58
59              wpfph.ClickMenuItemFileLogout();
60
61              wpfph.ClickMenuItemFileExit();
62
63              Utility.ReportResult();
```

```
64              }
65              catch (Exception exception)
66              {
67                  Utility.ReportExpectedVsActual(Utility.↵
                        ↪ TestName, "Exception: " + ↵
                        ↪ exception.ToString());
68                  Utility.Log.Error("Exception: " + ↵
                        ↪ exception.ToString());
69                  throw exception;
70              }
71          }
72
73          [TestMethod]
74          public void WpfAdminLogin()
75          {
76              Utility.Log.Info("Starting Test ***** " + ↵
                    ↪ Utility.TestName + " *****");
77
78              try
79              {
80                  Utility.LaunchWpfApp();
81
82                  pageWpfHome wpfph = new pageWpfHome();
83                  wpfph.ClickMenuItemFileLogin();
84
85                  pageWpfLogin wpfpl = new pageWpfLogin();
86                  wpfpl.LoginUser("Admin", "Admin123");
87
88                  pageWinMessageBox winmb = new ↵
                        ↪ pageWinMessageBox();
89                  winmb.ClickOkButton();
90
91                  wpfph.ClickMenuItemFileLogout();
92
93                  wpfph.ClickMenuItemFileExit();
94
95                  Utility.ReportResult();
96              }
97              catch (Exception exception)
98              {
99                  Utility.ReportExpectedVsActual(Utility.↵
                        ↪ TestName, "Exception: " + ↵
                        ↪ exception.ToString());
100                 Utility.Log.Error("Exception: " + ↵
                        ↪ exception.ToString());
```

```
101                    throw exception;
102                }
103            }
104
105        public TestContext TestContext
106        {
107            get
108            {
109                return testContextInstance;
110            }
111            set
112            {
113                testContextInstance = value;
114            }
115        }
116        private TestContext testContextInstance;
117    }
118 }
```

◈ Lines 56 and 88: Note the reuse of **pageWinMessageBox** logic.

10.2.6   Executing Tests

Execute the test **WpfAdminLogin** and you will see an output as shown in Figure 10.5. The test should execute successfully.

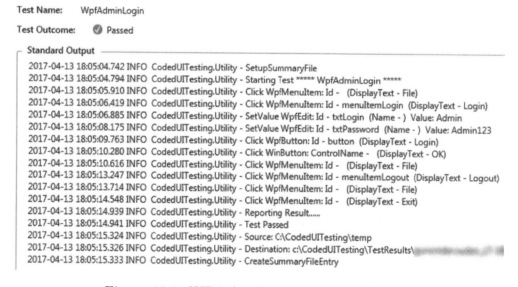

Figure 10.5: WPF Application - Login Output

10.3 WpfControls - Verify Employee List With Excel Data

We will perform the following Test Scenario to demonstrate the use of `WpfControls` in the *Employee List* functionality:

- Launch the demo WPF Application.
- Click the menu item *File ⇒ Login.*
- Login with the user 'Admin'.
- Click the menu item *Admin ⇒ Employee List.*
- Verify the employees' list with the data read from a file in XLSX format.
- Click the menu item *File ⇒ Logout.*
- Click the menu item *File ⇒ Exit.*

10.3.1 Configuration Parameters

Add Listing 10.10 code to the 'Config.cs' file.

Listing 10.10: 'Config.cs' - Parameter for WpfTree

```
1 public const string WPF_TREE = ↵
     ↪ "Microsoft.VisualStudio.TestTools.UITesting. ↵
     ↪ WpfControls.WpfTree";
```

10.3.2 Object Repository

Let's note down all the controls on the *Employee List* window.

WPF Application - Employee List Controls			
Control	*Type*	*Property*	*Value*
Employees Window *Parent: NA*	Window	TechnologyName ControlType Name	UIA Window Employee List
Employees *Parent: Employees Window*	Tree	TechnologyName ControlType AutomationId	UIA Tree treeViewEmp
Close *Parent: Employees Window*	Button	TechnologyName ControlType AutomationId	UIA Button btnClose

Add a new class 'repWpfAdminEmpList.cs' to the *Repository* folder and insert the code as shown in Listing 10.11.

Listing 10.11: 'repWpfAdminEmpList.cs' - Repository for WPF Admin's Employee List

```
1   /*************************************************
2    * All rights reserved. Copyright 2017 Arkenstone-ltd.com *
3    *************************************************/
4   using Microsoft.VisualStudio.TestTools.UITesting;
5   using ↵
        ↪ Microsoft.VisualStudio.TestTools.UITesting.WpfControls;
6
7   namespace CodedUITesting
8   {
9       public static class repWpfAdminEmpList
10      {
11          private static WpfWindow mEmployeesWindow;
12
13          private static WpfTree mEmployeesList;
14          private static WpfButton mCloseButton;
15
16          public static WpfWindow SetBaseWindowScope()
17          {
18              mEmployeesWindow = new WpfWindow();
19              mEmployeesWindow.SearchProperties[WpfWindow. ↵
                    ↪ PropertyNames.Name] = "Employee List";
20
21              return mEmployeesWindow;
22          }
23
24          public static WpfTree EmployeesList
25          {
26              get
27              {
28                  if (mEmployeesList == null)
29                  {
30                      mEmployeesList = new ↵
                            ↪ WpfTree(mEmployeesWindow);
31                      mEmployeesList.SearchProperties[ ↵
                            ↪ WpfTree.PropertyNames. ↵
                            ↪ AutomationId] = "treeViewEmp";
32                  }
33
34                  return mEmployeesList;
35              }
```

```
36          }
37
38          public static WpfButton CloseButton
39          {
40              get
41              {
42                  if (mCloseButton == null)
43                  {
44                      mCloseButton = new ↵
                          ↪ WpfButton(mEmployeesWindow);
45                      mCloseButton.SearchProperties[ ↵
                          ↪ WpfButton.PropertyNames. ↵
                          ↪ AutomationId] = "btnClose";
46                  }
47
48                  return mCloseButton;
49              }
50          }
51      }
52 }
```

10.3.3 Utility Functions

Add an additional case statement in the GetTableData function in the 'Utility.cs' file as shown in Listing 10.12.

Listing 10.12: 'Utility.cs' - Additional case statement in the GetTableData function

```
1  case Config.WPF_TREE:
2      Log.Info("GetTableData WpfTree: Id - " + ↵
           ↪ ((WpfTree)obj).AutomationId + " (Name - " + ↵
           ↪ ((WpfTree)obj).Name + ")");
3
4      rowCount = ((WpfTree)obj).Nodes.Count;
5      Log.Info("rowCount - " + rowCount);
6      Array.Resize(ref tblData, rowCount);
7
8      int g = 0;
9
10     foreach (WpfTreeItem item in ((WpfTree)obj).Nodes)
11     {
12         Log.Info("item.Name - " + item.Name);
13         Mouse.DoubleClick(item);
14         int colCount = item.Nodes.Count() + 1;
```

```
15      Log.Info("colCount - " + colCount);
16      Array.Resize(ref tblData[g], colCount);
17
18      tblData[g][0] = ExtractData(item.Name);
19
20      for (int j = 0; j < (colCount - 1); j++)
21      {
22          Log.Info("item.Nodes[j].Name - " + ↵
                ↪ item.Nodes[j].Name);
23          tblData[g][j + 1] = ↵
                ↪ ExtractData(item.Nodes[j].Name);
24          Log.Info("Row: " + g + "  Col: " + (j + 1) + ↵
                ↪ "    Value: " + tblData[g][j + 1]);
25      }
26
27      Mouse.DoubleClick(item);
28      g++;
29  }
30
31  break;
```

◇ Line 10: Loops through each node of the `WpfTree`.
◇ Line 13: Expands the node by double clicking it.
◇ Line 18: Extracts the first data item.
◇ Line 20: Extracts the rest of the data items.
◇ Line 27: Collapses the node by double clicking it.

We need to define a new function in the Utility file as follows:

ExtractData - Extracts data from a string separated by colon		
Input Parameters	*stg*	String to extract data from
Return Value	*data*	Returns the data

Add the new function to the 'Utility.cs' file as shown in Listing 10.13.

Listing 10.13: 'Utility.cs' - Code for ExtractData function

```
1  public static string ExtractData(string stg)
2  {
3      string[] tmp = stg.Split(':');
4      return tmp[1].Trim();
5  }
```

◈ Line 3: The `Split` function returns a string array whose elements contain the substrings that are delimited by colon.

◈ Line 4: Returns the second substring.

10.3.4 Page Logic

The *Employee List* window of our demo application will have the following action:

Action	Description
VerifyEmployeeListXLSXData()	This action will verify the employees' list with the data read from a file in XLSX format.

Add a new class 'pageWpfAdminEmpList.cs' to the *Pages* folder and insert the code as shown in Listing 10.14.

Listing 10.14: 'pageWpfAdminEmpList.cs' - Code for WPF Admin's Employee List

```
1  /*******************************************************
2   * All rights reserved. Copyright 2017 Arkenstone-ltd.com *
3   *******************************************************/
4  using Microsoft.VisualStudio.TestTools.UITesting;
5  using ↵
        ↪ Microsoft.VisualStudio.TestTools.UITesting.WpfControls;
6  using System;
7  using System.Linq;
8
9  namespace CodedUITesting
10 {
11     class pageWpfAdminEmpList
12     {
13         public pageWpfAdminEmpList()
14         {
15             repWpfAdminEmpList.SetBaseWindowScope();
16         }
17
18         public void VerifyEmployeeListXLSXData()
19         {
20             String[][] empList = ↵
                    ↪ Utility.GetTableData(repWpfAdminEmpList. ↵
                    ↪ EmployeesList);
21
```

```
22          String[][] xlsxData = ←
              ↪ Utility.GetSpreadSheetXLSX( ←
              ↪ @"C:\CodedUITesting\CodedUITesting\ ←
              ↪ TestData\UserData.xlsx", 1);
23

24          for (int ii = 0; ii < empList.Length; ii++)
25          {
26              Utility.ReportExpectedVsActual( ←
                  ↪ empList[ii][0], xlsxData[ii + 1][0]);
27

28              Utility.ReportExpectedVsActual( ←
                  ↪ empList[ii][1], xlsxData[ii + 1][1]);
29

30              Utility.ReportExpectedVsActual( ←
                  ↪ empList[ii][2], xlsxData[ii + 1][2]);
31

32              Utility.ReportExpectedVsActual( ←
                  ↪ empList[ii][4], xlsxData[ii + 1][3]);
33

34              Utility.ReportExpectedVsActual( ←
                  ↪ empList[ii][3], ←
                  ↪ Utility.FormatDate(Utility. ←
                  ↪ ExcelDateParse( xlsxData[ii + ←
                  ↪ 1][4]).Substring(0, 10)));
35

36              Utility.ReportExpectedVsActual( ←
                  ↪ empList[ii][6], xlsxData[ii + 1][5]);
37          }
38

39          Utility.Click(repWpfAdminEmpList.CloseButton);
40      }
41  }
42 }
```

10.3.5 Creating Tests

Add a new test to the 'WpfTests.cs' file as shown in Listing 10.15.

Listing 10.15: 'WpfTests.cs' - WpfAdminVerifyEmployeeListWithXLSXData

```
1 [TestMethod]
2 public void WpfAdminVerifyEmployeeListWithXLSXData()
3 {
```

```
4       Utility.Log.Info("Starting Test ***** " + ←
            ↪ Utility.TestName + " *****");
5
6       try
7       {
8           Utility.LaunchWpfApp();
9
10          pageWpfHome wpfph = new pageWpfHome();
11          wpfph.ClickMenuItemFileLogin();
12
13          pageWpfLogin wpfpl = new pageWpfLogin();
14          wpfpl.LoginUser("Admin", "Admin123");
15
16          pageWinMessageBox winmb = new pageWinMessageBox();
17          winmb.ClickOkButton();
18
19          wpfph.ClickMenuItemAdminEmployeeList();
20
21          pageWpfAdminEmpList wpfel = new ←
                ↪ pageWpfAdminEmpList();
22          wpfel.VerifyEmployeeListXLSXData();
23
24          wpfph.ClickMenuItemFileLogout();
25
26          wpfph.ClickMenuItemFileExit();
27
28          Utility.ReportResult();
29      }
30      catch (Exception exception)
31      {
32          Utility.ReportExpectedVsActual(Utility.TestName, ←
                ↪ "Exception: " + exception.ToString());
33          Utility.Log.Error("Exception: " + ←
                ↪ exception.ToString());
34          throw exception;
35      }
36  }
```

10.3.6 Executing Tests

Execute the test `WpfAdminVerifyEmployeeListWithXLSXData` and you will see an output as shown in Figure 10.6. The test should execute successfully.

Test Name: WpfAdminVerifyEmployeeListWithXLSXData

Test Outcome: ⊘ Passed

```
┌ Standard Output ────────────────────────────────────────────────────────────
 2017-05-14 17:27:48.155 INFO CodedUITesting.Utility - SetupSummaryFile
 2017-05-14 17:27:48.216 INFO CodedUITesting.Utility - Starting Test ***** WpfAdminVerifyEmployeeListWithXLSXData *****
 2017-05-14 17:27:49.478 INFO CodedUITesting.Utility - Click WpfMenuItem: Id -   (DisplayText - File)
 2017-05-14 17:27:50.266 INFO CodedUITesting.Utility - Click WpfMenuItem: Id - menuitemLogin  (DisplayText - Login)
 2017-05-14 17:27:51.030 INFO CodedUITesting.Utility - SetValue WpfEdit: Id - txtLogin  (Name - ) Value: Admin
 2017-05-14 17:27:52.847 INFO CodedUITesting.Utility - SetValue WpfEdit: Id - txtPassword  (Name - ) Value: Admin123
 2017-05-14 17:27:55.081 INFO CodedUITesting.Utility - Click WpfButton: Id - button  (DisplayText - Login)
 2017-05-14 17:27:55.779 INFO CodedUITesting.Utility - Click WinButton: ControlName -  {DisplayText - OK)
 2017-05-14 17:27:56.266 INFO CodedUITesting.Utility - Click WpfMenuItem: Id - menuAdmin  (DisplayText - Admin)
 2017-05-14 17:27:56.822 INFO CodedUITesting.Utility - Click WpfMenuItem: Id - menuitemEmpList  (DisplayText - Employee List)
 2017-05-14 17:27:57.322 INFO CodedUITesting.Utility - GetTableData WpfTree: Id - treeViewEmp  (Name - )
 2017-05-14 17:27:57.537 INFO CodedUITesting.Utility - rowCount - 5
 2017-05-14 17:27:57.727 INFO CodedUITesting.Utility - item.Name - Employee ID: 10001
 2017-05-14 17:27:58.785 INFO CodedUITesting.Utility - colCount - 8
 2017-05-14 17:27:59.092 INFO CodedUITesting.Utility - item.Nodes[j].Name - Title: Mrs
```

Figure 10.6: WPF Application - Verify Employee List Output

10.4 WpfControls - Verify Employee With Database

We will perform the following Test Scenario to demonstrate the use of `WpfControls` in the *Verify Employee* functionality:

- Launch the demo WPF Application.

- Click the menu item *File* ⇒ *Login*.

- Login with the user 'Admin'.

- Click the menu item *Admin* ⇒ *Employee List*.

- Verify the details of employee id "10003" with the data read from the database.

- Click the menu item *File* ⇒ *Logout*.

- Click the menu item *File* ⇒ *Exit*.

10.4.1 Page Logic

We need to define an additional action as follows:

Action	Description
VerifyEmployeeById()	This action will verify an employee's detail with the values in the database.

Add the additional action to the 'pageWpfAdminEmpList.cs' file as shown in Listing 10.16.

```
1  using System.Data.SqlClient;
2
3  public void VerifyEmployeeById(string empId)
4  {
5      String[][] empData = { };
6
7      foreach (WpfTreeItem item in ↵
          ↪ repWpfAdminEmpList.EmployeesList.Nodes)
8      {
9          if (item.Name.Equals("Employee ID: " + empId))
10         {
11             Utility.Log.Info("FOUND: " + empId);
12             Mouse.DoubleClick(item);
13             Array.Resize(ref empData, 1);
14
15             int colCount = item.Nodes.Count();
16             Array.Resize(ref empData[0], colCount);
17             for (int i = 0; i < colCount; i++)
18             {
19                 Utility.Log.Info("subItems: " + ↵
                      ↪ item.Nodes[i].Name);
20                 empData[0][i] = ↵
                      ↪ Utility.ExtractData(item.Nodes[i].Name);
21             }
22
23             break;
24         }
25     }
26
27     string stringSQL = "SELECT [EmployeeID], [Title], ↵
          ↪ [Name], [Gender], [DateOfBirth], [Email], ↵
          ↪ [ContractJob], [Postcode]" + "\r\n";
28     stringSQL = stringSQL + "FROM [dbo].[Employees] where ↵
          ↪ EmployeeID = '" + empId + "'";
29
30     Utility.Log.Info("SQL is: " + stringSQL);
31
32     String actEmpId = "", actTitle = "", actName = "", ↵
          ↪ actGender = "", actDob = "", actEmail = "", ↵
          ↪ actContract = "", actPostcode = "";
33
```

```
34      using (SqlConnection con = new ↵
              ↪ SqlConnection(Config.connectionString))
35      {
36          con.Open();
37
38          using (SqlCommand command = new ↵
                  ↪ SqlCommand(stringSQL, con))
39          using (SqlDataReader reader = ↵
                  ↪ command.ExecuteReader())
40          {
41              while (reader.Read())
42              {
43                  actEmpId = reader.GetString(0);
44                  actTitle = reader.GetString(1);
45                  actName = reader.GetString(2);
46                  actGender = reader.GetString(3);
47                  actDob = reader.GetDateTime(4).ToString();
48                  actEmail = reader.GetString(5);
49                  actContract = reader.GetString(6);
50                  actPostcode = reader.GetString(7);
51              }
52          }
53      }
54
55      Utility.ReportExpectedVsActual(empId, actEmpId);
56
57      Utility.ReportExpectedVsActual(empData[0][0], actTitle);
58
59      Utility.ReportExpectedVsActual(empData[0][1], actName);
60
61      Utility.ReportExpectedVsActual(empData[0][2], ↵
              ↪ Utility.FormatDate(actDob.Substring(0, 10)));
62
63      Utility.ReportExpectedVsActual(empData[0][3], ↵
              ↪ Utility.DecodeGender(actGender));
64
65      Utility.ReportExpectedVsActual(empData[0][4], actEmail);
66
67      Utility.ReportExpectedVsActual(empData[0][5], ↵
              ↪ actContract);
68
69      Utility.ReportExpectedVsActual(empData[0][6], ↵
              ↪ actPostcode);
70
71      Utility.Click(repWpfAdminEmpList.CloseButton);
```

72 }

◇ Line 7: Loops through each node of the `WpfTree`.

◇ Line 9: Looks for the specific node.

◇ Line 12: Double clicks the node to display details.

◇ Lines 55 - 69: Compare the expected values with the actual values and report the outcome.

10.4.2 Writing Tests

Add a new test to the 'WpfTests.cs' file as shown in Listing 10.17.

Listing 10.17: 'WpfTests.cs' - WpfAdminVerifyEmployeeByIdWithDatabase

```
1  [TestMethod]
2  public void WpfAdminVerifyEmployeeByIdWithDatabase()
3  {
4      Utility.Log.Info("Starting Test ***** " + ←
          ↪ Utility.TestName + " *****");
5
6      try
7      {
8          Utility.LaunchWpfApp();
9
10         pageWpfHome wpfph = new pageWpfHome();
11         wpfph.ClickMenuItemFileLogin();
12
13         pageWpfLogin wpfpl = new pageWpfLogin();
14         wpfpl.LoginUser("Admin", "Admin123");
15
16         pageWinMessageBox winmb = new pageWinMessageBox();
17         winmb.ClickOkButton();
18
19         wpfph.ClickMenuItemAdminEmployeeList();
20
21         pageWpfAdminEmpList wpfel = new ←
             ↪ pageWpfAdminEmpList();
22         wpfel.VerifyEmployeeById("10003");
23
24         wpfph.ClickMenuItemFileLogout();
25
26         wpfph.ClickMenuItemFileExit();
27
28         Utility.ReportResult();
29     }
```

```
30      catch (Exception exception)
31      {
32          Utility.ReportExpectedVsActual(Utility.TestName, ↵
            ↳ "Exception: " + exception.ToString());
33          Utility.Log.Error("Exception: " + ↵
            ↳ exception.ToString());
34          throw exception;
35      }
36  }
```

10.4.3 Executing Tests

Execute the test `WpfAdminVerifyEmployeeByIdWithDatabase` and you will see an output as shown in Figure 10.7. The test should execute successfully.

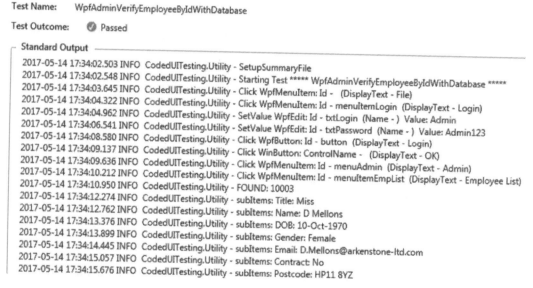

Figure 10.7: WPF Application - Verify Employee Output

Hopefully, now that you have learnt about how to hand code the Coded UI tests using our demo Website, Web Service, Windows Forms Application and WPF Application, you are feeling extremely comfortable using this Automation Framework and are now confident enough to be able to apply it to a number of different projects.

Happy hand coding of your Coded UI tests!

Index